No
Speed
Limit

NO SPEED LIMIT

SIXTY YEARS OF ROAD TESTING CLASSIC CARS

STUART BLADON

The History Press

To my wife, Jennetta, so often left looking after the children during my long absences abroad on international motor shows, rallies or new model launches, and to my daughter Rachel, an editor at Oxford University Press, who checked and edited the material.

All images are the author's own, unless otherwise stated.

Cover illustrations: front: The Jaguar XK150S instrument panel during maximum speed-testing in Belgium in 1959; inset: The Jaguar XK150; rear: A Sunbeam Alpine in which the author was injured when the photographer crashed in Greece. (Beaulieu Garage)

First published 2015

The History Press
The Mill, Brimscombe Port
Stroud, Gloucestershire, GL5 2QG
www.thehistorypress.co.uk

© Stuart Bladon, 2015

The right of Stuart Bladon to be identified as the Author of this work has been asserted in accordance with the Copyright, Designs and Patents Act 1988.

British Library Cataloguing in Publication Data.
A catalogue record for this book is available from the British Library.

ISBN 978 0 7509 6491 3

Typesetting and origination by The History Press
Printed and bound in Malta by Melita Press

CONTENTS

FOREWORD

BY LORD MONTAGU OF BEAULIEU

My first meeting with the author was in Monaco in 1959 when I had just completed driving in the Monte Carlo Rally, and Stuart Bladon was covering the rally for *The Autocar*; but I came to know him better when he came to Beaulieu in 1972 to cover the formation of the National Motor Museum. We were in a state of organised chaos, with step ladders and dust sheets everywhere, but Stuart and his photographer Peter Cramer produced a fine article in *Autocar*, 6 July 1972, introducing readers to the new museum and showing the variety of exhibits on display in those early days.

Since then he has been a frequent visitor to the National Motor Museum, and when he was chairman of the Guild of Motoring Writers in 1977 he organised an official visit to the museum for members of the Guild.

In his twenty-six years on the staff of *Autocar* he has driven and tested many thousands of cars, and this book relates some of the fascinating experiences and sometimes harrowing adventures in the life of a road-tester. The story of the Simca 1000 is sure to bring a laugh from anyone on reading it to the end, and one may be amused at the account of sinking a Singer Gazelle in the military vehicles' deep wading trough.

Even more exciting is the report of the race to catch the last available ferry to get back to the Italian mainland from the Isle of Elba in a Lamborghini Miura, and another hair-raising adventure was bouncing a Rover 3.5-litre across a railway line where there was no level crossing, in a bid to escape the Swedish police.

I am sure you will enjoy reading *No Speed Limit*, which will take you back to the days when there wasn't one outside built-up areas, and it charts the development and history of motoring over sixty years with graphic accounts of such landmarks as the arrival of the first parking meter in London, the Suez oil crisis, and the imposition of the 70mph speed limit in 1965.

Montagu of Beaulieu

INTRODUCTION

In June 2015, I completed sixty years as a motoring writer, having started work on *The Autocar* in June 1955. I have enjoyed a lifelong passion for cars ever since a fond aunt started teaching me to drive, working the steering and gear change from the passenger seat at the age of 7, and in my job over the years I have driven and tested almost every car on the road. An important part of car testing was always finding out how fast they would go, and in 1970 with a colleague in Italy I set what was for a long time *Autocar's* fastest road-test maximum speed, at 172mph. I left *Autocar* in 1981 and set up as a freelance motoring writer, contributing to a wide range of motoring magazines.

As well as driving fast, I have long been fascinated by economy driving, squeezing the maximum distance out of every litre of fuel, and set three world records for fuel economy listed in *The Guinness Book of Records* as well as driving fourteen trials observed by the RAC.

Many of the cars tested over the years became involved in great adventures such as the opening of the first major length of the M1, the switch to driving on the right in Sweden, the car that went into the wrong water trough at the Motor Industry Research Association proving ground, and the attempt to drive a Rolls-Royce through a wood to escape the German police.

Each chapter deals with one or two cars of special interest, recounting the events with which they, and I, were involved.

Stuart Bladon

ONE

VAUXHALL 14 J-TYPE

Out of the back window I saw huge flames leaping into the sky from the city

Water was running somewhere and keeping me awake. It could have been a tap left on at the hotel we were staying in at Barmouth in North Wales, or perhaps rain overflowing from a blocked gutter. But it didn't matter, I was too excited to sleep anyway – I had driven my first car, and I was only five! It wasn't a real car, of course, it was an electric bumper car in the amusements area on Barmouth seafront, and I had to stand up to be able to put my foot on the little shiny button on the floor that made it go; but it had kindled an excitement in feeling the response of the steering and the movement of the little vehicle which was to dominate my life.

My first memory of a real car was my father's Vauxhall 14, which he had purchased in 1938 after seeing it at the Motor Show in London, and it was quite advanced for its time, with a 6-cylinder engine and independent front suspension. It was in this car at the end of August 1939 that we went up to Scotland for a short holiday, and

An early addiction to cars.

the car was well filled, having me and my sister plus my grandmother and the maid in the back, and my father driving with my mother in the front. We never travelled light, so all the baggage was in a trailer towed behind the Vauxhall.

In Scotland it rained every day for several days, but then on a Sunday the rain had stopped and the sun was shining. There was great excitement after the boring few days in the house, and we were going down to the loch. There was not much to do except throw stones in, and then on the way back there was a sudden drama, which I didn't understand at the time. We stood outside a little cottage where the window was open and the wireless, as they were called in those days, was on. The news we were hearing was the outbreak of war on Sunday 3 September 1939. It prompted the immediate decision to return to our home in Coventry, amid horrendous fears of what the next few days may bring. My father thought that petrol might become unobtainable, and that road transport would be stopped, although as a doctor he would have had priority.

The return journey was very fraught. There was no wireless in the car, of course, so the grown-ups were full of anxieties and out of touch with developments, perhaps imagining things to be worse than they were, and then a disaster occurred: the trailer broke loose from the car, and I remember seeing it bounding like a mad thing across the moorland before the tow bar dug into the ground and it came to rest.

Somehow my father managed to connect it to the car with wire, and it was towed very slowly to the next town where everything was emptied out of it and the trailer was left at the station to be transported back to Coventry by rail. A little hole existed between the piled up luggage on the back seat and the roof, where my sister, three years older than me, and I were to squeeze in. At Edinburgh my grandmother baled out to continue the journey by train, but there was still not much room in the car.

Fortunately, my father was too old for war service, and as a doctor he was needed in Coventry, and able to get E (for Emergency) petrol coupons. Foreseeing that Coventry would be a target for enemy bombing he bought a caravan and arranged to have it kept in a field at a farm near Kenilworth, 3 miles from where we lived at Earlsdon on the outskirts of Coventry. The plan was that if things got very bad we would take refuge in the caravan.

The other common precaution taken was to have an air-raid shelter built at the bottom of the garden. I had seen my mother smoking and was fascinated by what she did, and one day I took the packet of cigarettes and matches to experiment in the garage, which was at the bottom of the garden. The men building the air-raid shelter thought this was a great joke, lit one for me and put it in my mouth and told me to suck in. I promptly did so and was sick on the garage floor. I was 6 years old, and never smoked again. I think every child should be made to do this!

The first time the caravan was used in earnest was in November 1940, and when we returned to the house next day it was to find that a landmine had gone off not far away and blown in most of the windows. Criss-crossed brown paper strips were glued to all windows in the war to prevent the danger of flying glass, and many of the shattered windows in the house were swinging on the paper. With the destructive element of all children, my sister and I enjoyed running from room to room, calling out 'Look out below' and knocking the broken glass out.

In one room – my parents' bedroom – the door would hardly open, and a black triangle of metal no bigger than a hand was sticking out of the wood. On the other side, a huge piece of metal from the landmine was wedged in the door, having passed completely through the window.

I have much more vivid memories of the second big air raid on Coventry in February 1941. A few days earlier I had been sent to take the entrance exam at what was to be my next school, King Henry VIII School in Coventry, the result of which was never heard because it was a casualty of the blitz.

When the bombing started in earnest we were pulled out of bed, dressed and told we were going to the caravan at Kenilworth, always an occasion of great excitement, and we stood in the hall of the house in Earlsdon waiting for what was called a 'lull' between the waves of bombers coming over with the monotonous and frightening drone of their engines. My father went down the garden to the garage, to bring the car round to the front of the house. On his return we were about to leave when the phone rang; it was an urgent message calling all doctors to report to the Coventry and Warwickshire Hospital in Gulson Road.

Another lull came, and we scuttled out to the Vauxhall and began the precarious drive with no lights on, by moonlight out to the caravan. As we drove along at very low speed I looked out of the back window and saw huge flames leaping into the sky from the city. We were dropped hastily at the caravan, and my father then drove off into the night to go bravely into that appalling holocaust of fire and bombs in the city. I still have the letter written by the mayor of Coventry thanking him and all doctors for the work they did that night, and for their courage in venturing into that maelstrom of fire, falling buildings and destruction.

Caravans in those days had no insulation or heating, and it was bitterly cold. My mother discussed with the maid how everything containing liquid had frozen solid and broken the bottles it was in. My sister and I were bedded down but woke to hear a car arriving. It was early morning, about 5 a.m. I was told later, and I remember the maid, Gertrude, saying excitedly: 'He's in your car, madam, what's happened to his car?'

It was only later that I learned what had happened. My father arrived at the hospital and saw all the cars in the car park, lit up by the bright moonlight, and thought they would be a prime target for the bombers, so parked his Vauxhall 14 at the back of the hospital. After doing emergency surgery until well after three in the morning he was told to go and rest, but said that he must go back to his family. He was told that he wouldn't recognise Coventry and wouldn't know the way, to which he replied that this was nonsense, he had worked there for years and knew

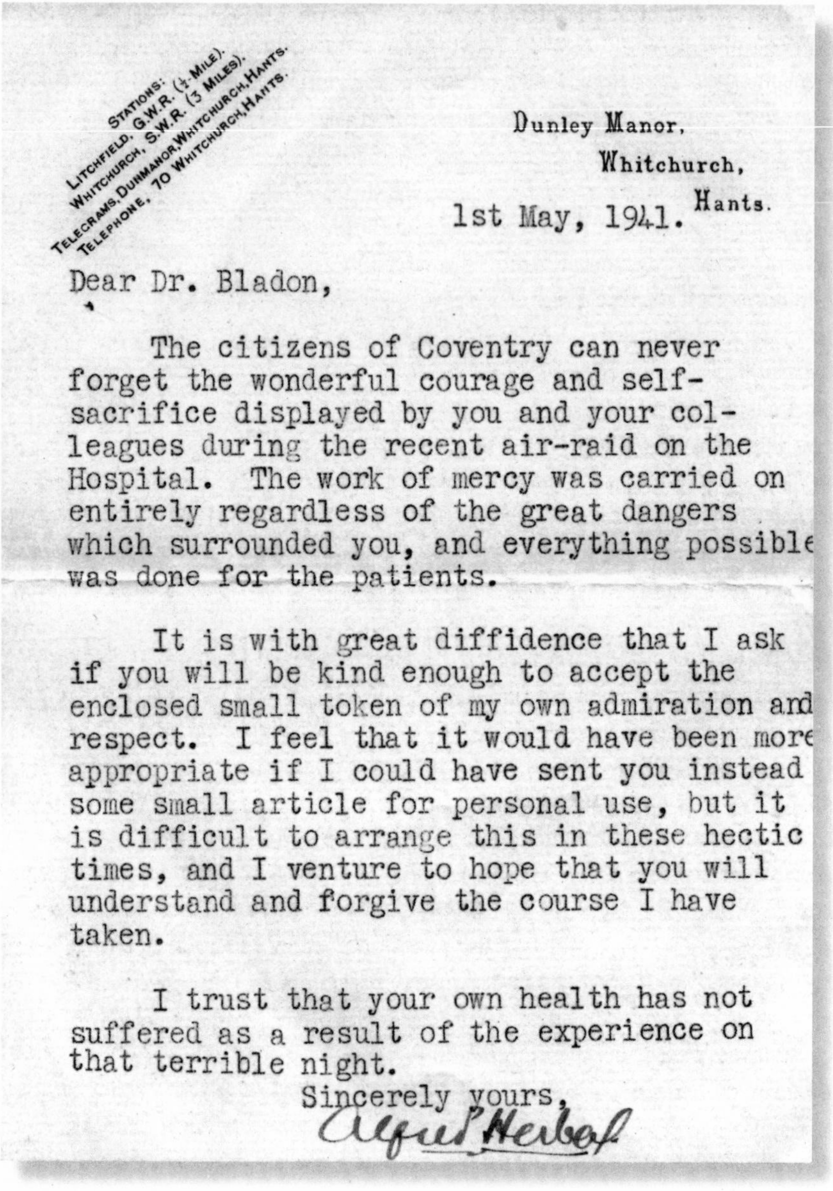

STATIONS:
LITCHFIELD, G.W.R. (¼ Mile).
WHITCHURCH, S.W.R. (3 Miles).
TELEGRAMS, DUNMANOR, WHITCHURCH, HANTS.
TELEPHONE, 70 WHITCHURCH, HANTS.

Dunley Manor,
Whitchurch,
1st May, 1941. Hants.

Dear Dr. Bladon,

    The citizens of Coventry can never forget the wonderful courage and self-sacrifice displayed by you and your colleagues during the recent air-raid on the Hospital. The work of mercy was carried on entirely regardless of the great dangers which surrounded you, and everything possible was done for the patients.

    It is with great diffidence that I ask if you will be kind enough to accept the enclosed small token of my own admiration and respect. I feel that it would have been more appropriate if I could have sent you instead some small article for personal use, but it is difficult to arrange this in these hectic times, and I venture to hope that you will understand and forgive the course I have taken.

    I trust that your own health has not suffered as a result of the experience on that terrible night.

Sincerely yours,

Alfred Herbert

After the second Coventry Blitz my father received this letter of thanks from Alderman Herbert for the work done on that terrible night in February 1941.

every street, but he was to find out how true this advice was. He went out to find that the unfortunate Vauxhall had taken a direct hit. He was able to get in, not realising in the dark how bad the damage was, and even started the engine, but it wouldn't move. Both rear tyres had gone, the back of the car was on the ground, and when I saw the wreckage, still there weeks later, I wondered how he had even managed to get into it.

He had then run and sheltered, run and sheltered, sometimes wondering where on earth he was, and realised that the advice he had been given, that Coventry was unrecognisable, was very true. At one point he took shelter under a railway bridge, and next day it wasn't there. Two hours after he left, a time bomb went off in the wing of the hospital where he had been working and many of the patients and staff in that wing were killed. He had a lucky escape.

Eventually he reached our house at Earlsdon, and got out my mother's car. When he had ordered the Vauxhall 14, he also ordered a new Vauxhall 10 for my mother, and they came with consecutive registrations: DKV 744 was the 14, and DKV 745 was the Vauxhall 10. He drove out to the caravan in my mother's 10, and later received war damage cover for the cost of the destroyed 14. 'Your new school's gone up in flames,' he told me. I was very disappointed because I had looked forward to going there, having presumed that I had passed the entrance test.

The morning found everything covered in heavy frost, and the journey back to Coventry took ages, with many roads closed by unexploded bombs, and at one time what few vehicles there were on the road were diverted into a field and out at the other end.

By the time we reached home, having taken over two hours for the 3-mile journey, I was suffering badly from the cold, and went down with pneumonia.

Many days later, when my father made one of his frequent visits to see how I was getting on, now well on the way to recovery, he said: 'Of course, you haven't seen the new car, yet, have you? It's this colour.' And he picked up a little grey aeroplane with which I had been playing on the bed. I thought it was a disappointing colour, and was also disappointed to hear that the new car was going to be exactly the same as the old one. In fact, it wasn't new at all, because you couldn't get a new car any more. It was a second-hand one, but in good order, and cost the same as the war damage settlement for the old one, £280. He later received a gift (I never heard what it was), sent to all doctors after their work at the hospital on that terrible night, with accompanying letter from Alderman Alfred Herbert.

Much later it was decided that with my baby brother now on the way, and to get away from the risk of further bombing at Coventry, I should be evacuated to my grandmother's house at Llanbedr in North Wales. My grandfather had died just after the war broke out, but my favourite aunt Gynny was also living there. It's no surprise that the awful train journey, alone with my gas mask and a little case of clothes, was enough to put me off trains for life. I remember being terribly thirsty but had been told on no account to drink the water from the tap in the toilet, and was so grateful when a lady in the carriage took pity on me and kindly provided a cup of tea from her thermos flask.

Gynny was doing war work, managing the canteen at Cook's explosives factory at Penrhyndeudraeth, about 10 miles from Llanbedr, so she was able to get the invaluable E petrol coupons and keep motoring in her little Morris 8, in which they met me at Dolgellau station. Gynny played an important part in my motoring life, introducing me to car control and allowing me to hold the steering wheel from the passenger seat. Each afternoon I would walk along the deserted road from Llanbedr until I saw the little Morris coming along, so that I would be able to get in and steer. Later I was able to work the clutch with my right foot and change the gears – an amusing co-operative effort with Gynny officially in charge of the car but operating only the brake pedal and accelerator.

My father's 1948 Vauxhall 14 in which I gained early experience of driving on Black Rock Sands in North Wales.

She taught me a lot about car control and safe driving, passing on the messages that had been drummed into her by her driving instructor many years before: 'Expect a fool round every corner' and 'never put your head into a hornets' nest' meaning that if there's a congestion ahead such as a narrow gap with a big vehicle coming through, hang back early and keep out of the problem.

In 1941 we had a lovely hot summer, and when term time came I was enrolled at a small school at Harlech, where I made friends and had a lot of fun, as well as beginning to take an interest in learning. Then came that terrible day on 13 August when I learned that my mother had died in childbirth. In those days for a woman to have a baby at over 40 was very dicey. The only good news was that I now had a brother, albeit one eight years younger than me. We packed rapidly and began the long 140-mile journey to Coventry, and I didn't see Wales again until we went there by train in 1943, losing all our luggage and my bicycle on the way. It all turned up after the first week.

My new school was Emscote Lawn at Warwick, to which I commuted by bus until later I was able to cycle the 7 miles to school. On one foggy morning I was waiting for the bus and heard it coming before I could see it. At the same moment an army truck came the other way going towards Coventry, and as the bus emerged from the fog the two vehicles collided. Bits flew off the vehicles and I saw the bus swerve and come towards me so I turned and ran across the grass, but in my haste I tripped and fell headlong, which was just as well as the damaged bus careered closely past me and into the ditch where I had been planning to take refuge. Later, when statements had to be filled in, I didn't make a very good witness because how could I possibly say which vehicle had been over its half of the road?

My time at Emscote Lawn was fairly uneventful, but the school was keen on making all the boys become proficient at boxing. One day I was sparring with a boy older and bigger than me, and was taking quite a beating when I managed a hefty punch to his face. There was an ominous 'click' and blood spurted from his nose, all over his vest. The fight was stopped and I was declared the winner, which left me quite elated. But next term he didn't come back to school and I was absolutely appalled when I learned that he had contracted some horrible disease which made his blood turn to water. I felt enormous guilt, thinking that he was losing his blood and I had wasted some of it. Worse, could it be that the hefty punch on his nose had caused his blood problem? In modern times no doubt I would have had counselling, but you didn't get that at the height of the war in 1943. It came as an enormous relief when years later I learned that his loss of blood after my successful punch would not have made any difference – he had been a victim of that terrible child-killer, leukaemia.

My great interest in driving, kindled in Wales, continued and after we had moved to a larger house farther out of Coventry on the Kenilworth Road, one day I plucked up courage and reversed the Vauxhall out of the garage and brought it round to the front door all ready for my father to get into and drive off to work, but my clutch control with the cold engine was not very good so it came out of the garage in a series of kangaroo leaps! Although my aunt had taught me the elements of steering and braking, no one had explained about how to work the choke and ease the clutch in after the first start of the day – I just did what I had observed. Being only 10 at the time I could hardly reach the pedals, but the technique improved and this became a daily routine. No public roads were involved. However, I did have my first highly illegal drive on the road with the window cleaner, Mr Flood, who came every other Sunday to clean my father's car. He took me out for a short run at the wheel of his little Austin 7 van, which I found very exciting. My father always said it was bound to rain when Mr Flood came!

After the war ended in 1945, car production slowly restarted, and the rush to buy cars became a tremendous scramble with desperate motorists happy to pay far more for second-hand examples than they had cost new. Doctors were given priority ordering, and in 1946 my father's new car arrived, a Vauxhall 14 again but in an attractive shade of light blue. By agreement with the distributor, W. Brandish of Coventry, the car stood in the showroom for a week covered in bunting and floral displays, as the first new Vauxhall to be delivered to Coventry since the war. In this year also, at the age of 13, I moved on from Emscote Lawn to Malvern College.

My father ran this car until 1948, when he was able to take advantage again of the priority ordering for doctors, and another Vauxhall 14 arrived, this time boasting a radio and a heater. The price obtained for the 1946 car was £650, nearly twice the cost of the new one.

It was in this car that I gathered quite a lot of driving 'practice' on holiday in Wales, on the concrete strips of an abandoned wartime establishment near Harlech and on the beach at Black Rock Sands, so I arranged to take the driving test on the way back from school at the end of the term at Malvern. The nearest driving test centre was at Worcester, so rather grudgingly my father agreed that he would come to the school to collect me, take me to Worcester and wait while I underwent the test.

I thought I was doing quite well, having managed the three-point turn very neatly and responded quickly to the emergency test, but when the examiner told me to take the next right turn I did exactly what he said, realising too late that I was about to go past 'No Entry' signs, the wrong way down a one-way street. The resultant fail was well-deserved, and being only four days past my 17th birthday I'd had hardly any experience in complete control of a car on the public road – that journey from Malvern to Worcester had been my first real drive. In those days you could take the test again almost as soon as you wanted; I did so within a few days and was the proud holder of a driving licence when I went back to school for the next term.

There was an exciting change of plan in 1950: instead of going to Wales on holiday as usual, we would take a couple of weeks at a rented seaside house at

Porthleven in Cornwall, and on the way down we would break the journey at Lynmouth to show solidarity after the disastrous floods three months earlier. The scenes of devastation – wrecked buildings and cars, and the high-water mark some 15ft above the ground in places – were appalling. But we were to have our own small disaster.

We all went down to Lynmouth Harbour, and then my stepmother, sister and brother opted to go up to Lynton on the gravity water-powered cable car, while my father and I would drive up in the Vauxhall. About halfway up Lynton hill, the car suddenly lost power and came to a jerky halt, well out in the middle of the road. My father revved the engine, but the car wouldn't move either forwards or backwards. He trudged off up the hill to get help while I remained behind doing a traffic patrol job, halting the down-coming cars and giving priority to the ones grinding their way up the hill. Cars didn't make light work of Lynton Hill in those days.

Eventually the breakdown truck arrived, connected up the tow rope and at first couldn't move the car, but then with lots of revving and smoke there was suddenly a tremendous bang and the car started moving. We were towed to the garage at Lynton, where in due course the verdict was that the gearbox had no oil in and had seized up. My father had taken the car in for a service before the holiday, and the garage to which he had entrusted it had drained the gearbox and forgotten to refill it.

We were confined to Lynmouth for an extended stay, as it was Easter, and a car had to be sent to Barnstaple to collect a replacement gearbox. My brother and I took the opportunity to stand for hours watching the hill climb, which was one of the tests for the Land's End trial. Eventually we were under way again, but the journey to Cornwall was very tedious as we were told the new gearbox needed to be run in almost as carefully as a new car, with 30mph not to be exceeded for the first 250 miles.

In subsequent school holidays I enjoyed driving my father on his rounds, though he was always a very nervous passenger and I suspect did not enjoy this very much. I would read while he was in the patient's house, and one day he asked what I was reading and I showed him the cover, *Memoirs of a Fox-hunting Man* by Siegfried Sassoon. He then said that he always thought someone must be very egotistical to write the story of his own life. I took this very much to heart, so this is not intended to be a book about me. No one but my nearest and dearest would be interested in that. Instead, it's about the cars and the wonderful – sometimes exciting, sometimes amusing – motoring adventures that it has been my good fortune to experience over more than half a century.

T W O

MORRIS 8

Ξ I noticed the clouds of blue smoke trailing along behind us

When my mother died in childbirth in 1941, my aunt Gynny sold the Morris 8 in which I had 'driven' so many miles steering from the passenger seat and working the clutch pedal with my right foot, and she took over my mother's Vauxhall 10. After the war she was able to get priority car ordering because of her essential work running the Coventry chain of British Restaurants and purchased a 1947 Vauxhall 12. After I had passed my driving test there were many opportunities when I was allowed to drive the little Vauxhall 12, which seemed to me at the time an absolutely delightful car. It had a 4-cylinder 1.5-litre engine and three-speed gearbox, and like the bigger Vauxhall it was unusual in having torsion-bar independent front suspension.

After waiting five years, her pre-war fiancée was demobbed and she married. Subsequently I was saddened to hear that the little Vauxhall was to be sold and the money was to be used to purchase two second-hand cars, one for the two newly-weds, now living in a bungalow in Matlock, Derbyshire, and the other for my grandmother to use. She had now moved back from Wales to the Midlands and taken over the house of a deceased recluse relative in Rowington, near Warwick. As she couldn't drive, and had no intention of learning, a retired handyman living nearby would drive her, and – joy of joys – I would be able to do so during the school holidays.

But first we had to sell the Vauxhall 12, and I was asked to get it ready for auction. I was appalled to see the decrepit, filthy state into which the Vauxhall 12 had been allowed to fall. It was also neglected mechanically, as I found when I used the brakes for the first time and found that the pedal went almost down to the floor.

But I worked away at it and made its black paintwork shine like new, while half an hour's work with a screwdriver on the ratchet adjusters all round made a tremendous difference to the brakes. The result of my efforts, combined with the shortage of cars, was that it fetched £750 at the Measham car auction, more than twice what it had cost new, and I was rewarded with a most welcome and generous cash present for my work.

I was now eagerly looking forward to acting as buying agent to acquire a suitable car for my grandmother, and thought we could do quite well with half the proceeds – around £375; but it was not to be so easy. Gynny was now supporting a husband who had effectively gone back to school to make up for his lack of education, with the ambition – later achieved – of becoming a schoolmaster, so no more than £200

My aunt's 1949 Vauxhall 12 provided valuable driving experience until sadly it was sold in 1951 for over twice the price of a new one.

was to be spent on the replacement car, and it was felt that a Morris 8, like she had run before, would be ideal. After all, I was told, the Morris had been very well built because Bill Morris, later Lord Nuffield, had been determined to make it better than the Ford 8.

Adverts were duly scoured, and dealers visited, as I cycled all over Coventry to track down something that would meet the constraints, and eventually found a 1936 Morris 8 with an asking price of £175, advertised privately by a sheet-metal worker. He agreed to the car being taken to Rowington for the approval of the lady, and his son came with me. My grandmother was immediately happy with the deal and wrote a cheque for the car straight away. But I was secretly worried about the amount of oil it was using, having noticed the clouds of blue smoke trailing along behind us.

One didn't have to wait for a cheque to be cleared in those days, and after dropping off the son at his terraced home in Coventry I drove back home for a late lunch. Insurance was arranged with a quick telephone call and there was a bit of tax still to run. I felt quite elated that I had my first car at the age of 17, although of course it wasn't mine at all. Responsibility began to dawn when I pulled out the oil dipstick and found just a little bit of black sludge on the bottom.

Frequent journeys followed, and on return from school for the holidays always one of the first expeditions was to cycle over to my grandmother's, get the little Morris out of the garage, and take her to the shops at Shrewley, about 3 miles away. There was a garage there, and petrol rationing had ended though it was still 'pool' petrol. National Benzole used to advertise that 'The return of the branded spirit is a thriller which has yet to be written'. After these expeditions it would always be: 'Oh dear, it looks as if it's going to rain; perhaps I could leave my bike here and take the Morris and then I'd be able to take you shopping again next week!' There would also be the occasional excitingly long journey to Matlock to see Gynny and the new husband. The Morris trailed smoke all the way, and a fully topped up sump always needed 2 pints of oil for the 70-mile journey back.

The Morris 8 not only had a sunroof, but you could open the windscreen letting in a lovely stream of cool air, and on one occasion when I was driving along with the screen open a wasp came in, hit me on the face and then started buzzing furiously around me. I learned the hard way that a driver must never allow attention to be diverted from the road, and after frantic efforts to fend the wasp away I looked up just in time to avoid mounting the kerb and possibly hitting a lamp post. The little Morris was not the most stable car in which to make a violent swerve, but it didn't roll over as seemed likely at one stage.

On another occasion I noticed that the brakes seemed very spongy, and next time I used them the pedal went nearly down to the floor. Investigating at home, I felt that there must be a master cylinder somewhere, but couldn't find it anywhere under the bonnet. Carefully following the course of the brake pipes I located it, under the floor on the driver's side with a small access hole above. Topping up and bleeding to get air out of the system returned the brakes to their normal, rather borderline adequacy. The oil-consumption problem remained, although I tried a Holts product called Piston Seal, intended to bridge the gap of worn-out cylinder bores; it made no difference. The Morris ran on for several years, always trailing oil smoke, but was eventually sold.

Long afterwards, on one of our visits to the old family home at Llanbedr in North Wales, we found it abandoned on the road from Llanbedr to Mochras, still bearing the registration BRR 74, which in later years might have had a lot of value. How it had come to finish up there I never learned, but it was extraordinary that the same make and model of car should have finally come to rest so near to where I had enjoyed my first experiences of car control more than twenty years earlier.

THREE

AUSTIN 10

As we came down the hill towards Bellevue Terrace, the headlights lit up a policeman sitting on the wall. I was terrified

In my five years at Malvern College I am afraid I did not shine very well, my most notable achievement being that I was the first – perhaps the only – boy to be beaten by the headmaster for the heinous crime of driving a car.

On the rather rare occasions when my parents came up to take me out it was an established routine that I would take the Vauxhall 14 back to the school on the Saturday evening, which saved my father from the two-way trip of taking me there and then driving out again on the Sunday morning to collect me to join them for breakfast. They always chose to stay at the Broomhill Hotel on the other side of the Malvern Hills, my teetotal father valuing the fact that it was unlicensed.

In my last term at Malvern a nasty little directive from the headmaster appeared on the notice board to the effect that 'No boy may drive a motor car during term time.' It was generally felt that this was a mean, jealous reaction to the sight of my friend the Earl of Suffolk and Berkshire – always called simply 'Suffolk' – who had been seen driving his mother's magnificent Rolls-Royce in the previous term. Suffolk's father had been killed while trying to disarm an unexploded bomb during the war. It was a ridiculous restriction to impose on young men who were then 17 or 18 and old enough to serve their country driving army lorries or even flying aircraft.

I never found out for certain who it was that had spotted and reported me, but I suspected the culprit was a master by the name of George Chesterton, who was a stalwart supporter of Malvern. He died at the age of 90 in November 2012, so all is forgiven!

The headmaster was an unimaginative, miserable man with the appropriate name Gaunt, always given the equally apt nickname 'The Goat'. The beating when it came was not severe, and I came out of the headmaster's study thinking what an absolute prat he was.

I would have deserved the punishment much more, and even no doubt expulsion, had an earlier exploit been discovered. It involved me and my close friend, Don. We jokingly modelled ourselves on characters in the *Daily Mail* cartoon strip Rip Kirby. Don always called me 'The Boss' and he was the sidekick 'Curtains'. The exploit was all very secret, but the date and time were agreed.

At 1 a.m. I slipped out of bed, went to the washrooms and put on the dark trousers, gym shoes and jumper I had put ready, and went down to my study. There was a short wait and I thought Curtains had chickened out, but he was reliable and silently sidled into the study. The plan had been agreed, and the first thing to check was the side door out of School House. The main doors and gates at the back were always locked at night, but the one and only alternative access was the side door, also bolted and locked by key. When we crept up the side stairs we found the huge iron key still in the lock – so the plan was on. We slipped the noisy bolts across, took the key with us and locked the door from the outside so that anyone trying it from inside would hopefully not feel it necessary to pull the bolts across, and stepped out into the moonlit night. It was June, so it was not cold.

Keeping close to the wall and not making a sound, we slipped past the front entrance of School House, then along the pavement past No. 9 House and the music centre. We had agreed to try the Abbey Hotel first, and if no luck there, Malvern offered many more possible hotels to visit. But we were in luck, and when we reached the Abbey Hotel after only about five minutes with the streets completely deserted, Curtains whispered to me: 'The keys are in this one.'

It was an old Austin, I think 8 or more likely 10hp, parked on the hotel forecourt nose on to the wall. I climbed in, ran a quick check on the controls, pulled out the choke and released the handbrake. With awful crunching noises of the tyres on the gravel, the car started to move backwards with Curtains pushing, and I steered it out into the middle of the road. There was a junction to the right, where the road ran steeply downhill – Malvern is all hills – and as I steered down there the car quickly gathered momentum. A bump start in gear was the plan, but when I tried to move the lever into top gear there was the most awful noise of grating gears. A quick try into third had the same effect. I braked quickly to a halt and Curtains came running up to the driver's door, which I still had not closed to avoid the noise.

'We've picked a dud 'un, Boss,' he exclaimed, but I said: 'No, it's alright, we're well away from the hotel; I'll try the starter.' The engine fired immediately, and Curtains ran round to the passenger side and jumped in. We moved gently off down the hill and after a little while closed the doors.

It wasn't the intention to go far – just a quick circuit of the town, now with the headlights on, but as we came down the hill towards Bellevue Terrace, the lights shone on a policeman sitting on the wall. I was terrified – if he signalled us to stop, what should we do? Drive on and make a run for it, or stop and try to bluff it out with the story we had rehearsed about borrowing the car from our Aunt, Mrs Lauderdale who was staying at the Abbey Hotel. We had also agreed that if we looked like being arrested, I would wait for the most hopeful opportunity and then say: 'It looks like curtains', which would be the signal for us both to try to break free and run for it. We were both good runners and reckoned we could shake off any pursuit. We would head uphill, away from the school.

Fortunately it did not come to that; the policeman remained sitting on the wall and we motored quietly past and on down the hill towards the Abbey Hotel.

Just before we reached the hotel I stopped the engine, doused the lights, and we coasted straight in by moonlight across the forecourt and into the same space the car had been in before. I left the car exactly as it had been, in neutral with the handbrake lightly applied and the bunch of keys hanging from the ignition switch. We tried to close the doors quietly by pushing them to, but had to slam them, which we did in unison making only one sharp clunk.

There was still no sign of anyone and we hurriedly made our way back to School House. On the way we discussed what would await us. Will the Erg – Mr Erskine, our dour Scottish housemaster – be standing there with arms crossed saying: 'Well, Bleed'n, and what have y' bin up to?' So it was with trembling fingers that I inserted the great key into the lock, turned it, and pushed the side door open, to find with enormous relief that there was no one there. We returned the key to its rightful position, locked and bolted the door, and shook hands before returning to our respective dormitories. 'Not a word to anyone,' I whispered, and Curtains nodded. Often such escapades had been revealed to the authorities by careless bragging about them. In the washrooms I changed back into my pyjamas and crept back to bed. Almost at once, I heard the school clock strike two. We had been away less than an hour, but it seemed as if we had been out all night.

Later, after I had left the school, I learned that Curtains did tell a few trusted friends about our little act of bravado, and I learned that someone's opinion of me had risen enormously on hearing about it. It was one way to achieve fame!

FOUR

HILLMAN 10 CABRIOLET

≡ This car nearly killed me twice

As schooldays came to an end and I had to choose a career, jobs which I wanted to do – notably journalism or engineering in the motor industry – were dismissed as inappropriate and I found myself remorselessly nudged into following my father to be a doctor. But my heart was never in it, and although I gained the necessary Higher School Certificate, the equivalent of later A levels, and admission to King's College, London, and Westminster Medical School, it all fell apart after I failed the first MB exam. I was then 19, and too old for deferment of call-up for National Service, which was at that time absolutely compulsory.

By mistake, everyone on the course at King's had been issued automatically with a certificate of deferment of call-up for a further year. Whoever sent out these

The hood on the Hillman Cabriolet could be folded fully down or in the De Ville position.

certificates had not anticipated the possibility that some students – like me – might fail the first year exam. The result was that, although too old for the course, I had been given deferment from National Service, but by the time this mistake was noticed I was going over the whole first year course again at Coventry University. The authorities wrote to me saying that I should take the medical, which was essential to see if one was fit enough for National Service, then apply for delayed call-up. I was very suspicious about what that implied. Each letter took about three weeks, and my reply always at least four, each time pointing out that on the strength of the certificate of deferment it was too late to talk of rescinding it and making me give up my studies.

I was wrongly advised that I had better submit, so I took the medical and was passed as A1 fit. Events followed exactly as I had feared. I had already passed the physics and chemistry sections of the exam, and felt pretty certain to pass the biology, which was my strong subject. My father was furious and submitted an appeal, which was heard at Birmingham and turned down. The very next day the call-up papers arrived, and I had to report to RAMC Crookham two weeks later. This was the very day that I should have been sitting the final exam of the first-year medical course, after which I would have been under the age limit for the next stage of the studies. The absurdity is that within months the government cut the period of National Service from two years to one, and made it much easier for anyone with a reasonably valid reason to apply for exemption. Shortly afterwards, National Service was abolished. But for me it came too late.

The basic training in the RAMC convinced me that I wasn't cut out to be a doctor anyway, and certainly didn't want to go back to all that study when I came out of the army. What I really wanted to do was journalism. I had always enjoyed writing and had a keen interest in English.

After basic training I was posted to Southern Command Headquarters at Wilton, near Salisbury, where I was appointed assistant to Major General Murphy, the Deputy Director of Medical Services for Southern Command. It was very much a clerking job, which I had achieved because of my ability to type and write shorthand, and I quite enjoyed my time there. However, I was keen to try for a commission; at the same time I applied for transfer to the Royal Army Service Corps, which meant transport and was where my real interests lay.

There had been a competition in a now-defunct newspaper called *The Recorder*, inviting students to write attacking a university resolution that if another war came students would refuse to fight for their country. I won the prize, which helped to boost the funds in my Post Office savings account, and I was eager to buy my first car; but although I had £65, which was quite a lot of money in those days, you didn't get much of a car at anything less than £100. Each Saturday afternoon was spent, usually with my friend Alan Crost, going on the bus to Salisbury, only 3 miles away, to see what the dealers had on offer. For several weeks there was nothing any good that I could afford, and then one day the dealer who by then knew me by sight, called out: 'Terraplane' and pointed to a huge American monstrosity, which I wouldn't have wanted at any price. But I was interested in the car behind it.

First registered in 1934, it was a Hillman 10 Cabriolet in yellow and black. You could fold the hood back to the main support rail in what was known as the De Ville position. Then, using a winding handle not unlike a starting handle, the hood could be fully wound down behind the rear seat. The price was £55, and in those days one didn't bargain with the dealer. I agreed to have it and would pick it up the following Saturday. This car would nearly kill me twice.

One of the formalities was that I needed official permission to keep a car at the quarters, and I duly submitted an application to see the Regimental Sergeant Major. When I explained that I wanted to apply for permission to keep a car at the barracks, he exclaimed: 'What are you, Private Bladon? Are you a man of private means?

First you want to be made an officer, and now you want to have a car here.' I explained that I just had a small amount of savings and wanted to spend it on a car.

Permission was granted, and the great day came when I was able to drive back to Wilton on the strength of an insurance cover note, and tax application 'in post'. The little Hillman went quite well, but the worst feature was the terrible brakes. They were cable operated and 'self wrapping', which meant that the rotation of the wheels pulled the brakes on harder. Probably when new and well adjusted the system worked well, but on an old, worn-out car they always pulled unevenly and I never knew which way the steering would pull when the brakes were used. Also terrible was that when applied while reversing the whole brake assembly would revolve and lock the back wheels with a sickening thump.

The barracks in which we were billeted at Wilton were absolutely frightful. The main building, Fugglestone House, had been built as a workhouse in Victorian times, and later what we would now call a hospital for people with special needs or a psychiatric hospital. Our sleeping quarters were in corrugated-iron Nissen huts with a coke-burning brazier for heating. When it rained, water leaked in, and when it was cold it was freezing even though we stoked up the brazier till the top of it was red-hot. But all the time there was talk of a move up to the new billets. I didn't hold out any hope for this to happen, but it did. A day was fixed when all personnel would parade on a Saturday morning and be marched up to the new quarters. A small amount of personal possessions could be stacked up to be moved by lorry. I asked the RSM what I should do about my car, and he evidently thought the idea of one of his privates having a car was a great joke, so I was told that I would drive along following the parade. Because the new billets, only about a mile away, were being promoted as the excellent new pattern for military quarters, the parade was marched on a roundabout route through Wilton village. I duly followed the column in first gear, with the engine getting rather hot.

Whenever I pass through Wilton and see the narrow bridges with a warning sign, 'Caution, oncoming vehicles in middle of road', I recall the appalling accident that happened when the GOC's driver, travelling at enormous speed, met a bus in the middle of the bridge. The driver, a sergeant, was killed and I believe there were some fatalities on the bus, and the Humber staff car was comprehensively destroyed.

Soon after taking possession of my proud new car, the tax disc arrived and was in the car ready to be put on the windscreen. Driving to Salisbury I passed a police car parked facing me on the left of the road, and noticed a policeman in the passenger seat taking great interest in the Hillman as I went by. I bet he's noticed there's no tax disc, I thought, so I quickly tore off the perforated surrounding, stuffed it into the licence holder and shoved it back on the screen all while driving along. Sure enough the Wolseley police car soon came tearing past with its ominous bell ringing, and an arm out of the window giving the imperious 'slow down' signal. I duly stopped and switched off the engine, and the policeman got out and started walking towards

The brakes of the Hillman 10 Cabriolet had become very dangerous.

me, then stopped halfway and did a sort of double take. 'I thought,' he said, 'that you didn't have a tax disc.'

'Well, I do,' I replied, which wasn't a lie, 'and if that's all you've stopped me for could I ask you to give me a swing?' The Hillman urgently needed a new battery, so it was often essential to use the starting handle, which I passed through the window to the policeman. He gave a sharp pull on the handle, the engine fired up, and he passed the handle back. I thanked him and drove off, hoping he did not notice the smirk on my face.

October came, and my friend Alan Crost, who was as mad on cars as I was, put up an interesting proposition: if we left after parade on Saturday we could drive to his aunt's house at Chesham Bois and stay the night. She would kindly give us supper and breakfast next morning, and then we could go to the London Motor Show at Earls Court. It was a great idea, and he offered also to share the petrol cost.

We were very late starting and were flying along in the dark when I saw a red light in front with something round and black above it. The 6-volt headlights on the

Hillman were pathetic but as we came nearer I suddenly realised that it was a huge transporter with a tank on it, and the round thing I had seen was its gun pointing towards us. With more experience I would have steered safely past it, since there was nothing coming the other way, but I was only 19, with somewhat limited driving ability, and in panic I smashed my foot down on the brake pedal. Immediately the Hillman went into a violent spin. We went round twice, though it seemed more, and finished up on the other side of the transporter, having missed it by amazing good fortune, and facing back in the direction from which we had come. There was a terrible smell of burnt rubber from the tyres, and the engine was roaring because my foot had slipped off the brake pedal and was hard down on the accelerator; the gear had jumped out or been knocked into neutral.

Two men came running up from the transporter and exclaimed: 'We thought you'd had it.' All I could think of was to say lamely, 'So did we.'

Alan took it very well, and we agreed to go a bit more steadily from then on. We had been doing about 55mph. We reached his aunt's house in Chesham Bois, there was no sign of her but a pleasant meal was laid out, and next morning being Sunday we motored quietly to Earls Court, parked on one of the many empty bomb sites left over from the war, and enjoyed several hours looking round the 1953 Motor Show. It was the third time I had been to the British Motor Show, and I never missed one since until they stopped.

After our return, I was determined to do something about those awful brakes, and on a bright Sunday in early November I took the car up to some waste ground above the new quarters, which I tended to use for routine service on the little car, such as changing the oil and greasing its enormous number of grease points. I had the car jacked up and standing on piles of bricks, with all the wheels removed so that I could adjust the cable lengths and get them equalised. All was going well, but I needed another spanner and rolled out sideways from underneath to get it. A few seconds later the car suddenly slid forward and crashed down on to its brake drums. One of the bricks I had been using had pulverised into fragments, which had set the whole pile tumbling at each corner. The good Lord had really taken care of me that day, as if I had still been underneath I would have been crushed by the car and even if I had survived I was too far away from the billets for anyone to have heard my screams. I never again went under any car without being absolutely certain that it could not possibly fall off its supports.

The winter of 1953–54 was quite severe with occasional snow and a lot of frost. I did not put antifreeze in the Hillman because the only way to start it on a cold morning was to pour hot water into the radiator; the routine every night was to drain it so that it wouldn't freeze.

The offices in which we worked were also very cold, being heated only by braziers fed with briquettes made from coal dust. The resulting sulphurous smoke emitted by these over the whole of Southern Command headquarters on a cold morning was absolutely shocking. But the worst thing of all was the guard duty, which came round about every ten days. Two hours on – which meant wandering round the camp armed with a pickaxe handle – and four hours off. Whenever possible I contrived to be on the same roster as Alan, because he had a key to one of the office huts where we would go in and get the fire going, so that we could sit around it in reasonable comfort.

Another chore that had to be taken in turn was the job of returning the Secrets, as they were called, to the strong room. The Secrets were several box files and thick ledgers detailing all the mobilisation plans for Southern Command in the event of a national emergency. They were consulted by the officers working under command of my general, Major-General Murphy, and were entrusted to the chief clerk, a staff sergeant. At the end of the day he would give his bunch of keys to whoever was due to take the Secrets down to the safe in the strong room, and then the keys had to be handed back to him.

One evening I had gone to the pictures in Salisbury, and was astonished to see my name on the screen in the middle of the film. Then I read the legend: 'If this person is in the auditorium please see the manager' and underneath in hand writing was 'Pte Bladon'. Suddenly I knew what it was all about: the chief's big bunch of keys was still in my pocket, which meant not only that I had access to the Secrets but that he couldn't get into his room in the Sergeant's Mess. I tore out to the Hillman, which mercifully started straight away, and hurried back to find him sitting on the floor in the corridor outside his room. I expected the most tremendous dressing down, but in fact he took it in a very resigned way, almost like Captain Mainwaring saying 'You stupid boy.' Only later did I realise that the reason why I wasn't put on a charge was because he was not supposed to entrust the precious Secrets to a mere private.

At last I was allocated a date for my WOSB – the War Office Selection Board exam, which would determine if I was to be accepted for a commission and go to Officer Cadet School. But before that, there was more good news. An officer was wanting to sell his 1937 Vauxhall 14 DX. This was the previous model to the one my father had bought, but it sounded too good to be true when I learned that he would be happy to take £50 for it, and I was already in touch with a sergeant who was keen to buy the Hillman. I had warned him about the brakes, but he wasn't worried about them and said he knew someone in Transport who would sort them out for him. With another friend, Roy Alton, who was a driver in the RASC, I went to the barn where we had been told we would find the Vauxhall, and took it for a quick run.

'You can tell it's a f------- Vauxhall, can't you?' said Roy, as it emitted the characteristic Vauxhall whine in first gear. I was sold immediately, and the very next day the deal was done. I was paid £60 for the Hillman, so it left me with £10 over, which was a valuable bit of spare cash in those days.

FIVE

Vauxhall 14 DX

≣ While in my care for a year this unfortunate car was to be involved in
≣ three accidents

My first reasonably long journey in the big 1937 Vauxhall 14 DX series was to drive to Barton Stacey in Hampshire to attend the day of torture known as WOSB (the War Office Selection Board for candidates wanting to go for a commission). I was allowed a small mileage allowance in lieu of a railway warrant. The journey gave plenty of opportunity to assess the new car, and in most respects it was a vast improvement on the old Hillman. In particular, the 6-cylinder 2¼-litre engine was an absolute joy. It started always reliably at the first pull of the T-shaped starter control, was very quiet and gave far better performance. I could actually overtake things that were travelling in the same direction. The fact that it gave only about 27mpg instead of 34 with the Hillman was of no great consequence with petrol at 2s 3d a gallon. It was also far more comfortable with its independent front suspension by coil springs contained in an oil bath each side, all suspended from the kingpins and revolving with the steering. Although pretty worn, the pleated leather armchairs were also much more comfortable. But while in my care for a year this unfortunate Vauxhall was to be involved in three accidents.

The downside again was the brakes. At least they didn't pull erratically or wrap on with a horrible thud when reversing, but efficiency was terrible and one had to press very hard on the pedal. Again they were cable-operated. With the next model of the 14, of which my father had four, the coil-spring front suspension was replaced by short torsion bars, and the brakes were hydraulically operated.

Mingled with the satisfaction of driving a much better – and cheaper – car was my anxiety about the WOSB. It was vital not to make a mess of it and finish up spending the rest of my two years' National Service as a private doing mundane clerical work. I arrived at Barton Stacey, was checked in, met the other candidates, and was given a meal; then we all retired to bed early ready for a crack-of-dawn start. It was an exhausting day of interviews with senior officers, interspersed with all manner of practical tests.

There would be a small stream with a load to be taken across, but the planks provided were just too short, and the vital rope needed was on the other side. We each had to take it in turn to command the squad. 'Right,' said the one whose turn it was to lead, 'who's a good swimmer?' Several hands went up – never volunteer for anything in the army, but at WOSB always be keen to show enthusiasm. 'Right, I want you to strip off and swim across to get the rope.'

'Oh, just a minute,' interjected the supervising officer, 'I forgot to tell you there are alligators in the river.'

Undaunted, the candidate responded: 'Right, you and you run over there and catch a couple of those sheep. Then throw them in the river here and there, and while the alligators are enjoying them, you,' pointing to me, 'swim across and get the rope.' I think he earned quite good marks for that. Fortunately the whistle went before the plan was put into action!

Another test was the stamina and courage stage, with various tests to be accomplished in no more than five minutes. One was easy – just jump over a rope about 3ft high – but it only gained two marks. The clever thing was to include it on the way to something else. The most frightening task was to climb a tree using the footholds provided, get on to a platform about 15ft off the ground, then launch out to grab a rope that was well out of reach and climb down. It was a big earner in points, so I was determined to do it, but when I leapt off the platform with my hands open to clasp the rope, I hope I didn't look as terrified as I felt. I often wondered if anyone missed the rope and broke anything falling to the sand at the bottom.

The interviews seemed to go fairly well, and I was absolutely elated at the end of the day to learn that I had passed. All seemed well with the world when I climbed into the old Vauxhall and headed back to Wilton. A short time later my posting to Mons Officer Cadet School at Aldershot arrived.

I think General Murphy was quite sorry to see me go, and on the last day the buzzer went, calling me in to his office. I presumed that he had one final letter to dictate before my escape, and was surprised instead to find three more of the senior medical officers there, including Lieuenant-Col Humphreys and Major (Miss) Morrell who had always been very friendly towards me.

'We all wanted to wish you the best of luck in the next stage of your military career,' said General Murphy. There was a short discussion about the future, some questions about my past, where I had been to school and why I had given up medicine, and so on. Finally, he said: 'Well good luck, work hard and make sure you get your commission.' Having no headdress I couldn't salute, but did a smart move to attention, thanked them for their good wishes, assured them that I would do my utmost to achieve it and to be worthy of it, and left the room; and I jolly well will, I thought, as I closed the door. I wondered if any other would-be cadets had been given a send-off by a major general, a lieutenant-colonel and two majors. It was quite humbling and the chief clerk said: 'At least you won't be here to forget my keys again, will you?'

I was determined to do my damnedest to succeed at Mons. The thought of being among the quite high proportion rejected as not attaining the required standard and being RTU'd (returned to unit) was horrifying. Mons was six weeks of pretty fearful hell, with drill parades, platoon attacks tearing about on the Aldershot plains with rifle or Bren gun and full kit, interspersed with lectures and tests. At the end of the six weeks I certainly felt that I would never again in my life be as fit as I was then.

All the time we were under the watchful eye and roaring voice of Regimental Sergeant Major Brittain. After I had been at Mons for about a fortnight I realised that I should have requested permission to keep the Vauxhall at the barracks, so I applied to see the commanding officer (CO), and made sure that on the day I was to report, the car was parked on a street outside the barrack limits. In those days you could park a car almost anywhere without fear of theft, vandalism or as yet uninvented clamping. It was a lovely sunny morning at the end of March, and I was leaning on the balustrade outside the CO's office, chatting to another officer cadet when suddenly this terrifying roar started. 'You idle officer cadets, what do you think this is, a mother's tea party. Lounging about like a couple of old women having a nice little chat over the fence …' and so it went on.

We immediately smartened up, stood stiffly to attention, and I muttered out of the side of my mouth: 'Where the hell is he?'

A Canadian driver forgot what side of the road to use in Great Britain.

'I don't know,' said my friend. 'Can't see the devil.' Then equally abruptly he emerged from between two of the barrack huts, marching stiffly as always with his great yardstick under his left arm. He went on yelling at us until he was right behind us, and it was quite deafening.

Eventually he departed with curses about the standard of would-be officers: 'You want to be in command of men? I wouldn't put you in command of washing up at the Women's Institute!'

When my turn to see the adjutant came, I was marched in, stated my request, and was asked: 'Where is it now?' Fortunately I was able to reply that it was parked outside the barracks.

'Taxed?'

'Yes, sir.'

'Insured?'

'Yes, sir.'

'Permission granted.' Immediately the roar from the sergeant who had marched me in: 'Salute. Right turn. Quick march, left-right-left-right …'

That's how it was all the time, the only concession being that on parade, officer cadets were addressed as 'sir', so the sort of ridiculous conversation with the RSM standing behind during parade inspection went:

'Ham I harting you, sar?'

'No, sir.'

'Well I should be, sar,' almost in a whisper, 'because,' now in a roar, 'I'm standing on your back hair. Get it cut, sar. March 'im down to the barber's shop.'

RSM Brittain had the remarkable ability to single out an individual on a big parade. On one occasion a cadet had an insect land on his face. He tolerated it for a bit, then quickly put a hand up to his face to flick it off, hoping the movement wouldn't be noticed.

'Sergeant Cullam,' the great voice roared.

'Sir!' And then the instructions: 'Sergeant Cullam, two paces step forward, *march*. Sergeant Cullam, left turn, *quick march*.' Then after a while: '*Halt. Left turn.* Now, the officer cadet in front of you there, picking his nose on parade. Tike 'is nime.'

That was always the big threat – take his name, which meant one would be on a charge resulting in some trifling but irritating punishment. And the threat always was that if one did this or that you would 'lose your name', meaning that your name would be taken.

After six exhausting weeks at Mons, it was all over, and with immense relief I heard my name among those listed as 'posted to Buller'. This was the next stage of the commissioning process where we were to spend ten weeks at the Royal Army Service Corps (RASC) barracks named after a famous officer, General Sir Redvers Buller. The actual barracks was only about a mile from Mons, and if the wind was blowing the right way we could hear RSM Brittain's voice booming across from the parade ground.

The sergeant major at Buller Barracks was always immaculately turned out, and this applied also to his Hillman 10 saloon, which never had so much as a speck of dirt on its glistening black paintwork.

I enjoyed the ten weeks at Buller, where there was much less of the frantic discipline but still a lot of hard work with lectures about RASC procedure, night operations, convoy runs and lessons on camouflage, supplies for the troops, defensive positions, battle attacks and so on. There was still plenty of shouting, but it was mainly from the excellent Captain in charge of us, whose famous command was: 'Get your bloody head down, there's no divine right of commanders.' In other words, just because one was giving orders one was just as likely to be shot as anyone else. On journeys out to the battle training area he would often follow our truck in his beautiful Daimler convertible.

In the middle of the course came 1 May, and my twenty-first birthday. We never knew whether we would be given the weekend off from Saturday parade, or kept in for extra work. I think we always tried our damnedest, but sometimes we were 'an idle lot of gentlemen, not fit to carry the Queen's commission', and at other times we were 'beginning to get there', and 'I might be able to make something of you yet.' As it turned out 1 May was one of the good days, so I was able to get into the Vauxhall and drive home to Coventry to find quite unawares that a small party had been arranged to celebrate the occasion. They were a bit shocked to hear that if things had turned out badly I might have been unable to get home.

The build-up to commissioning came gradually, with the arrival of tailors to measure us for our new uniforms, and interviews as to where we would like to be posted. Unwisely in retrospect, I missed the chance of an interesting overseas posting and asked instead for a UK position, and was allocated to 20 Company RASC at Shorncliffe near Folkestone. Then came the final week, and we were told that the GOC was going to take the passing-out parade. 'How lucky you are, you officer cadets, to have the General Officer Commanding for your passing-out parade,' roared the sergeant major. But we groaned inwardly, knowing that we weren't lucky at all because it meant the turn-out would have to be specially sparkling.

Parents were invited to attend the passing-out parade, so my father and stepmother came down to see it on a lovely afternoon in May, after which I packed everything into the Vauxhall and we set off to return to Coventry in convoy. Within half an hour my unfortunate Vauxhall 14 DX had its first accident. We were on a secondary road and I came over the brow of a small hill to be confronted by a black car on my side of the road. With more experience I might have avoided the accident with a last second swerve, but all I could think to do was to steer to the left giving the oncoming car more space, and brake as hard as possible. The Vauxhall stopped quite effectively, but skidded once it was on the grass, and there was a sickening crunch as it hit the oncoming car head on. It was an Austin A40 Somerset, and my car's front bumper went over the top of the Austin's and made a frightful mess of the front. The impact speed was not very great so neither I nor the driver of the other car was hurt.

'What the hell were you thinking of?' I yelled to him, as I got out of the car.

'Wait a minute, wait a minute,' he kept saying. It turned out that he was a Canadian over here on holiday, had hired the Austin, and temporarily forgotten what side of the road to drive on.

His car had a smashed radiator and was a tow-in job, but my faithful Vauxhall had taken it quite well and was still roadworthy. After getting all the details from the other driver I was able to continue on my way. One would have thought it was a clear-cut case, and the repairs to my car were only about £100, but it was a terrible battle to get the money out of the hire company's insurers. The pictures taken at the scene showed pretty conclusively that the impact occurred well over on the grass verge on my side of the road.

The Vauxhall was still at the Vauxhall dealer in Coventry, when my two weeks' posting leave was up, and I was due to report first to the area commander near Hounslow, and then to my new unit at Folkestone. So I went by train, travelling in uniform and very self-conscious, in first class. A staff car met me at Folkestone station, making me feel very important, and after introduction to the CO, Major Touzell, he took me on a tour of the company and its vehicles. He seemed to be impressed by my knowledge of cars, because he decided to put me in charge of the 'staff car platoon' instead of the 'transport' one. It meant that instead of having some thirty trucks, mainly 3-ton Austin lorries, I had a mixture of cars and eight ambulances under my command. It was a much more interesting assignment, and I enjoyed my time at Shorncliffe.

After the crash the Vauxhall 14 looked sad, but was still driveable.

One of the first things Captain Oddey, who was second in command to Major Touzel, demanded was that all his officers should be able to ride motorcycles, so we had some training time set aside for motorcycling and when he was satisfied that we were good enough he signed 'pass' certificates for me and the other subaltern. We were able to have our driving licences upgraded to include motorcycles. I then found that motorcycling counted as 'recreational exercise' so every Wednesday afternoon instead of playing football or rugger I went off on a motorbike, sometimes with a corporal who was equally enthusiastic for riding, and sometimes on my own. Much preferred was the Norton 350, but if this was not available I would have to take one of the BSA 500s, which had a side-valve engine and a rigid frame with no rear springing.

Armed with the OS map I would ride all over the little lanes and tracks of Kent. On one afternoon I stopped the Norton engine and climbed off to open a gate but couldn't restart it. Miles from anywhere I wondered what to do; inevitably there was no toolkit in the box where it should have been. I trudged on up the hill, and over the brow I saw a lone cottage. To my great joy there was a man in the front garden working on a motorcycle. The great camaraderie of all motorcyclists applied, and he came back with me to the abandoned Norton where it was the work of a moment to get the spark plug out, remove the whisker that had formed over the electrode and get the engine running again.

Many of my vehicles were on detachment at places such as Dover Castle and Canterbury, and it was an essential part of the job to drive over and inspect them, always using a staff car, sometimes with a driver and sometimes alone. I used the Wolseley 1800 quite often, or the Austin 16, but preferred the Vauxhall Velox. This had a later version of the 6-cylinder OHV (overhead-valve) engine that was in my car but of course was far better although only with a three-speed gearbox and column-mounted gear change.

I had two of these in the platoon, but one of them was constantly VOR (vehicle off road) being worked on at the LAD (light aid detachment). 'Water in the bloody fuel,' I was told. 'Can't find how it's getting in there.' Then one day when it was my turn to be duty officer and my tour of inspection took in the NAAFI, I saw one of my drivers in a clinch with one of the NAAFI girls. My suspicions were aroused when I realised that this was the driver allocated to the Velox, which was always having water-in-fuel problems. So when it came out of the workshops I posted a corporal to keep watch from a nearby barracks when the driver washed the car. Sure enough when he came to the back of the car he looked around, then flipped open the filler cap and squirted the hose into the fuel tank! He was duly charged, and was taken off driving and put on cookhouse fatigues for a long time.

A big inspection was due with a visit by an RASC brigadier, and we had to have everything in tip-top condition including two vehicles for him to inspect. One of these was selected as the better of the two Veloxes, and by the time my team had finished working on it its condition was absolutely brilliant. You could have eaten your sandwiches off the engine, but to my utter dismay it was failed. Later, when the brigadier was being entertained in the officers' mess I had the opportunity to ask him what had been wrong with the Vauxhall.

'Suspension,' he replied, 'wrapping up underneath. Every time you put the brakes on, the front of the car goes up.' I found it hard to conceal my contempt for an officer claiming to be an engineer who didn't know that this was a characteristic of every Vauxhall with Dubonnet independent suspension. The torque reaction on the wheel carrier arm under braking had the effect of making the front of the car lift instead of depressing. Much later cars have what is called anti-dive engineered into their suspension design. What a clot, I thought, that he didn't know that.

In the autumn we had a fortnight's training at the army's battle exercise area in Norfolk, which was quite instructive. On the return convoy run to Folkestone I was one of the last to leave, with a corporal to share the driving, in a Humber staff car. It had a 4-litre side-valve engine, and huge balloon tyres, but it went quite well and on one of the straights out of Norfolk with little traffic around on Sunday morning I managed to wind it up to nearly an indicated 90mph, the fastest I had ever driven.

After going round the North Circular Road and then down on to A20 – there being no Dartford Tunnel then, of course – we came across one of our 3-ton Austin trucks stationary beside the road. On stopping to find out what was up, I was surprised to learn that it had run out of fuel, since we had calculated that all the vehicles should get back to Folkestone without a fuel stop, but just in case, each vehicle carried a 20-litre (we called it then 4½-gallon) jerrycan of petrol. The driver had already started pouring the fuel in, and succeeded in spilling it everywhere because of the poor access. Then he got back into the cab and, before I realised what he was going to do, tried to start the engine. Immediately the whole of the front of the truck was engulfed in flame, and our Humber was not far away, too. One thing the army was very good about was the provision of fire extinguishers in vehicles, and I grabbed the one out of the Humber and was impressed to find how quickly and effectively it put the fire out, even though it meant squirting it up from underneath. The corporal tried to open the bonnet and burnt his fingers.

When we did get the bonnet open we found that the metal petrol pipe had fractured, and when questioned, the gormless driver confessed that, yes, they had been smelling petrol as they drove along. It had been quite a close call because the jerrycan, still half full and with its cap open, was standing by the roadside awash with spilt petrol. Soon the LAD back-up vehicle arrived and commenced repairs.

After home leave over Christmas, I returned to the unit and immediately fell ill with my old problem – sickness and violent stomach ache, which had dogged me repeatedly through my years at school. It was always any change of diet that brought it on, and it's amazing that with a doctor for a father the cause was not investigated. But now in the army, a new interest was taken in the problem. A lieutenant in the RAMC, who I learned had also been to King's London and Westminster Medical

School and was now doing his postponed National Service, took full details of the history of my repeated stomach problems. I told him how there had been three new matrons at School House during my five years at Malvern, and for all of them I had been their first patient, falling ill at the very beginning of term. He referred me to the district medical consultant, who confirmed his view that I should have my appendix removed.

I was duly given a date to report to the Royal Herbert Military Hospital at Woolwich with a first-class rail warrant, which I was able to change for a mileage allowance to go up by car. When I arrived at the Royal Herbert and turned in towards the parking area, a soldier came out of his little hut, lifted the pole, saluted and then exclaimed: 'Good God, Bladon; sorry, sir.' Immediately I recognised him: it was Roy Alton, who had been with me at Southern Command headquarters and had come with me to advise on that first trip in the Vauxhall.

It was strange being admitted to hospital while feeling perfectly fit, but next day the operation was carried out, and I felt fine again provided I didn't laugh; if I did there was an excruciating pain. One of the officers in the ward, a Captain who had been very seriously injured in a car crash in Malta, had a great sense of humour and found innocent merriment in making me laugh. When he heard that I had driven myself to the hospital and that my car was in the yard he was beside himself with excitement. If I would drive him to London, along with two other officers who were also recovering from various injuries, we could have dinner at the Savoy and all I would have to pay for was the petrol to get them there and back. The Savoy responded magnificently, and provided staff to carry him and one of the other disabled officers from the car to a wheelchair, and I was allowed to leave the Vauxhall in the reserved area at the front of the Savoy, adjoining the Strand. We had a great evening, although I didn't have much appetite and had to keep pleading, 'please don't make me laugh, it's killing me!'

On the way back to Woolwich, the Vauxhall suddenly conked out, only about 2 miles from the hospital. It was most embarrassing for me with three officers, two of whom were unable to walk. Fortunately, a car stopped and gave the three of them a lift, and I said I would walk, after running the car back on to the verge and leaving a little notice on it to explain that it had broken down. It was a cold, crisp night, and although the operation scar was giving me some discomfort I managed to reach the hospital alright.

'What sort of car is it?' one of the other officers in the ward asked next day. 'Well,' came the reply, 'it's as only an RASC officer's car can be!' and I knew what that meant. I was informed that the appendix that they removed had indeed been badly diseased, and afterwards I never had any recurrence of the stomach problem, which had plagued me for years. So this was another good thing I obtained from my National Service. I also cured the problem with the Vauxhall, on finding that fuel was not reaching the carburettor due to a faulty fuel pump. I had earlier had suspicions about it and managed to get hold of a service kit of replacement valves for the pump, so all I had to do on a very cold morning was remove and strip the mechanical pump, fit the new valves, and it then ran perfectly back to Folkestone.

A few weeks later towards the end of February, I went home to Coventry for the weekend – a long drive that involved going all the way up the A20, right across London and then through Radlett, where I was later destined to live for thirty-three years, and up the A5. During the weekend it snowed. Unlike many people I always relished the challenge of driving on snow, and was quite disappointed when it started to thaw and turned to sleet for my journey home. There was very little traffic because of the weather, but on the A45, before it joined the A5 at Daventry, I caught up a lorry. It was throwing up a lot of slush and grit, so I decided to overtake, but the road at that time was only a single-carriageway three-lane road, and when I was in the little-used centre lane I was ploughing through a lot of rutted slush and the whole car began to snake. There was suddenly a terrific thump at the back and I knew I had hit the lorry, but at least the gyrations stopped. I looked in the mirror and at first saw no sign of the lorry, then moved my head and saw that it had gone right off the road.

I stopped, got out in the wind and sleet, and heard the lorry driver yell what sounded like 'Halt!' but might have been 'Help!' He became quite frantic when I got back in the car, but I had no intention of driving on and leaving him, and reversed back. I apologised – something one was later told never to do – and asked how I could help. 'Take me to the Blue Boar,' he said. 'My mates there will soon get me back on the road.' My Vauxhall had a nasty crease on the left rear wing, which had contacted his front offside wheel, but there was no damage to the lorry, which had just sunk into the soft grass verge and come to rest. At the Blue Boar café he refused any further help, and I continued on my way.

One morning I went out to parade and noticed a lot of damage to the rear of the Vauxhall parked at the back of the officers' mess and after lengthy enquiries learned that it had been hit by the duty ration truck during the night, and that the army driver knew he had hit a car but did not report it, hoping to get away with it. He was duly charged, punished and had ten days' loss of pay. I submitted a claim to the War Office but had enormous difficulty in getting settlement. It was only after some quite furious correspondence that a War Dept cheque arrived to settle the unfortunate Vauxhall's third accident, and I was able to get repairs carried out at Folkestone including the crease on the rear wing on the other side, which cost a few pounds extra.

With the arrival of April I became increasingly uneasy about the future. My two years' National Service were drawing to a close, and I was due for 'run out', as they called it, in May. I had been writing to everyone I could think of in the hope of a job connected with cars, journalism or the motor industry. All sorts of firms were written to: the AA, Ferodo, Rootes, *The Motor* and *The Autocar*, Shell and so on.

The ritual of opening 'sorry, no vacancies' letters became a source of merriment at the breakfast table in the officers' mess. *The Kent Messenger* drew a blank, but I was offered an interview at *The Kentish Express* at Ashford. The result left me very despondent on hearing what was on offer in both terms and salary. I began to reconcile myself to the fact that I could do worse than apply for a short service commission, giving me a further three years in the RASC. Then one day there was a more encouraging response. Arthur Bourne, the editorial director of *The Autocar* wrote that there were 'one or two opportunities for some first class young men on the staff of the journal', and advised me to make contact with his assistant, Mr Jarvis, to arrange a mutually convenient appointment for me to attend their offices near Waterloo for an interview. In the meantime would I submit some samples of the kind of article I thought would be of interest to readers of *The Autocar*.

I worked late into the night on them and sent articles on running cars on a minimal budget, and how the vehicles of the army were maintained and controlled. The day agreed for my interview was the Thursday before Easter, and I was allowed to take a day's leave tacked on to the Easter holiday. I drove up in the Vauxhall and parked right outside the offices of Iliffe & Sons, Dorset House in Stamford Street. A car parked there now wouldn't last five minutes! Smartly dressed in my best suit, I reported to reception.

The editor, Maurice Smith, soon put me at ease though he had a daunting way of talking very rapidly, asking several questions all at once, and then hardly waiting for the answers before chattering on again. Suddenly he said: 'I don't think old Bourne will frighten you, let's see if he's there.' He grabbed the house phone and quickly dialled a number, and then I heard him say, 'I have young Bladon here, would Mr Bourne like to see him?' Then I could hardly believe my ears when he said that if Bourne agreed to take me on to the staff I would probably be started on about £500 a year, subject to six-monthly review. My pay at the start of National Service had been £1 5s a week (about £60 a year), and after commissioning it was still only around £270 a year.

It became better. When I was taken up to see Arthur Bourne and sat in his plush oak-lined and carpeted office, the interview went well. He wanted to know in particular what I thought about motorcycles, and I was able to respond with enthusiasm, telling him that army officers were encouraged to ride motorcycles and that it was accepted as recreational training on Wednesday afternoons, in lieu of playing football. Only later did I discover that he had been editor of Iliffe's other publication *The Motor Cycle* for many years. Without saying so in so many words, he made it pretty clear that I could have the job on *The Autocar* at a salary of £600 a year, and the prospect for the future was 'salary of around £1,500 a year and your car provided by the age of 35'. A letter would be sent to confirm the arrangement, and when I said that I was going on north from here to my home at Coventry, I was told to give the address to 'Jarvo', as he called him – his industrious assistant Mr Jarvis.

Repairs left the Vauxhall looking better than it was before.

There was no post on Good Friday, but the letter duly arrived on the Saturday and I was absolutely elated: I was appointed to the editorial staff of *The Autocar* on a starting salary of £600 a year. On Bank Holiday Monday I had to drive back to Folkestone, and was descending the A45 down the hill into Daventry when a policeman decided to stop the traffic and let the bottled-up column out from the A5 junction on the left. With those awful cable brakes I knew there was no way I could stop, but what the Vauxhall lacked in braking it made up for in having very powerful horns. I blasted the horn and the policeman jumped back on to the pavement, saving his life!

As I drove on to London I realised that this had been a very narrow escape. I wouldn't have hit him, but it would have been a frightening incident, and now that I had good job prospects I must trade the Vauxhall in for something better. The following weekend I made a trawl of the Folkestone car dealers and found a Morris Minor Tourer for sale at £375. It seemed a hell of a lot of money but spread over two years with hire purchase it wouldn't be too bad, and the dealer allowed £75 for the Vauxhall. Later I saw it with a price of £100 displayed on the windscreen.

On the last night before 'run out' an officer was allowed to order drinks for himself and any fellow officers without charge, and stupidly I drank far too much, leading to a terrible hangover next day. The army didn't let one sneak away unnoticed, and there had to be an interview with the commanding officer, with such questions as why one was deserting the service, what job was lined up, and how would the pay compare? Eventually it was over and I threw my kit into the little Morris and set off for London. In some ways I was sad to be leaving the army job, which I had enjoyed for a year, but I was eagerly looking forward to the new one.

S I X

FRAZER NASH

He lived only long enough to give his name and say he was
from *The Autocar*

I was interviewed by the editorial director, Arthur Bourne, before being taken on to the staff of *The Autocar*. After asking me a wide range of questions, he suddenly asked if there was anything about the magazine that I wanted to know. I asked about a number of detail matters and then, since it showed that I had read the magazine, asked how the accident had happened in which John Cooper had been killed. Bourne gave what was probably the most accurate answer: 'Nobody really knows.' Then he went on: 'I was only once a passenger in a car when he was driving, and on that occasion he was driving fast but very ably, so it's a mystery to know what went wrong.'

But later I heard more about it and was able to put together the likely picture of what happened on that fateful day in March 1955. John Cooper was the sports editor of *The Autocar*, but he also took a keen interest in the road-test side. When a Frazer Nash came in for road test and the test team reported that its top speed was 'only' around 95mph, Cooper declared that it should surely do more. For any high-performance car in those days a top speed of more than 'the ton' was an important credential. So at the weekend he took it away in quest of the magic 100mph.

In 1955 there were not many places where such a speed could be attained. Another three years would pass before the first mile of motorway was built – the Preston bypass, opened by Prime Minister Harold Macmillan, and later to become part of M6 – and what few dual carriageways there were tended to be short and full of traffic. The best chance was the A11 road to Newmarket, which offered many long and level straights, and it's generally thought that Cooper was headed there. On the way, he took the A505 road from Baldock to Royston, and may have seen an inviting clear stretch and decided to have a go.

In those days, parking restrictions, clearways, open-road speed limits and yellow lines were all unheard of, and the British motorist of the 1950s had no qualms about stopping anywhere. People could and did even stop their cars, sometimes on a blind bend, and have a picnic. As bad luck would have it, on this occasion they weren't having a picnic, but two cars were stationary, one on each side of the road facing in opposite directions, and a car was coming through the gap between them when Cooper arrived at what is generally thought to be enormous speed. The 'speed kills' lobby would have had a field day.

There was nowhere for Cooper to go and, although the Frazer Nash would have had good brakes, disc brakes and anti-lock control were years away. I understand that a woman, possibly in the process of getting into one of the parked cars, was killed outright, and Cooper lived only long enough to give his name and say he was from *The Autocar*.

When the message came through that one of the staff had been killed driving a silver sports car, people were mystified at first. Later it turned out that the impact had been so severe that most of the green paintwork had shattered off the aluminium bodywork making it look like a silver car instead of a green one.

In the aftermath, life had to go on, and production of the journal had to continue. A short news item, which I had read, announced with regret the death of Cooper, and a little later it was declared that his position as sports editor was to be taken by Peter Garnier, who had been employed in the news and general features section. It meant that there was a vacancy at the bottom of the staff register, and my letter on headed notepaper of the officers' mess, Shorncliffe, seeking a position on the staff, could not have landed on the editor's desk at a more appropriate time.

SEVEN

MORRIS MINOR TOURER

If I thought I was going to the Le Mans 24-hour race, I was doomed to disappointment

Shortly before I was due to leave the army, the breakfast table at Shorncliffe officers' mess, so accustomed to my despondent groans on opening yet another letter saying 'no vacancies for unqualified ex-National Service officers', were startled to hear me yell, 'Whoopee, I'm going to Le Mans.'

'What's Le Mans?' enquired one officer.

The letter, on the notepaper of Iliffe and Sons, publishers of *The Autocar*, had at first filled me with dread; surely they hadn't changed their minds and didn't want me after all? But when I read the contents, signed by the editorial director, Arthur Bourne, I was elated. 'When I suggested that you should commence work for *The Autocar* on 8th June, 1955,' he wrote, 'I had overlooked the incidence of Le Mans. It would therefore be better if you would start on Monday, 1st June, 1955.'

But if I thought I was going to the Le Mans 24-hour race, I was doomed to disappointment; I wasn't even going to start on *The Autocar*. The editor, Maurice Smith, had been appointed only a few months earlier, and he was already editor of Iliffe's sister magazine *Flight*, a job he was eminently qualified to do as a former RAF bomber pilot awarded DFC and Bar. He felt that his new title *The Autocar* was a shambles and he didn't want me to pick up bad habits. So to start with I would work on *Flight* as assistant to the sub-editor, Roy Casey.

Although I was desperately keen to begin on *The Autocar*, it wasn't a bad move, and I learnt a lot about journalism and publication from Roy. I was writing from press releases about high-duty alloys, the structure of aero-engine turbo fans and all sorts of things that I didn't understand, but it was good practice, and my speed of typing accurately, acquired in the days long before computers made it easy for everyone to produce clean copy, was appreciated.

The mechanism of publishing a weekly magazine was every bit as impressive as I had expected. I would be given a press release or other document and told to write a news piece from it. My typescript – 'always double-spaced, please, and on only one side of the sheet; oh, and always keep a carbon copy otherwise you'll be crying your heart out if it gets lost' – would be handed to Roy, who would read it and perhaps make a few changes before giving it back to me so that I could see what had been altered and learn from the mistakes. Then I would put it in one of the 'copy to printer' folders and drop it in the 'post out' basket. About every hour one or two girls would come in, pick up the folders and drop another lot in the 'post in' basket. Within an hour or so I would have the 'galley' – the proof from the printer of what I had written, now set in type. The galley was a long sheet, later to be cut up, stuck down in the appropriate place on the make-up page. The speed of the operation was owed to the fact that the printers, Cornwall Press, were in an adjacent building and connected by vacuum tube. The girls who took and delivered the copy folders took them to a central office, put them in a transparent cylinder and fed them into a suction tube. As a 4-year-old boy I had watched with fascination a similar arrangement when my mother took me to the grocers in Coventry, and put her money in the tube which went up to the accounts department, returning a minute or so later with the change. The make-up page showing the printers where the pictures would go, with appropriate captions, was sent back the same way, and in due course a proof of the page would arrive.

Pictures in those early days were also an elaborate system. The photograph would go first to 'the retouchers' who would use airbrush and other implements to make it sharper. Then it went across the road by messenger to the block makers who would use the old-fashioned acid-etching technique to make a copperplate mounted on a piece of wood, which then went to the printers. How very much easier it is now, with digital printing, but we didn't have such facilities in the 1950s. What we did have was a process called photogravure, which was a photographic system giving better quality but taking longer. While the letterpress pages of the journal went from writing the copy to seeing it in the published magazine only three days later, the gravure sections went to press about a week earlier.

I was keen to learn all this but was also anxious to meet my future colleagues on *The Autocar* and begin writing about something that I understood. The only one I had met so far was the editor, Maurice Smith, who frequently came up to the *Flight* offices, and on the Monday of my second week he gave graphic accounts of the terrible accident that had happened at the Le Mans 24-hour race when the Mercedes-Benz of Pierre Levegh had crashed and somersaulted into the crowd, killing eighty-three spectators. Twelve more died later in hospital, bringing the fatality total to ninety-five.

At about that time a railway strike was called, and a notice was put up listing employees who drove to work with their offices, home addresses and car registration numbers so that those who normally came up by train could make contact and perhaps get a ride to work. It was a valuable list for me, enabling me to find out who they were and go down to the car park to see what cars they had. Maurice Smith had the best of all, of course, an Aston Martin DB2/4 convertible. The associate editor, Michael Brown, had a Riley 1½-litre, and I admired the Sunbeam Talbot 90

With no parking controls, I was able to work on the Minor in Beaufort Gardens.

of Peter Garnier, the newly appointed sports editor. Up in the main car park above the covered area was my humble Morris Minor Tourer.

My friend from prep-school days, David Dixon, had completed his National Service in the Navy, and now had a job at Dunlop's head office in Piccadilly. He was in digs in Beaufort Gardens, Knightsbridge, close to Harrods, and was able to find me a room in the same building, with the advantage that I could park the little Morris outside. Beaufort Gardens was a no through road with a pleasant open garden area in the centre. Those were the days of easy parking in London.

After an instructive but slightly frustrating couple of weeks, two members of the staff of *The Autocar* spoke to me at lunch in the canteen, and asked when I was going to join them. Harold Holt was a pompous but friendly little Yorkshireman and was *The Autocar's* sub-editor, equivalent to Roy Casey. The other, tall and always untidily dressed, was John Davey, who wrote the ever popular feature called 'Disconnected Jottings' as well as being responsible for the feature dealing with new products and accessories. I replied that I was eager to join them and they said they

A chilly morning in February 1956, and the Minor had no heater.

would see what they could do to 'spur Maurice on'. Shortly afterwards I was told to leave *Flight* and start next week on *The Autocar*.

At first I was very much underemployed, working on the News and Views pages in the same office as Harold Holt, and all the time asking if I could help on this or that, gradually getting more and more work. I was also entrusted with assignments that involved using my own car. The first time I did this I was advised by colleagues to put in expenses for an outrageous amount of petrol and oil, but it came back with a note from the director, Arthur Bourne, saying 'please advise engine capacity so that I can allocate a mileage allowance'. I learned that this was fixed in three stages: 5½*d* up to 1,000cc, 8½*d* up to 1,600cc, and 10½*d* over 1,600cc. I realised I would have done much better to have a car with a bigger engine, which would almost double the mileage allowance yet wouldn't cost twice as much to run.

As the months passed rapidly I managed to get more involved with work on the journal but also became caught up in the absurd working hours. We didn't start the day until about 9.30 a.m., but on press days (Tuesday and Friday) we were invariably still hard at it at 9 p.m. The worst time came just before the London Show in October, when the editor had left rather vague directions as to what he wanted for the big show number and then disappeared to the Paris Show. We were all still there at 11 p.m., but earlier we had gone down to the car park to get our cars out before they became locked in for the night. The printers emerged from the adjacent Cornwall Press and made envious comments about our fleet of interesting cars, and I was flattered to hear one of them exclaim: 'I'll settle for the little Minor Tourer.'

However, I was becoming disenchanted with the Morris, which, as I had found on that first long journey from Folkestone up to London, was desperately slow. Its little 903cc side-valve engine gave no power for overtaking, and the maximum speed was only about 60mph, but it was certainly a joy to have at last a car with decent hydraulically operated brakes.

One concern was the terrible rattle from the front suspension over the slightest bump, and when talking to colleagues about it I learned that there was a modification. The very simple suspension of the Minor, which had been so praised for its good handling, was by torsion bars connected directly to the lower suspension arm, and the upper arm comprised a lever-arm shock absorber – or, as I was now being told to call it, suspension damper. This incorporated a housing with internal screw thread, which allowed the vertical wheel carrier to turn with the steering. They had been made of bronze, which wasn't strong enough and wore rapidly. I purchased new ones made of steel, and, working in the open in Beaufort Gardens one weekend, unbolted the old bronze ones and screwed on the new steel ones. The result was a big improvement.

Encouraged by my success with the front suspension, I decided that the Minor might perform better if it were given the process known as decarbonisation –

long since discontinued – and John Davey put me in touch with a firm that would machine the cylinder head for me at no great cost, to increase the compression ratio. I found the Morris Minor's side-valve engine was certainly easy to work on, as I removed the cylinder head on a Saturday in Beaufort Gardens, and carefully cleaned the pistons and valves. On Monday morning I went to work on the Underground with the cylinder head in a carrier bag, and had it back a few days later, ready for fitting the following weekend. It made a substantial difference to the performance, but I thought the Minor was still awfully slow, and was anxious to change it for something else. The problem was that I was tied into two years of hire purchase, and was still a long way off accumulating the money to pay it off. I would have to keep on saving, which I was able to do quite well since my £600 annual salary left a lot of cash over at the end of each month. I think the rent at Beaufort Gardens, which included breakfast brought up to the bedroom by a servant girl, was only about £2 per week. The generous expense allowances were helping, and the time would soon come, I felt, when I would be able to settle the hire purchase money and buy something else.

E I G H T

SINGER HUNTER

Now adopted as Peterborough Airport, Glatton was an abandoned airfield used for testing

Road tests always involved two members of staff, one to do most of the driving and write the report about the car, which usually ran to about 2,000 words, and on the day of testing a second person to read the instruments and write down the data figures recording what the car achieved. I was tremendously keen to be involved in this, and delighted when I was told to go to Coventry station early in the morning in July 1955 and meet up with Charles Haywood to help him with a road test. Although I would have loved 90 miles at 5½d, I was to go by train because I was to bring the car back to London for the rest of the road-test staff to try it.

An ex-army major, Charles was tall and very expressive, always saying what he thought, garnished with suitable swear words. Everything was 'oh, that bloody game of soldiers!' He was *The Autocar's* Midlands editor, based at our Coventry office, and we met at Coventry station and then drove to Glatton. I had heard a lot about Glatton and was keen to see it, though somewhat disappointed when we got there. It was one of the many aircraft runways hurriedly laid down at the beginning of the war, but since abandoned, and the journal paid a rent of £100 a year to be able to carry out testing on it. Nowadays it has been smartened up and adopted as Peterborough Airport.

Before we went there, the first port of call was the small garage of W. Ratcliffe & Son on the A1 trunk road, where we were welcomed and Charles set to installing the fifth wheel. This was a rather crude device comprising the wheel of an auto cycle driving a small generator by cable, and the generator gave impulses to a large electric speedometer, guaranteed to be dead accurate. I would sit in the passenger seat with this speedometer, mounted on a wooden board, on my lap. Then there were the stopwatches – two of them, each with a split hand so that each watch would give two time readouts.

With everything installed, the rear bumper of the car removed and left propped up in Ratcliffe's garage and the fifth wheel frame bolted to the bumper bracket, we set off, hopefully to the Glatton airfield – but no, we stopped at the Railway Arms pub, where again Charles was greeted like an old friend. After beers and sandwiches we at last made our way to Glatton and testing started.

First it was straightforward acceleration testing and I soon had the hang of working the stopwatches which enabled me to do 0–30, 50, 60 and 70 acceleration times all in one run. Then we turned round to do the run the other way, cancelling out the effect of wind. The published figures would be the average of runs in opposite directions. I made the obvious comment that the runway was by no means level and we were now testing uphill. Charles agreed, but said that it averaged out. We then had to repeat the runs but this time I had to be looking out for the quarter-mile and kilometre markers. A lot of importance was attached to the standing quarter-mile figure. What about 0–10 and 0–20? I asked. 'Oh, we don't do those,' I was told. 'We used to do just 0–30 and 0–50, because that was all that most cars could manage, but recently it has been decided that we will soon take in 0–40 as well.'

Then came the accelerations in the gears. 'Let me see the speedo, and give me the watch,' said Charles, so I tilted it towards him, and at exactly 30 or 40 he would click the stopwatch to start it running at the precise moment when he put the accelerator down to the floor, and then hand it to me to stop it 20mph later. The idea was that we were timing acceleration from, say, 40 to 60mph, but this was the last time it was done this way. On all future tests the car was timed already in flat-out acceleration in the chosen gear, from the lowest speed which it would pull, usually as little as 10mph, to the last 10mph increment before maximum revs.

There were other tests to be done: tractive effort or torque, with a Tapley meter, and braking efficiency using a strange Mintex U-tube fixed to the windscreen.

It went on for what seemed like ages, and then it was back to Ratcliffe's to dismantle the fifth wheel and put the bumper back on. Finally we were back to the Coventry office, where Charles climbed out saying that he had another test car there to go home in, and I set off for London.

The car we had been bullying all afternoon was a Singer Hunter, which impressed me quite well. It had a kind of horse's head mascot on the bonnet, and with a 1,497cc OHC (overhead camshaft) engine it motored along very well – anything seemed fast after my Morris Minor – and I had a good journey down to London at the end of a long and rather exhausting day. But the wonderful thing was that it was Friday, so I had the use of the Hunter until Monday morning. On Saturday I drove it down to Reigate and took my old school friend Alan Davies for a ride in it. In one way it was like being in the army again with the free use of a car but with the difference that I could take this one wherever I liked.

I had enjoyed working with Charles Haywood, and I realised that he was a very competent driver. The miles that he drove me that day were to be the first of many, but he never made a mistake and never gave me an anxious moment.

NINE

SUNBEAM MARK III

If any drivers are sticking rigidly to the 30 limit with a string of traffic behind trying to get past, we would fail them for lack of consideration

'We get an awful lot of these things,' said Michael Brown, 'and very often they come to nothing. But this one may succeed because there are some good people behind it. So go down and check it out. They'll probably want you to take their new advanced driving test,' he warned.

Brilliant journalist, industrious and a very good driver, Michael Brown was associate editor of *The Autocar* when I joined the staff in 1955, and I learned much from him. He should really have been appointed editor after the abrupt departure of the former editor, H.S. Linfield, but Maurice Smith, son of Iliffe director Geoffrey Smith, was appointed editor of *The Autocar* in addition to the editorship of *Flight* magazine, which he already held.

The job Michael was giving me was to cover the formation of the Institute of Advanced Motorists, and the date was Thursday 21 June 1956. Armed with the invitation to 'find out all about the new Institute', I went down to a hotel near Putney and sat in the back of a Sunbeam Mark III to await my turn. In the driving seat was Richard Bensted-Smith, who was on the staff of *The Motor*. Dick was later to become editor of *The Motor* and then left to set up the huge organisation Newspress, which now handles most of the publicity for the motor industry. He unfortunately died in 2011.

We had a long conversation about the new IAM project with the person in the front passenger seat, who turned out to be George Eyles, the newly appointed chief examiner of the fledgling IAM. George was the owner of the Sunbeam Mark III in which we were sitting. One comment made by George stuck in my memory: 'If any drivers are sticking rigidly to the speed limit with a string of traffic behind trying to get past, we would fail them for lack of consideration.' How times have changed! But you must remember that in 1956 we had only one speed limit, the random 30mph restriction dictated solely by the presence of street lighting, and many such limits were totally unrealistic and upgraded later.

Eventually Dick left and my test started soon after 11 a.m., taking a good hour. The Sunbeam was a car I greatly admired and I was later to buy one, though my example was a neglected Sunbeam-Talbot 90, which proved a heap of trouble, unlike George's lovely Mk III. In future, I was told, candidates would use their own cars for the test – a sensible move, greatly reducing costs, but we early runners were privileged to use George's Sunbeam.

I enjoyed driving it, despite the floppy, four-speed steering-column-mounted gear change and rather heavy, woolly steering, and just followed the route as directed, driving swiftly and – as one always did in those carefree days – taking little notice of speed limits.

When we returned to Putney and I learned that I had passed the test, I was told: 'If you would like to wait for a while you can meet famous rally driver Sheila van Damm, because she is taking the test next.' It then emerged that she had been taken off to lunch (no such favour for the gentlemen of the press!), and in any case I had met her already several times on rally coverage, so I didn't wait as I had to get back to the office to write my account of the IAM and my experiences on the test.

Michael Brown was not too pleased to hear that *The Motor's* man had taken the test before me, especially as they published on Wednesday and we on Friday, so they would beat us by two days. In those days there was great rivalry between the two leading car magazines, and we were scarcely allowed to talk to the opposing staff. Perhaps the management was afraid we would catch something, like the discovery that we were not as well paid as they were!

After a few weeks my test certificate arrived and my short article about the formation of the IAM and experience of the test was published in *The Autocar*, Friday 29 June 1956.

At an annual dinner of the Guild of Motoring Writers, forty-nine years later, I happened to be seated next to the IAM's chief executive, Christopher Bullock, who sadly died in 2007. When I told him that I had been the second person to take the test he responded that I should take it again in 2006, the Institute's bicentenary year, and I readily agreed to do so.

It would have been good to have done it in June, fifty years to the day since the original, but I was away in France at the time, so a date was fixed for 26 July 2006.

The day dawned warm and sunny so I decided to use my Triumph TR7, ignoring my wife's well-meant advice that it would be much easier in our Audi A4. Assistant chief examiner Steve Mead arrived promptly, and after a quick check of documents – insurance, MoT, driving licence – and preliminary briefing, we set off.

The whole approach of the IAM has changed dramatically since those formative days – and quite right, too, many would say. You can't ignore speed limits, as was encouraged when the Institute was founded, so I had to be on best behaviour in this respect. But one or two things seem now to be also in need of updating, especially the requirement to keep in gear at all times. No one would advocate freewheeling down a steep hill as is often done by economy drivers when there is no supervision, but I can't see anything wrong in slipping into neutral when you see an obstruction ahead, such as a traffic light just changed to red, or a stop sign. It enables the car to roll much farther than it would if left in gear with the engine holding it back. Cars such as the Volkswagen Passat are indeed being developed now to do this automatically in the interests of economy, and to switch off their engines on coming to rest.

I followed strictly to the rules laid down in the IAM's very good guidebook and was pleased to learn from Steve Mead that I had passed again. We then sat out in the sunshine and had a fascinating discussion about all aspects of my one-hour test drive. It all brought home to me the important fact that learning to go on driving ever better and more safely is a never-ending process.

After further discussion it was suggested that I should take it again when I reached the age of 80, which happened in 2013. By then I had moved from Hertfordshire to the south coast, and a date was fixed for me to drive up to London, again in my Triumph TR7, and I took the test for the third time on 20 June. On this occasion I was tested by the chief examiner Peter Rodger, and taken on a very well-chosen one-hour route, which took in all kinds of traffic conditions. After it was over, and I was told I had passed for the third time, I was kindly taken to lunch with Peter and the chief executive of the Institute, Simon Best. I felt that I had at last caught up with Sheila van Damm.

TEN

AC ACECA

☰ We could have been doing 100mph with no brakes

After a few months at the digs in Kensington my friend David Dixon and I found new and cheaper accommodation just off the Bayswater Road. It was a bit farther for me to drive to the office, involving going through Hyde Park, but that didn't matter, and in any case often one of the days each week was spent away from the office on road-testing. We no longer had breakfast brought up to our rooms by a girl but had breakfast in a small dining room on the ground floor. After some weeks there we moved again, and joined up with two other friends to share a flat at Hampstead. The rent was £7 a week, which the four of us paid in turn, and we also took turns to be duty cook and washer-up in the evening. The arrangement worked well, and it was a happy time for several years, though the friends sharing the flat with me changed from time to time.

Just before Christmas 1955, I was told that my provisional appointment to the staff was confirmed, and shortly afterwards came a welcome letter from the director confirming that the annual Christmas bonus, comprising one week's salary, would be paid to all staff. I had also been moved from the sub-editor's office to what was effectively the road-test office, shared with Mike Clayton, John Davey and the secretary, Fay Tatham. All three of them smoked, and the atmosphere in that office was sometimes like a pea-souper London fog.

One day, in June 1956, Mike asked me: 'Have you got a passport?'

'No,' I replied.

'Well you'd better get one quick because we're going to Belgium on Wednesday for a road test.'

The formalities of getting a passport from an office in a road called Petty France in London were fairly quick in those days, and I was then allocated a cash advance in French and Belgian francs, with the details entered in the back of the new passport to comply with the currency controls then in force. The car we were to test was the AC Aceca, a very stylish coupé with a 2-litre 6-cylinder OHC engine.

The Autocar staff in those days knew of no other way to take a car to the Continent than to fly from Lydd to Le Touquet with the car loaded on board a Bristol freighter of Silver City Airways. It cost quite a lot more but was a great time-saver compared with the boats, which in those days were very slow.

We set off very late, but after frantic driving on the road to Lydd, near Dover, it looked as if we would make it, when Clayton suddenly announced that there was 'just time for a quickie' and pulled into a pub where he ordered the inevitable pint and then used the phone in the pub to call up Silver City Airways and warn them that we might be a bit late. We were the only customers so it was not surprising that the aircraft and staff were waiting patiently for us when we arrived, about twenty minutes late.

Passengers travelling with cars were not allowed to drive them on to the aircraft. This task was entrusted to a Silver City official, and we then walked over to the steps to go on board. I had never flown before but sat on the plush but well-worn leather seat, fastened the seat belt and enquired in all innocence where the parachute was.

The traditional running up of the twin engines was a little disconcerting, then the aircraft set off along the runway and soon we were airborne, looking down at the waves of the Channel. In later years, when we were supposed to be impressed by the speed of the hovercraft and later the Channel Tunnel, they all paled into insignificance in comparison with my first trip to France in 1956, which took exactly twenty-two minutes.

As we walked to the airport building at Le Touquet, we saw the AC being reversed down the ramp and driven round to the arrivals area, where we were quickly checked through. The elaborate *carnet de passages* document, which had to accompany all cars being taken temporarily to the Continent, was stamped and the tear-off section removed, and we walked out to the car, whose key was in the ignition, and drove off. But as we passed through the entrance gates Clayton announced that he must have a quick pee before we set off, so parked the AC in front of the terminal building. That simple act could have saved our lives.

Mike returned to the car, pursued by one of the airport officials, who was chattering away in French and gesticulating. He pointed to the front right wheel. I got out of the car, and both Mike and I looked underneath and saw brake fluid running out on to the road.

It turned out that the straps put over the wheels to hold the car securely in place on the Bristol freighter had moved the brake pipe and started a leak. The official gave us directions to a garage that might be able to fix it for us, and we limped there very slowly with Mike using the handbrake. We both wondered why on earth the official had not taken the key out to make sure that we did not just drive off unaware of the brake-fluid leakage. In those days you didn't get split front/rear hydraulic circuits, nor on the Aceca a brake-fluid warning light. The garage responded very well, and the car was soon up on a hoist, where the brake pipe was retightened at the banjo union, and then all brakes were bled and the system topped up progressively.

With the car back on form we drove from Le Touquet ('le tucket', as Clayton liked to call it) to Calais, then had to stop at the Belgian border where the customs officials were more interested in the car than in us. The relevant tear-off sheet was removed from the *carnet* and we drove on to Ostend and then on to the autoroute, which one day would be extended to Brussels. I had never seen anything like it: dead straight and level dual carriageways carrying hardly any traffic. Not surprisingly this had been the venue for a number of high-speed record attempts and was known as the famous Jabbeke straight, that being the name of the nearby village that it bypassed. There were motorways in Germany, and had been since before the war, but this first stretch of motorway in Belgium was conveniently near, and as it was still some years off being extended to Brussels, it carried little traffic.

We stopped on the grass at the roadside and fitted the cumbersome fifth-wheel speedometer, then ran through all the speed tests, including acceleration runs

My first Continental road test, the AC Aceca 2-litre.

through the gears to 80mph and the maximum speed, which was 102mph (mean) with a best one-way of 104mph. A large patch of spilt tar by the roadside just happened to be in the right place to mark exactly a quarter of a mile to one of the over-bridges, which was used for our quarter-mile sprint, and similar random markers were used for the measured kilometre going towards Brussels and back. There was so little traffic either way that when we had finished each run we made a U-turn across the grass centre strip, which had only a few shrubs growing on it, later to become a hedge, and repeated the figures in the other direction.

Here and there were houses either side of the autoroute, with no protective fence to keep stray animals off the carriageway, and at regular intervals a large 'A' sign warned that this was an official animal crossing where we might expect a herd of cows to go plodding across. Clayton told me an amusing story about a former technical editor of *The Autocar* who had been testing a fast car there and measuring maximum speed when suddenly a man came running across in front of the car from a house at the side. He would obviously have passed in front well before arrival of the car so there was no need for panic action, but then suddenly a woman appeared from the same house, brandishing a frying pan and clearly chasing him. The test driver on this occasion was Gordon Wilkins, one of the longest-established motoring writers, who had been at the launch of the original Volkswagen Beetle in

My first trip abroad, was with the AC Aceca with 6-cylinder, 2-litre engine. This example is a later model with the Bristol engine. (Ray Potter)

the presence of Hitler in 1938. He sadly died in 2007, well into his 90s. If Wilkins had tried to brake from that speed, he might well have killed the woman, but with great presence of mind he swerved across the centre strip onto the west-bound carriageway, having noted that there was no vehicle coming towards him, then passed well in front of the running woman and swerved back on to the correct carriageway, all at undiminished speed. You couldn't do that now, with Armco crash barriers on the centre strip and non-stop traffic coming the other way.

When we had finished all the tests, we motored back to Ostend, checked into a rather dreary hotel where we had dinner, and then Mike wanted to go to his favourite pub, a small café called Chez Mouche, where we spent time talking to the locals in schoolboy French and drinking far too much beer. The hangover the next day put me off Continental lager for about fifteen years, during which if I ever drank it again I was promptly ill, so I always stuck to English beer, wine or cider. It was an allergic reaction, which took a long time to pass. My first adventure on the Continent had been exciting, though I felt it had been such a wasted opportunity for travel and exploring; but that would come later.

ELEVEN

VAUXHALL VELOX

≡ I could have had any of several pre-war Bentleys for less money

After more than a year on a salary that was roughly double what some of my friends were earning, with the addition of generous expenses, my finances had recovered to the extent that I could at last get rid of the disappointingly slow Morris Minor Tourer, in exchange for something with rather more steam that would earn the higher rate of mileage allowance available for anything with an engine over 1,600cc. I had formed great affection for the Vauxhall Velox when I was in the army and decided to try to get hold of this model.

Following the advertisements I tracked down several examples and finally found one at a dealer in Richmond. It was advertised at £375 – the same price that I had paid for the Morris the previous year – but first I had to get rid of the Morris. I advertised it free in *The Autocar* – one of the perks of being on the staff – and had a buyer very soon, who agreed to my price – exactly the same, £375. When he turned up with the cash he was a bit shocked to hear that the car was still subject to hire purchase, but I assured him I would be paying it off. It was a bit naughty, I understood later, to sell the car without first settling the hire purchase on it, and when I wrote to the United Dominions Trust to ask how much I owed I was shocked at the settlement figure. Paying up in advance would, I thought, cost less than the total of the outstanding payments, but instead it was considerably more due to 'administration costs'.

The dealer at Richmond, called Richmond and Jane, showed me some of his other cars in stock, and today one might be appalled to learn that I could have had any of several pre-war Bentleys at less money than I was paying for the Vauxhall. But who wanted a 1934 Bentley 3-litre saloon in 1956? They were going at rubbish prices and would have been a marvellous investment for anyone who had the cash to spare and the garage space available. The dealer demonstrated to me how you could restart the Bentley's 6-cylinder engine once it had warmed up simply by moving the ignition advance-retard control. There was always one of the six cylinders under compression with petrol-air mixture, and altering the timing triggered a spark which was enough to set the engine running.

I bought the Velox, subject to having a radio fitted. This was agreed, and the Richmond dealer simply installed a fine HMV set removed from one of the Bentleys. The Velox had been a BBC staff car, and had covered 75,000 miles when I bought it, with a new engine fitted at 48,000 miles. It twice needed a new water pump because the bearing failed and although the pump wasn't leaking it became very noisy; but apart from that, no major repairs were necessary. It served me very

The 1949 Vauxhall Velox proved reliable, comfortable and fast for its day.

well, and I always enjoyed driving it. Although it only had a three-speed gearbox with column-mounted gear change, the 6-cylinder 2¼-litre engine developed high torque at low revs. The natural cruising speed was about 60mph, which was fast for the 1950s, and it gave about 28mpg.

It wasn't until after I had bought it that I discovered how badly corroded the underbody was, but what I always used to do was to change the oil at the recommended 3,000-mile intervals and then use an oil can to squirt the old oil all over the underbody. This technique certainly prevented the corrosion from getting any worse.

In the second year with the Velox I took it abroad on my first foreign holiday with two friends, camping. We covered 2,500 miles through Belgium, Germany, Switzerland and Italy, finishing up at Le Mans for the 24-hour race. Perhaps unwisely, I allowed them to drive in turn, and on one occasion when David was driving I noticed a smell of hot oil, looked across and saw that the temperature gauge was almost off the scale and he hadn't noticed. We stopped in a cloud of steam, and found that the top water hose had split. We were in Italy, and there was a babbling brook nearby, but I insisted on a wait of at least an hour before trying to put water in. This was a wise precaution, because even the small amount of water poured in after the wait immediately came out boiling. But we managed to cool the engine without cracking the cylinder head, which was what I had feared, and then limped on to a garage. There was no chance of getting a new water hose with its

Waiting in the queue of traffic delayed by snow on the Gross Glockner pass.

odd shape, but they removed the thermostat and carefully bound up the split hose with adhesive tape, which lasted until the car was back in England. A proper repair and replacement of the thermostat put it all back into working order again, and the boil-up had not caused any harm.

On a drive from Coventry back to London the engine started to give a lot of clattery tappet noise. After ignoring it for a while I pulled into a garage and checked the oil, but the level was well up on the dipstick. However, a pint was poured in and the noise stopped, only to start again before reaching London. At the next opportunity I decided to take off the cylinder head and investigate, as well as checking the state of the valves. The cause of the noise was evident straight away: a blockage in the oil supply to the valve rocker gear was preventing any oil from getting through. It was a simple repair and the engine ran better after what was traditionally called 'a decoke' – removing all the accumulated carbon from the piston crowns and valves.

I ran the Velox for two years. It put me on to the higher mileage allowance of 10½d per mile, which did wonders for my finances, since the car hardly cost any more to run than the Minor had done. In my two years of ownership I took the mileage on to 96,000, and it still had not involved any major expense, but I felt it was time to move on to something a little more sporting and had my eye on the purchase of a Sunbeam Talbot 90. The Velox sold, once again for the magic figure of £375, so there had been no depreciation cost in two years. A long time later at a function in London I met the man to whom I had sold it and asked if he still had it. 'No,' he replied, 'I ran it for 10,000 miles by which time the mileometer had gone back to zero and then on to 6,000, and I felt it must be due for some expensive repair work soon, so I sold it.'

TWELVE

Jaguar Mark VII and 2.4

I was absolutely horrified; I had driven it only 10 yards and damaged it already

In those first two years on the staff of *The Autocar* I was only too happy to be used as what might be called the 'office tea boy' or 'dogsbody', though in this case it didn't involve making tea for everyone; instead I was always available for anything that involved driving some of the lovely cars that came to the journal for road-testing. One of the most exciting of these early drives came within my first year, when I was required to take the Jaguar Mark VII back to Coventry and hand it over to the Midlands editor, Charles Haywood for return to the factory.

This was the first Jaguar to be available in UK with automatic transmission, although it had been offered for some time in export markets. It was still powered by the famous 6-cylinder 3.4-litre twin-OHC engine developing 190bhp, and the BorgWarner three-speed automatic transmission made it even smoother than the manual version.

I took it back to my Hampstead flat in the evening, and next morning drove through Hemel Hempstead and up the A41. This was always the preferred route, the A5 alternative being beset with heavy traffic. Emerging from Aylesbury, I trickled through Waddesdon and then on to the long straight leading to Bicester. It was only a single-carriageway road, but by a lucky chance I had it completely clear of traffic in both directions, put the accelerator on the floor and watched, as they say, the interesting effect.

The rev-counter needle made its characteristic backward surges as the upward gear changes of the BorgWarner automatic took place, and the speedometer needle

The Jaguar Mark VIIM was the first car in which I saw 100mph on an ordinary road.

went marching on round the dial. It showed 103mph when a car in the distance and the approach to Bicester led me to ease up, but honour was well satisfied when study of the road-test speedometer corrections showed that the 103 indicated would have been exactly a true 100mph. When I told my flat mates that evening that I had driven at 100mph they were almost as impressed as if I had said I had driven to the moon. It was still regarded in Britain as an amazing speed.

On arrival in Coventry I couldn't resist showing the car off at the family home, and on leaving stopped with the nose of the Jaguar protruding through the gateway of my father's house on the Kenilworth Road and took a picture of it. This was much appreciated back at the office, and used as the heading picture for the road test, published in May 1956.

It was only much later when reading an article by Paul Richardson in *Triumph World* about the birth of the Triumph TR2 that I learned that the same Bicester straight where I had reached 100mph in the Jaguar Mark VII was also used repeatedly by his father, Ken Richardson, development engineer of Triumph, in preparing the TR2 for its attempt on the 2-litre production-car speed record. Ken reported: 'As the Bicester straight was open to normal traffic, the high speed tests with MVC 575 were undertaken just after dawn to ensure traffic-free runs.' Using the same Jabbeke straight in Belgium that *Autocar* also used for overseas maximum-speed runs, the Triumph TR2 achieved 124.095mph as the average of runs in each direction, to capture the up-to-2-litre speed record for production sports cars over the

Jaguar 240. (Works publicity picture)

measured mile. The date of the event was 20 May 1953, when I had just been called into the army for my National Service, but I remember reading about it at the time.

Nowadays, of course, that stretch of the A41 although bypassed by the M1, is beset with 50mph speed limits and speed cameras, and the sheer density of traffic makes any high speeds along there impossible.

Only four months after my memorable drive with the Jaguar Mark VII, I took on another very interesting assignment. Eagerly awaited since its launch at the 1955 Motor Show at Earls Court, the Jaguar 2.4 was coming in for road test, and an interesting plan was put into action to do the high speed runs on this car on the main runway of an air-force bomber station, thereby saving the cost and time of taking the car abroad. Jaguar said it would do 100mph; there were doubts, but it was important to know. I didn't let on that they might try on the straight stretch of the A41 south of Bicester, where I had reached a true ton with the Jaguar Mark VII!

The editor, Maurice Smith, DFC and Bar, was also still editor of *Flight*, and hence able to pull strings in high places. Yes, approval was given for the main runway to be used for the purpose, subject to all kinds of restrictions, one of which was that it would be available only on a Sunday morning. Immediately, enthusiasm of other members of the staff for taking the car to the American Air Force base diminished, especially since it also emerged that the venue was Wittering, and I keenly volunteered to do the run. Where was Wittering? I asked, and I was told, 'You'll find out; ask the boys on *Flight.*' When told where it was, I realised that I was in for a long drive up the A1, collecting valuable mileage allowance in my newly acquired Vauxhall Velox.

The scheme then expanded when it was learned that a second fast car was coming in for road test at the same time. It was a new version of the Austin-Healey with the C-Series 2.6-litre 6-cylinder engine. The logical arrangement was that just the high-speed runs would be done at Wittering, and all the fiddly work of acceleration testing, brakes and so on, could be done at our usual abandoned airfield site at Glatton.

A consequence of this plan to test two cars at Wittering was that I would have to drive one of them. It was goodbye to the hoped-for mileage allowance on my Velox, which would have brought much more than the petrol would have cost, but instead I had the prospect of driving the exciting new small Jaguar 2.4. It was never called Mk 1 at that stage; it was only after later introduction of the Mk 2 with wider wheel track at the rear that the original achieved the Mk 1 epithet.

Midlands Editor Charles Haywood would take the new Healey there, and he would leave the Jaguar for me to collect from Coventry station on the Saturday. I have no recollection of the railway journey from Euston to Coventry, but I very clearly remember stepping out of the station on that sunny Saturday in early September and seeing the beautifully sleek shape of the white Jaguar 2.4 standing there waiting for me. Like thousands of others, I had admired its graceful lines at the Motor Show when it was launched in October 1955, and now I was actually to drive the beauty. Trembling with excitement, I found the keys in the agreed hiding place, switched on, set the choke lever and pressed the starter button. The engine sprang to life with that sense of vitality and fabulous smoothness that was in such contrast to more mundane cars at that time, and I knocked the gear lever across into reverse.

The movement produced the ugly crunch of gears, which one learned later to avoid by waiting a moment with the clutch pedal fully depressed. I then reversed gently out of the place where it had been parked – nose into the wall outside the station (no parking restrictions in those days, of course). The car had almost come to rest preparatory to moving forward when there was a sickening thump and thud from the back end, and there was something white across the back window.

Knowing how important this Jaguar 2.4 test was to the journal, I was absolutely horrified; I had driven it only 10 yards and damaged it already! Dreading what I would find, I climbed out and went to the back where I realised that the whiteness I had seen across the back window was the boot lid, open and pointing to the sky. I then saw the cause: I had not noticed a low flatbed porter's luggage trolley, and it had struck the push button release for the boot. To my intense relief I found not the slightest mark on the back of the car, and most of the ominous noise had been made by the spring-loaded boot lid flying open. I made a mental rule in future always to 'weigh up' a car park before getting in and reversing out.

It was a sobering start and made me super-careful from then on, but it did not spoil my enjoyment of the extraordinary refinement that the new 'small' Jaguar provided. Its engine was so smooth and so fantastically quiet when cruising in overdrive that it was quite a revelation of motoring enjoyment. In those days even 60mph was quite a high speed and saw one flashing past other traffic, yet here was a car that would do more than that in third gear, with top and then overdrive to come.

Overdrive was selected by a strange sideways-moving switch on the facia; the column-mounted overdrive control came later. The big let-down of the Jaguar was its Moss gearbox, which had no synchromesh on first gear, and tended to crunch when hurried into any of the three other gears, which did have synchromesh.

Sunday morning's blissfully clear roads provided the right setting for a memorable journey from my Hampstead flat up to Wittering, where I arrived about an hour early and went off for a little drive around until the time for our meeting. When I returned I could see the red and black Austin-Healey 100 Six parked inside, so I obtained permission to go through, and found Charles in the control tower talking with the two senior American Air Force officers who would remain there while we were testing. They explained the emergency signals that would be given should the need arise for us to get off the runway.

We did the Healey first. Its 6-cylinder engine in that early form was not very high-revving, with the power peaking at only 4,600rpm. We soon knocked off its maximum speeds in top and overdrive. Both were unspectacular, giving just under 100mph in direct top, and a best of 107mph in overdrive.

When it came to the Jaguar it was not quite so easy. It accelerated well to 80mph, and soon enough reached 90; but then it became a race between the rather slow pace at which the speed kept rising and the increasingly rapid rate at which we were nearing the end of the main runway, well over a mile long. We made about 98mph before we had to brake and turn off on to the perimeter track. There was no wind, and almost exactly the same speed was reached in the other direction.

Deciding that we needed more distance, we evolved a new technique: the car would come in round the wide hairpin off the perimeter track at one end, which could be taken with determination at about 50mph, and go off at the other end on to the grass, which seemed firm and reasonably level, providing an almost unlimited stopping zone to ease the strain on the drum brakes with which the early 2.4 was fitted. The only hazards to be negotiated were the landing lights marking the end of the runway. Like big dustbin lids they were about 7ft apart and nearly 1ft high. We couldn't go round them, but only moderate skill was needed to pass between them, though it was vital not to hit them as they would probably have burst a tyre if not rolled the car.

This technique made all the difference. We saw 101mph one way, and a satisfying 104 in the other direction – ample to justify Jaguar's claim that the 2.4 was a 100mph car. All done, we returned to the control tower, where the American commandant expressed great interest in the new 6-cylinder Healey and jumped at Charles' offer of a quick ride in it. With equal alacrity the burly adjutant accepted my offer of a ride in the 2.4.

He would be used to flying, and speed would mean nothing to him, I reasoned, but I noticed that when I hauled the Jaguar round the tight bend on to the main runway, with the tyres squealing at 50mph, he grasped the lower edge of the polished walnut fascia panel with both hands. Wants to steady himself, I thought to myself.

It was a point of honour that he should see the 100mph demonstrated. This was a speed that in 1956 few people had experienced other than in an aircraft or a racing car, and I hoped he would be impressed; so I kept the Jaguar hard down through the gears and brought the overdrive in at the right moment as we had been doing on the test runs earlier. The fifth wheel was still fitted, so I picked up the electric speedometer head and handed it to him.

'There you are,' I said triumphantly, '100mph!' A few seconds later we reached the end of the tarmac runway. I could sense that he was moving about, but I had to keep my eyes on that rather narrow passage through the landing lights. Once we had safely traversed a gap between them and were slowing down on the grass I turned to see if he was impressed, but I could hardly believe what I saw. Despite his great bulk, the flying officer had ducked down under the fascia and had his left hand pressed to his head.

The other hand, with knuckles showing white, still gripped the electric speedometer!

THIRTEEN

Rover 105S and Aston Martin DB2/4

≡ Try as we would, the Rover would not make 100mph

Because I was so involved with the motoring scene, and taking on more and more work, I did not notice the worrying international situation towards the end of 1956 following Nasser's illegal decision to nationalise the Suez Canal. Suddenly, Suez was upon us. It looked bad at Christmas, and in the new year, 1957, came the dreaded return of petrol rationing. As a business dependent on the use of cars, *The Autocar* was able to get emergency petrol coupons, but they were strictly controlled for business use. I had my private allocation for the Vauxhall but had to keep it for important journeys and went back to commuting on the underground from Hampstead station. It was not only the rationing that was a problem – the price had gone up too, and a special surcharge called the 'Suez shilling' was added to the cost of a gallon of petrol, taking it to 6s per gallon.

Road-testing also had to continue – the weekly road test being an essential feature of the journal, and when a Rover 105S was delivered for test it came with a special plea from Rover that we would take it abroad and try to get a maximum speed of over 100mph. Rover had launched two versions of the 105 at the 1956 Motor Show, the 105R with automatic transmission and the 105S, which was promoted as a fast car for business journeys. It's fascinating to look back now from these days, when any three-figure speed is regarded as 'how shocking', to recall that a top speed above 100mph was considered an important sales feature even in a time of petrol rationing and uncertainty over the future of fuel supplies. To achieve this, we were told, we must increase the tyre pressures to those recommended for high speeds and run the car on 'super' five-star petrol. This was not available in Belgium, so it was decreed that the car would be taken over on the night ferry from Dover to Ostend with a full tank.

We had a cabin, but the ship docked at about 4 a.m., and Mike Clayton, the tester on this occasion although it was very much a Midlands car, was furious when the steward thumped on the door at 3.15 a.m. He shouted at him and refused to budge, so when we finally descended to the hold the Rover was standing there in solitary state, the only car left on board.

We stopped at Ostend station and went in to get some refreshment, and after a delicious fry-up of eggs with bacon I felt a lot better. Being January, we had to kill a lot of time before it was light enough to begin testing, but eventually we had

In Bruges after failed attempts to get 100mph out of the Rover 105S.

it all 'in the bag'. Try as we would, the Rover would not make 100mph. For mile after mile it was steady at 96mph, dropping back slightly on any upgrade but then recovering to the same speed.

The embarrassing thing was that Belgium had decided not to impose petrol rationing but instead declared a 50mph speed limit, and as we wafted along trying to get 100mph out of the Rover, we passed several cars sticking rigidly to the limit, imagining what their drivers were saying about the irresponsible British. It was quite a relief when we had finished all our high-speed measurements and could return to Ostend and Clayton's favourite café Chez Mouche before catching the night ferry back to Dover.

At the beginning of the oil crisis I had been taken to a firm called Southern Counties Car Auctions – later British Car Auctions – to report the devastating effect that the petrol shortage was having on car prices. A very smart-looking Bentley Mark VI, only 5 years old, went unsold having failed to reach its reserve of £850, and there were many fantastic bargains for anyone with the courage to foresee that the Suez crisis would not last long. Instead, many people bought so-called baby cars, such as the Messerschmidt, Heinkel three-wheeler and the Bond Minicar, so that they could at least remain mobile through the crisis. But it lasted only a few months; we were soon hearing of giant oil tankers, too big for the Suez Canal anyway, making the long journey round the Cape.

My used car tests also reflected the good value available, and I had a great time testing an Aston Martin DB2/4 offered for sale at £1,895. A friend said he could provide the petrol coupons if I could run to the cost of the petrol, and we had some lovely motoring enjoying the enormous performance of the Aston on roads carrying minimal traffic because of the crisis. I had to spread the fuel costs over three expense sheets so that each one did not have too many entries of 'petrol for Aston Martin used car test'. I did the acceleration tests to 100mph on the road leading to Datchet, long before the M4 was built alongside. That road now has a 50mph speed limit.

By March the situation began to improve, and in April I called at one garage, carefully poured in 4 gallons and then offered the requisite coupons only to be told, 'We're not bothering with those any more.' Rationing of petrol officially ended soon afterwards. It had lasted 148 days and cost £400,000 to administer. In spite of dark suspicions that the 'Suez shilling' would last forever, it was also cancelled. By the end of the year the cost of petrol had returned to its pre-Suez price of just over 4s per gallon.

One Sunday evening I was in the office waiting for the GP report to come through from the sports editor, to prepare it for press, and I was sitting at his desk. In an idle moment, looking for a ball pen, I pulled open his top drawer and was stunned to see literally wads of petrol coupons there. Through his sporting and rally connections he had contact with a large number of car dealers, who had all supplied him with coupons.

FOURTEEN

BOND MINICAR MARK D

☰ I was heading for a dead cert collision

It was inevitable that the 1956 imposition of petrol rationing because of the Suez crisis produced a rash of funny little economy runabouts, many of which were submitted to *The Autocar* for test. Among them was the Mark D version of the Bond Minicar, in February 1957. I had been on the staff for less than two years at the time and had been asked to take the Bond down to the public weighbridge at

Southwark to get it weighed, where it turned the scales at only 545lb (247kg). It had a single-cylinder two-stroke engine of 197cc, developing 8.4bhp at 4,000rpm, front-mounted and driving the single front wheel.

Returning to the office, which was in Stamford Street near Waterloo, I was driving north along Blackfriars Road when the little car suddenly conked out. It turned out later to be a fuel problem.

The Autocar in those days was part of the Iliffe company, and had its own garage for servicing the company's fleet of staff cars. It was located in a small road called Roupell Street, only five minutes away from where the little Bond had come to rest. I pushed the Bond into a side street off the Blackfriars Road, and phoned 'Roupell' – as the garage was always called – from a call box just round the corner. Ted answered.

'I can't fix it out there,' he said, 'I'll come out and tow you in.'

After a short wait I saw Roupell's trusty Standard Vanguard coming down Blackfriars Road, and waved to it. The Standard was used to recover the company's cars wherever they had broken down or been crashed, often bringing them back on a four-wheel trailer equipped with ramp.

Ted was at the wheel, and when he saw me he pulled across the road, and reversed into the side street. No time was wasted trying to get the engine to run; instead, we pushed and pulled the Bond to turn it round so that it was facing the right way, and Ted fixed a hefty tow rope to it. In his friendly north-country accent, Ted said: 'Right-oh, Stooart, if yer wan' me ter stop, 'oot yer 'ooter.'

With that he climbed into the Standard, took up the slack in the rope, and pulled me gently to the T-junction on to the Blackfriars Road. After a short wait for a break in the traffic on the right, he turned left into the main road, but when I came to turn the wheel I found to my horror that it was completely jammed. The Standard was accelerating away to the left, and I was going straight across the main road. Even worse, there was a bus coming down the road to my left, with a car rapidly overtaking it, and I was heading for a dead cert collision, broadside on to these two vehicles.

'Oot yer 'ooter flashed through my mind, and I hit the little horn button, producing a plaintive 'beep'. Just when a crash seemed inevitable, the front of the Bond seemed to lift up in the air and tweak round to the left. Like the hero of the storybooks, Jack, escaping from the pit full of snakes (you know, 'With one bound Jack was free') I had been miraculously saved from what would have been a horrible accident. The little Bond, hit side on, wouldn't have given much protection.

Frantic 'ooting of the 'ooter brought the Standard to rest, and as the Bond stopped behind it I leapt out and opened the bonnet. What had happened was all too plain to see: Ted had fastened the rope round the bumper, through the front of the engine bay, and then tied it. But in the Bond, the whole engine including the driven front wheel and the exhaust pipe swivelled with the steering. As luck would have it, the rope was to the left of the exhaust pipe, and there was insufficient clearance between the exhaust downpipe curving forward from the engine and the back of the bumper. The rope had effectively jammed the steering on a left turn.

If Ted had reacted promptly on the first 'oot of the 'ooter and braked sharply, I would have sailed on to certain disaster on the other side of the road, but instead the Standard Vanguard had literally hauled the front of the Bond up into the air and set it down facing the right way.

It had been a really close call and I was a bit shaken by the experience. Ted seemed unconcerned and fixed the rope to something underneath so that it wouldn't foul the swinging movement of the engine, and we completed the journey back to Roupell.

F I F T E E N

Jaguar XK150

≡ I couldn't repeat the names he called him, in a towering bluster of fury

Most people in Britain in 1958 drove fairly slowly, 40–50mph being the norm, with many cars unable to do much more than about 60mph. So it was an absolute education for me to be driven by the late Charles Haywood, the Midlands editor of *The Autocar,* at what seemed to me enormous speeds along the A20 from London. Other traffic seemed almost to be stationary as we flew past, yet our hurtling progress was always smooth, controlled and with never a moment of apparent danger. Charles was a very skilled driver indeed.

The car we were in was the XK150 supplied by Jaguar for road test, and we were on our way to Belgium where the high-speed testing would be carried out. I had been abroad twice with Mike Clayton, but he always wanted to stay in a dreary hotel in Ostend; with Charles, I hoped it was going to be different. We would stay in Bruges and, he assured me, see a bit more of the Belgian nightlife.

For £117 extra – quite a lot of money in 1958 – the XK150 was supplied as a special equipment model, with disc brakes, wire wheels, dual exhaust system and what was called the Blue Top version of the 3.4-litre 6-cylinder twin-OHC engine, developing 210bhp. The standard XK150 had drum brakes, disc wheels, and its less powerful engine produced 190bhp, but I doubt whether many buyers went for it in this form.

It was late January 1958, and the agonies of the previous year's petrol rationing were just an unhappy memory, with things now back to normal. As usual, we were headed for Lydd and the Silver City Airways service to take us to Le Touquet. As we turned into the airport there were many advertising hoardings, and Charles said

Jaguar XK150S waiting at Louis Blériot airport at Calais for the return flight to England.

he thought we ought to have a display there saying 'The Autocar wishes you bon voyage', but I don't think the management were into spending unnecessary money. The policy always was to keep a fairly low profile and not let the motor industry realise how much money the journal was taking from them.

Our journey started smoothly enough as we progressed rapidly through northern France and into Belgium with the customary admiring glances by the customs officials when we stopped at the Belgian border, and then it was on to Ostend and the Jabbeke straight for performance testing. The weather was dry, but the road surface was a bit damp following overnight frost. After removing the bumper overriders, we bolted a bar across the inner width of the bumper, fitted the cumbersome trailing fifth wheel to drive the electric speedometer and started our acceleration runs.

The standing starts were quite amazing, with the car letting out a shriek of wheelspin and rocketing away so that I hardly had time to click the stopwatch as the speedo needle flashed past the 30mph mark in under 3 seconds, and in little more than the half minute (33.5 seconds) we were doing 110mph. Slightly disappointing was that the maximum speed was a little lower than the 129.5mph obtained with the previous substantially smaller XK140 model. Our best figure one-way was 125.5mph, and 4mph less in the other direction.

Figure-taking took quite a long time, as the XK150 had a four-speed gearbox with overdrive operating on fourth, which meant that five sets of 'in the gears' figures had to be done. Charles thought we had finished but I said: 'No, we've got overdrive to do.' 'Oh,' he replied, 'all that bloody game of soldiers.'

We were so impressed by the smooth pulling of the engine that we did a special demonstration, starting in top gear with a little clutch slip to get the car moving, and then accelerating right through to 100mph, all in top gear, which was completed from rest in 36.4 seconds. Making full use of the four gears, it did it in 25 seconds.

It was eventually all over and we had done all the fiddly things like brake tests with the Mintex meter recording 94 per cent efficiency, and the Tapley meter to read tractive effort with the figures whizzing round the dial almost too quickly to be able to read them. Then Charles invited me to drive to Bruges, and I enjoyed every minute of it. It was a surprise to find that the steering was sensitive and not too heavy in spite of all that weight on the front wheels and, of course, no power assistance, and the brakes were excellent.

After checking in to a quite pleasing hotel Charles declared that it was 'time the bloody firm gave us a bite to eat' since we had not stopped for lunch in order to get the test figures in the bag before the onset of January darkness. A good restaurant was found, and although I don't remember what I had I will never forget the enormous lobster that Charles devoured. And when the chef arrived and asked if he wanted the other half, he immediately tucked in. We then walked to a succession of dreary pubs where Charles became more and more drunk. Eventually, when I declared that I was going back to the hotel, he pleaded: 'Don't leave me, I can't walk all that way. Go and get the car.'

Having driven the XK150 to the hotel I still had the keys, and before setting off I put the window down, reached out and locked the driver's door on the outside. It couldn't be secured from the inside, and I was determined that he mustn't be allowed to get in the driving seat. I noticed that the weather was getting more windy as I set off, but when I found him it wasn't the wind that was making him sway about. He was completely paralytic, and had been joined by two policemen who were debating whether to take him in.

I stayed in the car, and Charles came up to the door, tried the handle and then said: 'This door seems to be locked.'

'I'll drive,' I replied, 'get in and I'll take you back to the hotel.' At the same moment one of the policemen came round to the left door, then realised that it was a right-hand drive car, and came to my side, saying very firmly in French that I must not let him drive the car. I agreed, confirmed that I wouldn't, and then Charles said: 'Put the bloody bonnet up, Stuart; we'll show them a British engine.' I reached across to the left and pulled the bonnet release, and after a bit of fumbling Charles freed the safety catch and got it up. The policemen, even seeing it just by the street lighting, were plainly impressed.

'Come on,' I called. The bonnet came down with a clang, and the two policemen helped him into the car. Back at the hotel I had to reach out through the window with the key again to unlock the door, and then it was about a half-hour fight to get him into the hotel and up to his room. Several times he would be halfway up the stairs and then go tumbling down again, and I was amazed that he didn't hurt himself.

We slept in late next morning, and when he emerged for a late breakfast he confessed to 'feeling pretty awful' and suggested that I should drive to Le Touquet, which I was more than happy to do. The wind had now got up in earnest. Things were blowing about, trees leaning over, and the car, although responding beautifully, was being buffeted about on the road. We reached Le Touquet and were dismayed to hear that the afternoon flight was cancelled.

'The RAF wouldn't have been put off by a few puffs of wind during the war,' said Charles sarcastically. The comment was ignored, and the airport official suggested that if we went back to Calais, the boat was still running and we could get back to England that way. We made good time for the 50-odd miles back to Calais but were then in for a long wait. Eventually we were loaded on to the ferry bound for Dover. This was in the early days of Captain Townsend's ferry service, before the tie-up with the Swedish firm Thoresen.

We knew it was going to be a rough crossing. Charles disappeared to the bar where he met up with some of the British drivers returning from the Monte Carlo Rally. I went up to the top deck and out into the open where I was amidships, fairly immune to the violent motion of the boat, and although very cold I didn't feel seasick. At times, I saw the bows bury themselves into the waves and was just beginning to wonder if they would ever come back up, when with great relief I would see them surface again like a labrador emerging from a swim with water tumbling off in both directions.

On arrival at Dover I rejoined Charles and we went down to the car. He told me he had spent most of the crossing being sick but that he felt better now and would drive. We went quietly into the customs shed; the few other cars on the boat had already gone. After a while a small bespectacled customs officer appeared and the inquisition started: where had we been, had we bought any alcoholic beverages or cigarettes, what else had we bought; and then he wanted to see in the boot. Charles unlocked it and opened the lid.

'What is that?' he asked.

'Our fifth-wheel speed-measuring device,' replied Charles.

Maximum speed of 136mph (140 on the clock) in the Jaguar XK150S in September 1959, with the late Charles Haywood driving. Engine revs are at 5,150 in overdrive top, well within the safe limit.

'How does it work?'

'Well, you see, we've just taken this wheel from an auto cycle and it's connected by the cable here to a little generator, and that works this speedometer,' responded Charles patiently, as if explaining to an interested schoolboy.

'What is it worth?'

'Why, do you want to buy it? Ten bob for you, bargain price.'

'No,' said the customs man, 'I want to assess how much duty you'll have to pay for it.'

'How much *what?*' roared Charles. And then he exploded. The hangover from the night before, the rotten crossing, being ill all the way, and now this silly little man who could have been one of the stupid privates when he was a major in the army, were suddenly all too much. I couldn't repeat here the names he called him as he held forth in a towering bluster of fury, which concluded with: 'There's 210 horsepower under that bonnet. If you want to stand in the way of it you can, because we're leaving. Get in, Stuart.'

I closed the boot, jumped in the XK150 and slammed the door. Charles started the engine and then did one of the roaring, wheel-spinning standing starts that we had done so often the previous day. Fortunately in those early days they didn't have barriers, humps and other obstructions as they do now to stop anyone who just decides to drive through, but at the end of the long pierside driveway from the customs shed there was a barrier and an exit check. I was afraid the man would have phoned through to have us stopped, but Charles stopped the car, and called out through the window: 'There's a silly little man back there and I've just told him what I think of him. Now put the pole up or I'll do the same for you.' Even as he was speaking, the pole went up, and we were away.

Charles drove quietly for a while, then said: 'I think I've blown it, don't you. The balloon will go up tomorrow.'

'Don't worry,' I reassured him. 'He was completely in the wrong. Anyway, it's his word against ours, and I don't remember you using any obscene language. I've never heard such names before,' I added with a chuckle.

In fact, we never heard another word about it.

Less than two years later, in September 1959, Jaguar sent us a new and improved version of the XK150 for test. It was called the 150S, and had the new Gold Top engine, still only 3.4-litre capacity but with triple SU carburettors, compression increased to the then high figure of 9:1 and power output raised to 250bhp. I was again allocated to go to Belgium on the road test with Charles Haywood, and did all the pictures as well as taking the performance figures.

The more powerful engine gave Jaguar the 130-plus maximum speed they had hoped for with the previous car, and its acceleration took it to 120mph in 39sec. It was 6sec quicker from rest to 110mph. The best one-way maximum speed was 136mph, and in the other direction we reached 132, to give a very acceptable 134mph mean. I took a picture of the fascia panel with the speedometer at the end of its scale, on 140mph. It was 4mph overreading. Its overall fuel consumption was 17mpg, but one didn't bother about such things in 1958. The more important aspect was the need for 100-octane fuel, which was not widely available.

This later car was finished in red and, I thought, looked absolutely gorgeous. The only point for serious criticism was the weakness of the handbrake – an early problem with discs on the rear wheels. Although considerably faster and in many ways far better, this later model had a limited-slip differential, which prevented those wheel-spinning standing starts that had been so spectacular with the previous one, and this test in the summer didn't have the thrill and excitement of the 1958 adventure.

We flew out on the service with Silver City Airways going via the new Louis Blériot airport at Calais. As we approached Calais on the way back, I said to Charles: 'At least we won't have to face that dreary little customs man at Dover again.'

'Oh, that little ...'

'Now, now, Charles,' I interrupted.

SIXTEEN

ROLLS-ROYCE SILVER CLOUD AND VOLVO AMAZON

≡ Try as I would I just couldn't get it petrol-tight

Only four months after the exciting road test of the Jaguar XK150 on the Continent with Charles Haywood came the wonderful news that I was to go again as commander of the stopwatches on an equally thrilling road test. The car in question was the new Rolls-Royce Silver Cloud. I groaned a little at the knowledge that the tester would be Mike Clayton again, but at least this time there was to be more motoring. We were to cross on the night ferry from Harwich to the Hook of Holland, drive to The Hague and collect a Volvo Amazon. We would then take both cars to Belgium for performance testing on the famous Jabbeke autoroute, and then take the Volvo back to the dealer in The Hague and return. It had the makings of being a marvellous trip, and as the time was early May we would hopefully enjoy some fine weather.

As we set off to Harwich I was simply amazed at the luxury of that Silver Cloud. It was not only the superlative comfort of its soft pleated leather seats, the beautiful polished walnut fascia, the wonderful aroma of leather and carpet, but above all the astonishing quietness. I don't think that more modern cars with radial-ply tyres can ever quite match the silence of that Silver Cloud running on cross-ply tyres. I sat there in the front passenger seat gazing along that vast tapering bonnet with the rear view of the beautiful Spirit of Ecstasy mascot, and was completely overwhelmed by it all.

We made the ferry without drama – Clayton had by now given up his trick of stopping for a 'quickie' and then phoning the port asking them to hold the boat –

and landed at a fairly civilised hour after a quick breakfast on board. Then we made our way to The Hague and the private address of the agent. Even before we found his name on the list of flats and rang the appropriate bell, we saw the Amazon looking very smart at the roadside with its two-tone finish and whitewall tyres. Volvo at that time was a make almost unknown in Britain, and it was not listed on the market, but the Swedish manufacturer was very keen to begin selling in Britain, although at that stage it could come in only as a private import priced at 12,600 Kronor, equivalent to £868. The Silver Cloud, by comparison, was £5,694, with a formidable £165 extra to pay for the newly available power-assisted steering.

We knew that the Tulip Rally was on its final day, with high-speed runs at the Zandvoort circuit, so agreed to make our way there and watch the rally. Mike was very much addicted to the Silver Cloud, but I knew my turn would come and jumped eagerly into the Amazon. As we drove off I was impressed by the lovely crisp sound of the Volvo's 4-cylinder 1.6-litre engine producing 85bhp – a lot for those days.

The sight of the cars hurtling round the Zandvoort circuit was very exciting, and it was particularly appropriate that we should be testing a Volvo when the rally was won by an older model, the Volvo PV444. After the rally we made our way south towards Belgium where I had been asked by the editor to look in on the great Brussels World Fair. 'It might be worth a page or two,' he said. We spent the night at a pleasant country hotel, and I knocked off the interior pictures of the Volvo while Mike sat on the verandah enjoying the evening sunshine, drinking as usual, and writing his notes on the Silver Cloud.

It was another brilliantly sunny May day when we went into the Brussels Fair, and the arrival, walking down the great stairway from the entrance hall and seeing all the wonderful floral displays and fountains, was something I shall never forget; and down below was the extraordinary Atomium. It was originally intended to be dismantled at the end of the exposition but instead was left standing to this day. I couldn't find at first the British pavilion, my mediocre French failing to make me realise I should have been looking for *Royaume-Uni*.

We managed to park the Rolls-Royce with the Atomium in the background, and I took a picture with several passers-by turning to look at the beautiful car. It made a fine heading picture for the road test in the 16 May 1958 issue, though the caption that Mike suggested – 'Silver Cloud, silver balls' – was not used!

After the visit to the exposition we set off to Ostend to start doing the performance testing on both cars. Mike again insisted on driving the Rolls, and I began to wonder if I would ever get my hands on its lovely slender steering wheel, but he was due to write both road tests so it would have to happen soon. I had quite a job keeping up with the Rolls, which had a top speed of 106mph, a full 12mph faster than the Volvo, but was managing to keep it in sight quite well when suddenly I became aware of a strong smell of petrol.

Realising that there must be a leak, and remembering the experience I had witnessed with one of my lorries during my National Service in the RASC, I switched off the engine, and coasted quietly to a stop on the grass beside the autoroute, seeing the Rolls fade away into the distance.

It was as well that I had taken the precaution of stopping the engine while still motoring at speed; otherwise there would undoubtedly have been a fire. The whole under-bonnet area was wet with petrol, and the float chamber of one of the SU carburettors was hanging down. The screw-bolt that should have been securing it had gone and was nowhere to be seen.

I found a good pair of pliers in the Volvo's toolkit and nicked a length of wire from a nearby fence, but try as I would I just couldn't get it petrol-tight. The wire always snapped just as it was beginning to get adequately tight. I considered the possibility of blocking the feed to the carburettor and carrying on with just one carb, but as

With the newly built Atomium in the background and Belgian passers-by turning to look at the beautiful Rolls-Royce Silver Cloud, this made an ideal heading picture for the road test in May 1958.

luck would have it the fuel supply went first to the forward carb, which had lost its float chamber screw, and then by a connecting pipe to the second carb. But what I could do, I realised, was take the screw from the number two carburettor and put it on number one. Number two could then be blocked off.

It seemed a brilliant idea, but just as I was undoing the float chamber screw I heard the sound of a motorcycle engine, and looked up to see a patrolman from the Belgian automobile service walking towards me with a jolly salute. Like the British AA at the time, his transport was a motorcycle with sidecar, in which were all his tools and equipment. He quickly appreciated the situation, took from me the remaining float chamber screw, and said he would try to get one to match it. As he rode away I realised I now had no hope of doing a jury-rig repair.

There was nothing for it but to wait, and as it was a lovely sunny afternoon I lay on the grass soaking up the sunshine and hearing the occasional car or lorry go trundling past. You didn't get much traffic on that autoroute in 1958. All the time I kept wondering what was keeping Mike. Surely he would have realised something was wrong when I didn't turn up at the Jabbeke straight and come back to look for me?

My patrolman was away nearly two hours, but eventually with great relief I heard the engine of his motorcycle combination returning, and he climbed off the machine proudly holding up one carburettor screw in each hand. He chattered away in French telling me about the difficulty he had experienced in trying to find a match for it and how he had finally been directed to an SU supplier in Brussels. Both carburettors were fixed in a few moments, and the engine then ran perfectly. These were the days when the sterling exchange rate against the Belgian franc was very favourable, and he was evidently delighted at the generous tip I gave him – more than he earned in a week, he said.

There was no sign of the Rolls at the Jabbeke straight, so I drove on to Ostend and there it was, parked in the central square with a note under a wiper blade: 'Am at our favourite bar.' It was never my favourite bar, and I was pretty furious that Mike had just abandoned me, not knowing or caring what had happened, but there was no point in having a row. We eventually started doing the performance checks on the Silver Cloud, before returning to spend the night in the dreary Ostend hotel that he had chosen.

Next morning Mike enjoyed for the second time his party trick: getting the hotel porter to come out with us bringing the luggage to the cars, upon which he would quickly open the door of the Rolls-Royce, put down the window, then close it again and reach in to put the key in the slot and press the starter button. There was always a gentle 'clonk' as the starter engaged, and then the engine would be purring over. The porter would then come to the boot, notice the slight burble from the exhaust and exclaim: 'Il marche? C'est pas possible!' as he marvelled at the quietness of the engine. The way it would do this certainly was amazing and I don't suppose any modern Rolls-Royce or Bentley would quite achieve this today.

As elegant in three-quarter-rear view as at the front, the Rolls-Royce Silver Cloud was parked in Ostend.

When we had finished testing the Volvo Amazon, I said: 'Right, I'd better have the key to the Rolls. You'll be wanting to get some experience of the Volvo on the drive back to The Hague.' He was quite crestfallen, and I think he would happily have written the road test on the basis of just the performance testing, but he could see the logic of it. That first long drive I enjoyed in the Silver Cloud, marvelling at the lightness of the steering, the response of the brakes and the engine and the wonderfully smooth transmission, was a most memorable experience. But there was more to come: after the night crossing from the Hook back to Harwich, there was a problem, which I didn't quite understand, preventing them from craning the Rolls off the deck until they had cleared the hatch behind it. The enormously expensive Rolls-Royce had spent the crossing lashed to the deck with a tarpaulin over it, and they had – either thoughtfully or jokingly – cut a hole in the tarpaulin for the Spirit of Ecstasy mascot to protrude through it.

Volvo was very anxious to start importing to Britain, where the make was virtually unknown. I enjoyed driving this new model, called the Amazon, but was desperately keen to have my turn at driving the Silver Cloud!

We were warned that there would be a long delay, and Mike couldn't wait. He had to be back at the office to get the road-test copy written and ready to go to press the next day, so he took my films, the valuable road-test record cards, and set off by train to London. I was left eventually to drop my bag in the boot, climb into the driving seat, and once again press the silvery starter button ready for another lovely drive in this amazing car. There would be many more such experiences in the future, but this was the first and most vivid memory of what was then undoubtedly the best car in the world.

SEVENTEEN

Sunbeam–Talbot 90

It was the first car of all the millions ever to have a parking ticket put on its windscreen by a traffic warden

When I was living in Hampstead, I noticed one day a Sunbeam-Talbot 90 saloon parked half on the pavement with a 'For Sale' sign on the windscreen. It was a car I had long coveted, and I contacted the owner who wanted £350 for it. What I really wanted was the Mk III model, and preferably a convertible, but both were out of my reach financially, and as the owner was selling because he was soon going abroad I was able to negotiate the price down to £325, and probably could have made it even less. Whatever the price, it was a disastrous mistake.

The model had enjoyed great success in international rallies, especially in the hands of Stirling Moss, but my example had suffered a hard life and was in very poor condition. Early on I felt it was not steering as well as it should, and took it in to the Rootes service depot at Ladbroke Grove. The news was very disheartening: they reported that the car had a crack in the chassis, and it turned out that this was a weakness of the model.

'Get it away from there, or it will cost you a fortune,' I was advised, and my colleague, the late Ron (Steady) Barker, came to the rescue with introduction to a friend, Louis Giron, who had already repaired one of these cars and was prepared to do the same for mine at cost of £35. It involved quite a lot of stripping down, and then he would weld a steel 'fish plate' on to the chassis each side, and for a further £10 would do the same to the sound side to prevent the same trouble from occurring there. I felt quite humiliated to be the person involved in testing used cars for the journal, and to have allowed myself to buy a car with such a fault, so I made a new rule always to have each used car put up on the garage hoist for a check underneath as part of the test procedure.

After this work the steering was much better, though never good, being a rather vague steering-box and drop-arm system instead of the rack-and-pinion layout that was becoming much more widely used. There was also a lot of play in the four-speed steering-column-mounted gear change, and it had an irritating habit of jumping out of first gear. Otherwise, I enjoyed driving the Sunbeam and it had some good features including a sunroof, efficient brakes and much better roadholding than my rather dated Vauxhall Velox.

One day when I was driving it in the Manchester area I noticed a Rover 90 some way behind with the driver flashing his fog lamp at me. I wondered what was the matter and slowed down only to find it was an unmarked police car. The policeman was alone but in uniform and claimed I had been exceeding the speed limit – something which in those days one did almost as a matter of course. He apologised for the way in which he had to stop me, there being no blue light or other police sign on the car, and confessed that if I hadn't stopped he would never have been able to catch me with the old Auntie Rover. This being long before the points system was introduced, it cost me a small fine and an endorsement on the licence.

The Sunbeam's performance, however, was disappointing. It had a 2¼-litre 4-cylinder pushrod engine allegedly developing 90bhp, but it was a very heavy car and performance was not sparkling. Travelling as passenger in it one day, my always amusing colleague the late John Davey, who wrote *The Autocar's* Disconnected Jottings page, commented from the back, 'Ahm, you couldn't really call it acceleration, but it gathers way quite satisfactorily!' Then later, spotting my big Grundig tape recorder on the seat, he commented, 'Come now, Stuart, let's have a little music. I suggest *The Ride of the Valkyries* would be appropriate to our mode of travel!'

A respray in dark blue with grey above the waistline cost only £25 and transformed the appearance of my Sunbeam-Talbot 90.

The appearance of the Sunbeam was much improved by a respray, as described in the Rover 16 chapter, carried out by one of the used-car dealers who had supplied a car for test. Its dull light-blue finish was transformed to a two-colour scheme with dark blue below the waistline and grey above. The work was well done, and all for £25.

One small distinction won by my Sunbeam-Talbot was that it was the first car of all the millions ever to have a parking ticket slapped on its windscreen by a traffic warden. One of my regular tasks on *The Autocar* was to write the weekly News and Views pages, in which I had followed the progress of the plans to introduce control of parking in London, with meters charging 6*d* for an hour, or 1*s* for the maximum period of two hours. The proposals had been steamrollered through by the Transport Minister, Harold Watkinson, in the face of great opposition, and finally the scheme was to come into force on Thursday 10 July 1958. Mr Nugent, Joint Parliamentary Secretary to the Ministry of Transport, posed for photographers as he posted a sixpenny piece – he wasn't going to waste a whole shilling! – into the meter in Grosvenor Square. I was sent along to cover the event, but as it was the day before our press day I was very busy, and late arriving.

'Parking spaces will be reserved for the press' stated the invitation from the Ministry, but when I arrived in my Sunbeam-Talbot 90 they were all taken, so I parked as one always did in those days, in the first available space. On my return I was concerned to see a little gathering of bystanders around my car, and there in the middle of them was a man dressed in this ridiculous yellow and blue outfit, which we had been told the new breed of 'Traffic Wardens' would wear to make them distinctive. As I approached, I decided what I would do, and went straight up to the windscreen, removed the parking ticket – the business of sticking them to the windscreen only came in later – and screwed it up into a ball, then flung it away. This was also, of course, before anti-litter laws were introduced.

The warden was beside himself with rage. 'You can't do that,' he expostulated. 'I've given you a parking ticket. You're going to have to pay.'

'I've shown you what I think of your parking ticket,' I replied, and promptly climbed into the Sunbeam and drove away.

A long time later came a copy of the parking notice with a demand to pay the excess charge of 10*s*. I noticed that the ticket didn't have a significant number, like a row of 0s with 1 at the end, which might have given it some novelty value as a collector's item. So I wrote back explaining that I was there in my capacity as an invited member of the press and that all the reserved parking bays were taken up. The parking charge was duly waived.

I kept the Sunbeam for about a year but was spurred on to make a change and take advantage of the fact that I had now accumulated more funds. On hearing that I was anxious to dispose of the Sunbeam, the manager of my firm's company car garage agreed to take it off my hands for £350 – slightly more than I had paid for it, excluding repairs and improvements. For the next few days I would see him and other members of the garage staff working on it during the lunch hour, and I understand they were able to sell it for a handsome profit, though I never heard exactly how much. I felt they had earned it.

E I G H T E E N

SINGER GAZELLE IIA CONVERTIBLE

I knew it was a mistake as soon as the nose of the car plunged sharply downwards, and I hit the brakes, but it was too late

'This venue is not to be used forthwith.' The edict came in a memo to all road-test staff on *The Autocar* from Harry Mundy, technical editor, who had joined the staff shortly before me. Harry had been appalled at the casual way in which road tests were carried out, with fuel consumption based on mileometer readings scribbled on a cigarette packet, and performance figures measured on the abandoned airfield at Glatton, which was by no means level. After a lot of negotiation he obtained special permission for the journal to be allowed to test cars at the Motor Industry Research Association (MIRA) at Nuneaton. It was quite a coup, because previously no journalists had been admitted there because of the great secrecy attending prototypes in those days.

Mike Clayton, in particular, did not welcome the news at all because he was devoted to his routine of merging road-testing with visits to pubs, and I certainly did not relish the prospect of the awful journey up the A5 through Radlett, St Albans, Markyate, Dunstable and so on – a route I knew all too well from my occasional journeys to the family home at Coventry. So for a few weeks we didn't use the newly available MIRA facility, but after the Mundy directive there was no option in the matter.

By then – summer 1958 – I had been on the staff for three years, and had at last become a full member of the road-test team. I was still running my Used Car Test series but also now testing new cars. My first road test was the Austin A35, published in July 1958, and then I was allocated a much more interesting car: the Singer Gazelle IIA convertible. It was a very attractive four-seater open car, which looked very sleek and sporty with the top neatly folded away. The hood could also be fixed in the intermediate *de ville* position with the rear part still in position but the top over the front seats neatly clipped back. The interior was attractively finished with walnut panels across the fascia and console. Following the absorption of Singer Motors into the Rootes Group, the Gazelle IIA was fitted with the Rootes 1,494cc engine with pushrod-operated overhead valves instead of Singer's overhead camshaft unit, and we were interested to see how it would compare with the former Singer version.

It was not only the long and tedious journey that made MIRA much less welcome than the old Glatton venue, it was also the much more elaborate test schedule. Worst of all was the requirement to disconnect the fuel supply and install a fuel consumption meter, measuring the fuel passing in two thousandths of a gallon. Fuel consumption was to be measured for 2 miles at 10mph increments from 30mph up to just short of maximum speed. Some complicated sums had to be done to turn all the meter readings into mpg, and of course we had no calculators in those days.

After the Rootes Group took over Singer Motors, the pushrod OHV engine was installed in the Gazelle model, which made it even a bit faster than the OHC version.

Ron Barker, always nicknamed 'Steady', who sadly died in 2015 at age 94, was keen to come with me to MIRA for the first time and experience the new testing arrangements, but we were appalled at the schedule which seemed to go on and on. Ron worked the stopwatches and acted as road-test observer. We were interested to find that the Gazelle with its new pushrod engine was quite a lot faster than the previous OHC version, which should have been more powerful. It reached 70mph from rest through the gears in 35 seconds, where the OHC model had taken 36.9 seconds.

Then these other tedious tests followed, and time flashed by. Still to do were the *pavé* test, the cross-country circuit, the washboard surface, the undulation humps testing the firmness of the suspension dampers and finally the water splash.

We were running terribly late, and although it was July it was a horrid day – dull, drizzling, and quite cold, but at last there was just this water splash to do, and then we could be on our way for the laboriously long journey back to London. Little did we realise, as I drove off in search of the water splash, just how late we were going to be.

When we found it, there were two of them, side by side. We were not to know that we were at the wrong part of the proving ground altogether, and that these were not water splashes, for checking sealing and effect on brakes, ignition and so on, but were deep wading troughs for military vehicles. There was no indication of depth, nor anything to say that while one was only 9in deep, the other was 4½ft. There was just a notice reading 'Check brakes' and inevitably I chose the wrong one.

'How fast do you think we should take it? Is this about right?' I asked Ron as we headed towards it at about 15mph. I knew it was a mistake as soon as the nose of the car plunged sharply downwards, and I hit the brakes, but it was too late. Water burst over the bonnet, then receded as a tidal wave running the full 40ft length of the trough, then returned again, splashing up on to the windscreen.

For an agonisingly long time, the Gazelle floated and, like a boat, it gently nudged the side of the concrete retaining wall and then inched away again. All the time, water gurgled and bubbled in on my side, round the pedals, and I felt an inane desire to try to plug the leaks. After his initial cry of horror, Ron Barker wound the window down on his side and reached out, grabbing the top of the wall and slowly pulled the Singer 'boat' towards the side so that he could climb out through the window. I did the same, forgetting to rescue my camera from the glovebox.

Turning my back on the disastrous scene, I ran the few hundred yards to the control tower, with the idea of getting help, but it was well past 6 p.m., and they had all gone home and locked the door. For a moment I felt quite helpless, then I heard the sound of a car and remembered that we had seen someone going round the rough *pavé* track long after the others had left. It was the prototype for the future Rover 3-litre undergoing endurance testing with a full load. I ran across and flagged it down.

There were no passenger seats in the Rover – just bags of sand ballast, and I sat on these as the driver took me back to the scene, where the Gazelle was now looking very sorry for itself. But we had no tow rope, so I left the dejected Barker salvaging test gear, my saturated camera, and the still legible road-test data cards, while our friendly Rover test driver took me to the Research Garage, only a couple of miles along the A5, to enlist a breakdown truck.

You would never believe the sheer volume of water that a car – even a convertible – can hold. When the Gazelle was towed out backwards, it cascaded from everywhere. I opened a door and jumped back as more water gushed out; and then suddenly, as we looked at this pathetic sight in the gathering gloom, the interior light came on. It inspired new hope, and it was agreed that the car would be towed to the Research Garage. Ron sat on his mac in the driving seat, but had his feet soaked when water rushed through from the rear footwells whenever he used the brakes.

With the car on the garage hoist, we drained the fuel tank until what was running out seemed to be more petrol than water. The mechanic then positioned an oil catch tray beneath the sump. The drain plug was on the side of the sump, and the moment he unscrewed it a jet of oily water shot out horizontally and hit the wall of the garage, fortunately just below the calendar with the inevitable picture of a topless busty girl. Then the oil started to come out. We drained the gearbox as well, and there was the rather frightening moment when the mechanic plunged an electric drill into the water lying in the rear footwells, to let the water piddle out.

We then took out the four spark plugs. 'I'll try to see if there's any water in the cylinders,' said Ron, and holding a torch he peered in as I inserted the starting handle – those were the days of starting handles – and tried to turn the engine. At first, it wouldn't move at all, then as I pulled harder suddenly it gave and a gout of water erupted from the sparking plug holes, catching Barker full in the face. Not for the first time that day, he exclaimed: 'Oh you fool, Bladon,' and set to drying his glasses with a handkerchief.

Eventually we had dried what we could, changed oils, put more petrol in the tank, and with much trepidation I tried the starter. At first it just seemed completely lifeless, then suddenly there was a cough, a splutter, and then miraculously the engine was running. Water gushed from the exhaust as if from a garden hose, and then steam poured out.

I signed the bill from the Research Garage, thanked and tipped the mechanic for his invaluable help, and we set off for London. It was a miserable journey down the A5 – they had started building the M1 by then, but it was still over a year away – and we trailed steam, all the way. It poured from the exhaust, from the windows, and from the heater, which we had full on. The seats were saturated, and as we progressed we realised that the stitching of the seats was beginning to pop,

Whitewall side trims on the tyres were a not very satisfactory addition, and the Gazelle shed some of them at high speed, but it was a very pleasing car, both before and after its unfortunate dunking.

revealing the foam padding. Water oozed from the carpets, and splashed about in the doors and even half-filled the clock.

'I'm beginning to realise what it costs to dunk a car,' said the editor, Maurice Smith, a little later on, clutching a bunch of bills for renovating the trim, carpets, upholstery, radio, clock (£3 13s 6d), and the polished walnut fascia panels.

I expected a storm of retribution, but it never came. Perhaps it was felt that there should have been some sort of warning about the depth of the trough into which I had driven with such confidence. But I had learned the hard way about the hazards of driving into water of unknown depth.

NINETEEN

Mercedes-Benz 300B

≡ The headlights shone on a telegraph pole and I was heading straight for it

As well as being included in *The Autocar*'s road-test team in 1958, I was working hard to build up my series of used car tests, which was proving popular with readers. Some forty of these had been published since I took over the feature from Mike Clayton, and I tried to concentrate on the more popular models but also to include the occasional extravagance. So when my weekly study of the journal's used car advertisements revealed a Mercedes-Benz 300B for sale at Woking Motors, I made a tentative enquiry to ask if they would be interested to submit the car for a test report. The offer was eagerly accepted, and I arranged to go down to Woking on a Friday in September to collect it. Would they mind, I asked, if I did a long run in this important car, because I had it in mind to take it to North Wales for the weekend and join my parents, who were on holiday in the family home at Llanbedr, near Harlech. The sales manager at Woking Motors readily agreed to this, but I didn't get away from the office as early as I had hoped in the afternoon, with a long and arduous journey ahead. There were no motorways so I had to go up the A5 all the way to Shrewsbury, then across to Welshpool and Barmouth, a total of some 280 miles.

These were early days for Mercedes-Benz cars in Britain, held back by the imposition of import duty, and the 300B was priced at £1,750, which was an enormous price for a 3-year-old car in 1958, but it was not too bad in relation to the £3,300 it had cost new in 1955. With its imposing radiator grille and huge front wings swept back into the doors, it really looked quite magnificent, and it was in very good condition, having covered only just over 27,000 miles from new. It had a four-speed gearbox converted to floor-mounted change, and its power unit was a 3-litre 6-cylinder engine, which gave forceful acceleration to reach 80mph from rest in 30.1 seconds. Even modest diesel cars would shame that today, but it was impressive in 1958, and I wrote in the test that it would cruise at 80 and reach the occasional 100mph without need for miles of straight, though where I registered that driving in the evening traffic on a Friday in September on the A5 I don't quite remember.

It was after 6 p.m. when I set off from Woking, and traffic on the A5 was more than usually bad so that 10.30 p.m. found me only at Shrewsbury where I took the opportunity to fill the tank and have a quick snack, knowing that this would be the last chance because everything closed early in Wales. I enjoyed the smooth, quiet engine of the Mercedes, with a third gear that could be held to more than 70mph, but the steering was both heavy and low-geared, taking many turns from lock to lock, and I was appalled by the dead feeling of the brakes and the inadequacy of the headlamps. The halogen bulb was yet to be invented, and the glimmering Bosch lamps on the Mercedes were particularly feeble.

With the prospect of not arriving until well after midnight, and with my parents prone to get anxious if I was very late, I was pushing on hard towards Welshpool. I swept round a bend and accelerated on a long straight, noting the lights of another vehicle approaching from the left which I thought was on a minor road, so I was very surprised when this car made a wild swerve across the front of me and only then realised that it was on the main road and that a tight corner to the left was coming up. I applied the brakes hard and they responded for an instant, and then the pedal seemed to become solid. In rapidly mounting panic I snatched the gear down into third and hauled on the steering. The feeble headlights lit up railings and I realised that this was one of those acute S-bends for which Wales is famous, taking

Import duty made any foreign car hideously expensive, and the Mercedes-Benz 300B cost a lot in 1958, but it was a fine car spoilt only by its poor drum brakes and rotten headlamps.

the road over a railway line. I must get it round somehow, I thought, and hauled harder on the steering. At the same instant I took my foot off the useless brake pedal and stamped down on the accelerator in a desperate bid to bring the back round.

That did it. I had a fleeting moment of joy as the railings flashed past the front of the car, but the terrific relief on realising that I had managed to get it round the corner was short-lived because the headlights shone on a telegraph pole and I was heading straight for it, the road now cornering sharply to the right. As I wrenched at the steering the tail of the car swung furiously round, and there was a sickening thump as the back end hit the pole.

Next instant, the lights revealed a small hedge at the side of the road on the right. I had managed to get the car round the second tight bend but just could not unwind the steering fast enough to correct the tail swing. The hedge smashed down as the bumper hit it, and then the front of the car dipped down at a horrifying angle. Again I was pressing the brake pedal as hard as I could, but the car continued its terrifying descent down the railway embankment, and several small saplings went down as the Mercedes-Benz careered through them. Suddenly it was all over. The car stopped abruptly and I was flung forward against the steering wheel but wasn't hurt. I opened the door and climbed out.

It was a fine night, warm and dry. The air was filled with the stench of overheated brake linings, which had resulted in the brake fade leading to the disaster, mixed with the smell of grass burning under the hot exhaust. In the darkness I clambered round to the back of the car and felt the bodywork. Yes, the nearside back wing was damaged, but it didn't seem too extensive. I reflected how unlucky I had been; I must have been within a couple of feet of missing that telegraph pole, but then I realised that I had also been incredibly lucky. If I hadn't managed to get it through that first tight corner the car would have gone straight through the railings and crashed nose first 20ft down on to the railway line. You didn't get Armco barriers in Wales in 1958!

I knew it was hopeless, but I did climb back in and try reversing up that steep grass slope, but one try was enough. There might not be another vehicle along for ages – that car which had swooped off the railway bridge in front of me was one of very few I had seen since leaving Shrewsbury – so I trudged back down the road to where I had passed some buildings. There I found a telephone kiosk. A police sergeant came out from Welshpool in a little Ford van to inspect the excitement, and took me to the police station, where he kindly allowed me to ring home. It was then nearly midnight, and the policeman did exactly the wrong thing when he got through, guaranteed to throw my father into a panic. 'Hello, is that Dr Bladon? Just a minute, I'm afraid there's been an accident.' He then dropped me at a hotel in Welshpool, which was fortunately still open, where I spent the night.

They closed the road next morning for about half an hour while a heavy recovery vehicle pulled the Mercedes back up the railway embankment, and then it was towed very slowly to a garage, with the front on a wheeled drawbar. As well as the damage to the rear wing, there was a slight crease at the front on the right, where the nose had hit the ground at the bottom of the embankment, but it wasn't too bad considering what the car had gone through, and I could see no structural damage.

It took a lot of persuading before they would let me have the car lowered from the dolly wheels so that I could try it down the road. I think the garage had their eye on a lucrative charge for storing the car. Satisfied that it was still handling perfectly normally, and that the brakes, now cool again, were working no worse than they had been at the start of the test, I insisted on driving it away to continue my journey.

The confrontation with Woking Motors on completion of the test was not relished, but, learning that all was insured and that the test report would still be published, they took it very well. Since then, I have driven many times along that A458 road from Shrewsbury to Welshpool, and the S-bend at Cefn where the road crosses the railway line has been made much safer by realignment, erection of protective barriers, warning signs and double solid lines. As for me, I had learned the hard way the sort of lessons never to be forgotten – not depending on brakes and not driving faster than the range of safe vision provided by the headlamps. I was also determined to take things very carefully for a long time, as this disaster had followed fairly quickly after the expensive dunking of the Singer Gazelle and I didn't want to lose my job on the staff of *The Autocar*, which I had been so lucky to achieve.

TWENTY

ROVER 16

The motorist who achieves three figures on British roads does so only at a risk to himself and others that would be difficult to justify

'Don't ever get yourself caught up in the professional jealousies on this journal,' warned Michael Brown, associate editor of *The Autocar*. I knew there had been personality clashes between him and the sports editor, the late Peter Garnier – we had all heard the shouting. They hadn't actually come to blows, but there had been the childish business of tipping a desk up and hurling everything to the floor including Michael's portable typewriter on which he wrote all his thousands of words. I never found out what it was all about, and seeing Michael's eyes close to tears behind the green-tinted glasses that he always wore, I didn't like to ask.

The storm between them blew over, though there were always rows over nothing, but then in May 1956 Michael unwisely created the scenario for his own dispatch. The editor, Maurice Smith, was away in France enjoying, but not covering – that was

Peter's job – the Monaco GP. Michael Brown wrote the traditional front-page leading article, and chose the topic of 'high speed responsibilities'. It was a very well-thought out piece for its time, and today would be applauded, but this was over fifty years ago when we had only the 30mph speed limit indicated by street lighting, cars were getting faster, and we had an editor who used to boast almost every day that his Aston Martin DBIII was going well, and that he had managed to top 100mph on his commuting journey from Ashtead in Surrey to our offices in Waterloo.

So when the last sentence of Michael Brown's leading article condemned driving at 100mph anywhere in Britain, the balloon went up in the biggest possible way. Published on Friday 18 May 1956, it read: 'We would say that roads and traffic within 50 miles of a big city in Britain very rarely permit a safe 80mph, and that the motorist who achieves three figures on British roads does so only at a risk to himself and others that would be difficult to justify.'

Rover's 16 saloon with 2¼-litre engine had a freewheel that could be locked in by a hand-wheel control on the fascia, and then had the same effect as dropping into neutral on the overrun.

At one time it was thought that he would get the sack immediately, as this was absolute anathema to a motoring journal intent on promoting speed, even as the much less influential magazine still does today. But it didn't happen straight away, and it was not until a year later, in May 1957, that he was despatched to the company's northern office based in Manchester. He had formed a passionate fondness for the Bristol 405, and pleaded to have one as a staff car, but the firm wanted to favour the more valuable advertising outlet of Jaguar, and issued him an XK140. I know which of these two I would have favoured, and it would not have been the Bristol, good though that is. Michael took his lovely black Jaguar off to Manchester, where he became a vigorous agent and campaigner for all the company's journals, including *Bus and Coach* and *Automobile Engineer*.

A year later he suggested to me that I should go up and take a car for one of my used car tests from a northern dealer, and at the same time have a look at the Preston bypass, which was then in its final stages of construction, ready for opening in December 1958. The editor agreed to the project, and I set off in my Sunbeam-Talbot 90, heading first for Manchester for an earnest talk with Michael, who seemed reasonably happy in his new role. 'Of course,' he said, 'it's not press-work and, as you know, I enjoyed press-work. But I am getting more opportunities for writing.'

I then drove across to Sheffield where a Rover 16 awaited me. It had been built soon after Rover's resumption of car production after the war and was first registered in October 1947, when the total price including purchase tax was a formidable (at that time) £942. The inflation of prices due to the chronic car shortage had ended, and this 11-year-old example was going at Portland Autos for £225. It was in very impressive condition, with glistening black paintwork, and inside the traditional polished wood trim and leather upholstery were all very good for their age. The only major fault – to be rectified before sale – was that the speedometer was not working. This didn't stop me from driving it and estimating all the time how fast I was going, but it did put paid to the usual performance testing that was carried out to compare acceleration with that of the model when new.

This Rover had a 6-cylinder engine of 2,147cc, its very long stroke accounting for the low 16hp rating under the ludicrous formula applying at that time, which was based on cylinder bore diameter but not swept volume. It was an exceptionally smooth and quiet engine, and a special feature of the Rover 16 was the provision of a freewheel. Turn the knurled knob on the fascia and the freewheel would operate whenever the driver lifted the foot from the accelerator. It helped fuel economy considerably, and enabled clutchless gear changes to be made. I appreciated the system, and in later years couldn't understand how extraordinarily steamed up some readers would get whenever I suggested that they might slip into neutral to save fuel.

Portland Autos proved efficient dealers, and very friendly, and when they saw my Sunbeam they commented how much better it would look painted in two-tone, dark blue below the waistline and light grey above. 'We can do it for you,' they said, and a price of £25 was agreed for the work, which would be completed by the time I returned the Rover four days later.

I then drove up to Preston, spent the night in a hotel there, and next morning went to the new bypass where I was most impressed by what I saw. This was the first stretch of motorway to be built in Britain and was unlike anything we had seen before with its gentle curves, complex flyover junction linking with the A59 to serve Preston, and designed for a cruising speed of 75mph. I simply drove past the barriers in my stately Rover on to the still unopened motorway and took a lot of pictures before returning to the hotel. I wrote a detailed description of how this new road with its special blue signposts we had never seen before set the pattern for the motorway network, which was at last beginning to be built in Britain. Already, work was under way on the first section of the M1. The Preston bypass had only two lanes on each carriageway, but there were exceptionally wide centre strips to allow for the later addition of a third lane on each carriageway just in case – you never know – the growth of traffic might justify it!

I went out and dropped my package of copy and films into the nearest letter box, and as always happened in those days it arrived at the London office next morning. Maurice Smith was also impressed and found an immediate page for it in the following week's issue, just one week before the opening ceremony. The bypass was, of course, destined to become part of the M6, and had been built by Tarmac Civil Engineering for Lancashire County Council.

The following day I went back to have another look at it, and found that television were there with racing driver Roy Brooks. He commented that it was a pity there were no gantry signs, and I wondered what on earth he wanted those for, but of course later with the mass of lorries on the left lane these are often needed to be able to see the advance warning signs.

I finished the work on the Rover and drove it back to Sheffield where I was delighted to find the appearance of my Sunbeam transformed by its rapid two-tone paint job.

Next week, Maurice Smith drove up to Preston to see for himself, and to attend the important opening ceremony by the Prime Minister, Harold Macmillan, on Friday 5 December 1958. Macmillan was accompanied by Harold Watkinson, later Lord Watkinson, who was the Minister of Transport who finally got Britain's motorway-building programme under way.

TWENTY-ONE

Triumph TR3A

> I was absolutely stunned to see an empty space in the slot
> where I always parked it

It was quite a novel idea to stage a motor show entirely for second-hand or – as we preferred to call them – used cars, and such a show was arranged at the Olympia exhibition hall in London in September 1959. Wanting to encourage it, *The Autocar* gave it a lot of publicity, and it was also agreed in advance that the journal would select one of the cars displayed and take it away to be the subject of one of our popular series, 'Used Cars on the Road'. I hadn't been there long on the press preview day when my eyes lit on a very smart-looking Triumph TR3A, and the vendors, G.E. Harper Ltd of Stevenage, were very happy to have it removed from the stand and loaned to us for test.

A fault declared at the outset was that the starter motor sometimes would not engage, but this was no problem since most cars in those days had a starting handle. The Triumph was just a year old and had covered 15,000 miles. I added nearly 1,000 to this over the weekend and absolutely fell in love with the car, but the price was a formidable £865, only £237 less than it had cost when new. On the Monday morning I went to see my bank manager and a loan was arranged, enabling me to tell Harpers that not only would they get the publicity of the test report but also that I had decided to buy the car. My firm's garage staff paid a reasonable price for my Sunbeam-Talbot 90, and Harpers arranged for the problem with the starter to be fixed, so it was good not to have to keep using the starting handle.

I hadn't had the Triumph many weeks when Simon, sharing our Hampstead flat for a few weeks, said to me one morning: 'One of my friends killed himself in a Triumph TR3 last night.'

I thought he was just trying to tease me, and the story sounded highly unlikely, but he said, 'I'll show you where it was.' We went off in the TR3A and drove to Regent's Park where, sure enough, there were the unmistakable signs of a terrible accident. The car must have hurtled round one of the quite tight bends in the park, skidded across the road and mounted the pavement before crashing into the railings of one of the houses. The wrecked car had been removed, but the black marks were clear evidence of what had happened, and there were recognisable bits of Triumph lights and other parts all over the place. I vowed to learn from that experience and determined always to take it a bit carefully, bearing in mind that the TR3 had a reputation of being a little too fast for its roadholding capabilities.

The 1959 Triumph TR3A was transformed by fitting an overdrive, and provided lovely motoring, especially in summer when the hardtop could be taken off.

My car was finished in powder blue with a white hardtop, but there was no hood – a deficiency I would have to rectify when the spring came round. Also, when I could afford it, I added a Motorola radio installed on the hump over the gearbox, where it could be heard very well – though less easily once the summer weather and removal of the hardtop gave open-car motoring.

An unhappy event occurred soon after I had acquired the Triumph. Charles Haywood, with whom I had assisted on a number of road tests, came down to London for the Earls Court Motor Show in October 1959. He was widely known throughout the industry, and no doubt lavishly entertained on every stand. Then, unwisely since he could easily have stayed overnight in London and reclaimed the cost, he set off to drive home in his Austin A90 Westminster. Going along the A5 late in the evening, he caught up a column of slow-moving traffic, knocked the gear down into third and went storming past them all.

With nothing coming the other way, it was a perfectly safe manoeuvre, but it so happened that the queue was caused by a large indivisible load being transported north, and having a police escort. One of the police outriders set off in pursuit of the overtaking car with the idea of giving the driver a dressing down, to be more careful in future, but when the door opened, and Charles tumbled out hardly able to stand, he was arrested for drunken driving. They didn't have any breathalyser or other scientific way of proving drunkenness in those days, but with the state Charles was in, the visible evidence of the police officers was enough.

Back at the office, it was all hushed up, but when the case came up in June the following year and Charles Haywood was disqualified from driving for a year, he could no longer be Midlands editor of *The Autocar*. A small paragraph was published stating that he was being appointed 'assistant to Arthur Bourne, the editorial director'. It was made to sound like a promotion, but many knew that

When it was recovered after being stolen at Coventry, the TR3A had not suffered too much abuse and I gained two spotlamps, an ugly badge bar, which I removed, and a useful toolkit left by the thieves in the boot.

it wasn't. The arrangement also was not a happy one, and when Bourne said one day that he'd left his bowler hat at the Savoy and asked Charles to pop over and fetch it for him, his violent temper erupted as it had done that time with the nasty customs man down at Dover and he told Bourne in no uncertain terms what he could do with his bloody hat. It was 'the bowler' for Haywood, who was summarily dismissed from the firm.

Where this affected me was that I was asked to stand in as Midlands editor on a temporary basis, to hold the fort while a permanent appointment was made. I was to go up and spend three or four days there each week and the rest of the week in the London office. This was also not a very happy arrangement, though I enjoyed having some responsibility, closer contacts with the Midlands-based industry and a good office. I was also well placed for taking a more active part in the road-test programme.

With the opening of the M1 (see Chapter 23: Aston Martin DBIII) the journey from London to Coventry and back had become much easier, but it also brought to light the shortcomings of the Triumph's relatively low gearing. The ability to cruise at 80 or 90mph on the M1 meant that the TR3A's 4-cylinder Vanguard-derived 2-litre engine was turning at 4,500rpm, which it clearly didn't like at all, so I managed to get hold of a reconditioned Laycock de Normanville overdrive for £15 and arranged to have it fitted by Standard-Triumph while I was away on a holiday in 1960.

On return, and finding the work very well done, it was a joy to be able to switch into overdrive top and see the revs drop down to a much more comfortable cruising pace, but I was a bit shattered when the bill for fitting it arrived, charging £40 (the equivalent of some £600 today). Overdrive could be switched in on second and third gears as well as top. On one occasion when I was required to cover a local rally for the journal, I arrived in the Triumph and was told I should be a competitor, and a rally plate was thrust at me to stick on the front of the car. In the company of Sandy, my flat mate, we set off, with Sandy reading out the instructions, and for about half an hour we were flying along tiny lanes in the dark, using second and overdrive second nearly all the time, and trying to keep up an average of 30mph. On one corner I arrived much too fast, and the TR3A went nose first off the road and into the hedge. Fortunately we were able to back out and no damage had been done, and in spite of this delay we arrived at the control and were told we were on time.

'Here are your next instructions,' said the marshal, and handed a postcard on which were ten six-figure map references, all to be visited in any order. That was all very well, but unlike other competitors who had been following their progress on the OS map, we hadn't a clue as to where we were. After that experience, and recalling my earlier determination not to push my luck too hard with the Triumph, I decided that rallying was not for me, though I did take tremendous pleasure in covering and reporting rallies. It was much better, I reckoned, to describe how someone has crashed and finished upside down in the scenery than to be the unfortunate individual!

In September 1960, the technical editor, Harry Mundy, called in at the Coventry office where I was working, and after a cup of tea and a chat he announced that he was going over to Rootes to see the new models they would be introducing at the Earls Court Show the following month and asked if I would like to accompany him. I accepted eagerly, of course and, after a pleasant lunch at Rootes and detailed briefing on the new models, we returned to the office. While Harry was having another cup of tea, I went up to the nearby multistorey car park to bring the Triumph down. I was absolutely stunned to see an empty space in the slot where I always parked it.

Car theft wasn't as common as it became later, and it took some while for it really to sink in. Had I indeed left the Triumph there, or had I come up in something else? When the inescapable truth emerged I went back and told Harry what had happened. He commiserated and took me to my parents' house at Coventry, where I spent the night instead of returning to the flat I shared with a friend at Leicester. I informed the police and immediately notified my bank because my cheque book had been among personal documents locked in the boot.

What puzzled me was how thieves had managed to overcome my DIY burglar alarm, which sounded powerful Nanucci triple trumpet air horns if anyone switched on the ignition without first operating the secret turn-off switch. But other anti-theft measures such as steering column locks were yet to come, and car theft was easy. With the TR3A one had only to slide open the window in the detachable side-screen, reach in to pull the door release cord, note the key number stamped on the ignition key slot, and go off to Halfords to buy the necessary key.

Later, I learned that the air horns had indeed gone off, and if I had still been in the office I could not have failed to hear them, but unfortunately I had been several miles away at Rootes. The amateur thieves had gone away and reported to their boss what had happened, and he simply returned with them, opened the bonnet and pulled the wire off.

When I was an officer cadet in the army, I needed a bank account and opened one at Barclays in Aldershot. So when the thieves found my cheque book in the boot of the Triumph, with an Aldershot account, they drove to Aldershot in the Triumph on the following Sunday when the banks would be closed, bought a copy of the local paper, and went to visit various advertisers expressing interest in the cars advertised. The first prospect wisely refused to accept a cheque, but a Lieutenant Colonel selling his Morris Oxford Traveller was taken in by the apparent genuine interest in the car, and accepted a payment of £377 10s written on my cheque book. He was being posted abroad, wanted to get rid of the Morris before he went, and was tempted by the good price offered. In those days, cheques did not have the name of the drawer printed on them, so the thief was able to sign any name. With the same technique they also 'purchased' a Hillman Minx.

The colonel was a bit anxious about the cheque, and as soon as the banks opened on Monday he went round to Barclays in Aldershot, only to learn the dreaded truth that the cheque book had been in a stolen car and there was a STOP on the account. He went straight to the police and gave full details of the offence to a CID officer, Detective Constable Vincent. Then came an extraordinary coincidence. Vincent was off on another job, and on the way passed a used car dealer in Aldershot where he saw what he thought was the missing Morris Oxford Traveller. He checked the number and found, sure enough, that it was the colonel's fraudulently purchased car.

The dealer, of course, was the innocent party, having bought the car at the auction that morning. DC Vincent went next to the car auction where he learned that the cheques would go out on Thursday, and the address of a lodging house in Farnborough was given. The thief didn't risk going there to collect the mail on Friday morning, but got a soldier to go for him, who found DC Vincent waiting patiently for him. 'Where were you told to take it?' produced the answer that he was to hand it to a man waiting round the corner in his sports car. A police car was then called up, which boxed in the Triumph and the thief was arrested. Investigations then unearthed an elaborate car ringing operation, which had been going on in Coventry for weeks, and had already stolen sixteen cars. It was certainly bad luck for them that a car purchased with a dud cheque on the Sunday, sold 30 miles away at an auction on the Monday, should then be brought back to Aldershot and displayed for sale within a couple of hours, in time for the officer handling the case to spot it!

The case opened at Birmingham Assizes six months later and lasted a full week. The ringleader was sentenced to twelve years' imprisonment, subsequently reduced to eight on appeal. Four members of the gang, including the one who had stolen my Triumph, were given three years each, and a fifth, less-involved criminal received a two-year sentence.

Not long after the theft I went to Aldershot police station to recover the TR3A, which didn't seem to have suffered too badly, and I gained a rather good toolkit left in the boot. I had to get new number plates for the car, the original ones having been substituted, and at least there was the compensation that it hadn't been crashed by any of the various criminals who had been driving it.

In a quite separate incident, months later, I drove off in the morning, reached down to turn on the radio, and realised that my fine Motorola set had been stolen during the night. I was an early victim of what was to become the epidemic of car radio thefts. The next Motorola purchased to replace it had transistors, which didn't like the warmth from the heater directly above it and would cut out after about ten minutes. But by then my days with the TR3A, which I so enjoyed, were coming to an end when the firm decided it was time I was allocated a company car.

Towards the end, I had the TR3A resprayed in a darker blue by the same firm, Portland Autos of Sheffield, that had resprayed my Sunbeam-Talbot. With the hardtop in black instead of white, the combination suited it much better and it looked very good, but when I came to advertise it for sale with 50,000 miles behind it, response was slow except for endless calls from people wanting to buy the hardtop, which was offered separately at £20. I could have asked a lot more for the hardtop, but was content eventually to sell the TR3A for £460, representing depreciation of less than £130 a year.

T W E N T Y - T W O

Vauxhall Friary

☰ In Yugoslavia we were ordered to pay a fine of 10,000 dinars

After my earlier exploits abroad, which had always been followed by a touring article in *The Autocar*, manufacturers were always ready to provide a test car for a long Continental journey, and when I approached Vauxhall with a request to take one of their Velox estate cars to Yugoslavia – as it was called in 1959 – they responded with enthusiasm. The car's estate body was a conversion built for them by Friary Motors, and hearing that the car would be heavily loaded with my three friends and a mountain of camping gear, they thoughtfully provided a spare rear spring. The 6-cylinder 2¼-litre engine was also modified to a low-compression cylinder head in readiness for the poor quality Yugopetrol that it would have to suffer.

We crossed overnight on the Dover–Ostend ferry and then put 606 miles behind us, taking us to our first campsite in Austria. Unfortunately, hidden in the long grass was a tree stump, and as we went over it there was an ominous thump from underneath. Inspection showed that it had hit and bent the track rod, and the next morning the sound of squealing front tyres accompanied us the short distance down to a garage where we could speak no German and they no English, but they were quick to understand the problem.

I was guided on to an inspection ramp, and the mechanic went down and returned in no more than a couple of minutes with the damaged section of track rod. He then knocked it several times against the work bench, looking along it each time until he was satisfied that it was straight, and almost as quickly as it had been removed, it was refitted. We had paid the modest bill and were driving out of the garage within thirty minutes of our arrival, highly impressed at such efficient service.

As a car tester I was always keen to submit cars to every possible challenge, and after seeing in the AA book that the Loibl pass connecting Austria with Yugoslavia was the steepest in Europe, with gradients of 1-in-3½, I was keen to have a go at it. As we left Klagenfurt, the last town before the Austro-Yugo border, the downpour started, and we were clearly in for a soaking if the Friary refused on any of the steep

The Vauxhall Friary estate car stood up to the poor Yugoslav roads amazingly well, nearly all the time trailing clouds of dust behind it.

hairpins, but in spite of having only a three-speed gearbox with a very high first gear, it took the climb exceptionally well.

The Loibl introduced us to the appalling state of inland Yugoslavian roads back in 1959, always dirt surfaced with the constant din of stones flying up underneath. Traffic seemed almost non-existent, but one had to be ready for the occasional vehicle, usually an overladen lorry, coming the other way and inevitably the meeting would be on a blind corner. The car was soon covered in mud and dirt.

A dramatic change came when we reached the coast road at Crikvenica, the surface now being tarred and the road curving its way at times through steep cuttings where tons of bright red-coloured rock had been blasted away to make space for it. The rain had stopped at last but it was still very dark and cloudy.

The good road continued as far as Zadar, where as the map clearly warned, the tarred surface ended and we were back on stones and dirt. After passing through Sibenim and Split, we set up our fifth camp in a suitable green area just off the road near Makarska. Quite suddenly in the evening, a tremendous gale sprang up, and we didn't get much sleep as the wind bashed away at our ex-army tent, the seams of which opened up a bit but it stood up to the onslaught very gamely. Rather weary next morning we were settling down to breakfast when a jeep arrived with two policemen who demanded to see our passports. I gathered them together and handed them over, and was then shocked to see the policeman getting into the jeep and preparing to depart. I ran across and asked for our passports, but the only reply was 'Polizia Makarska'.

We packed up rapidly and drove the short distance to Makarska, and were trying to explain to someone that we wanted the police station, when a young boy asked: 'Can I help youse guys?' It turned out that he was a Yugoslav lad whose parents had emigrated to Australia, and he was back here on holiday. It was fortuitous, because he was keen to help and turned out to be a good interpreter. At the police station we learned that the chief police officer had gone fishing, and that we couldn't have our passports back until we had attended court next day on a charge of camping without registering at the local police station. This was a requirement not explained in any of the material the Yugoslav tourist office in London had provided.

Next day we met up with our young interpreter, always addressing us as 'youse guys'. He proved much better at translating than the old man the court provided, and in spite of putting up every avenue of defence we could think of and explaining that I was writing an article about touring in Yugoslavia, we were ordered to pay a fine of 10,000 dinars. Fortunately we had all ignored the regulation that no more than 3,000 dinars could be taken in, obliging one to change currency at the ridiculous official rate of 1,120 dinars to the £1. At banks in England we had been able to get 1,750 dinars to the £1, so the fine was less than £2 each, but was still highly resented.

We said goodbye to our young assistant, gave him some spending money and thanked him for his invaluable help, and drove on to Dubrovnik hastily overriding the demand from one of the party that he wanted to make a night raid at the police station and pour our sugar supply into the jeep's fuel tank!

The weather had now changed, and Dubrovnik was quite beautiful, but not so the campsite – we were now using official sites to avoid further trouble with the police. It was very messy, and became intolerable when the water supply failed, so we packed up and headed north-west through Banja Luka to pick up the Belgrade *autoput*. Although only single carriageway it was a good road, mainly carrying heavy lorries, and took us all the way to Zagreb and Ljubljana.

Instead of going back over the Loibl pass, we opted for the less severe Wurzen pass back to Austria at Villach, but the descent was to prove the most frightening experience of the whole trip. The drum brakes of the heavily laden Vauxhall Friary soon cooked up and provided hardly any braking, and the high first gear didn't hold the car back enough. I spared the brakes as much as I could but just had to use them really hard to scrub some speed off for each of the interminable hairpin bends, and would then release the pedal and fight the car round in a fusillade of flying stones and gravel. It was a great relief when the pass finally levelled out, the brakes could be spared, and gradually the stink of burning brake linings began to waft away.

Our troubles were not over, because when a tyre went flat we changed the wheel, took it to a local garage to be repaired, and it was found that the wheel rim had begun to split allowing the air to escape from the tubeless tyre. No replacement wheel was available, but on the suggestion of the garage staff in Germany an inner tube was fitted inside the tubeless tyre.

Later, in Belgium, the other tyre went flat, again with a split along the rim. The tubed original was fitted, and I took it carefully for the rest of the journey back to London, though the split became worse and towards the end one could see the pink colour of the inner tube through the crack.

Apart from this problem, resulting from the combination of heavy loading and the appalling Yugoslav inland roads, the Friary had served us very well and proved extremely comfortable. It consumed 6 pints of oil in the 3,000-mile round trip – good for those days – and overall fuel consumption was 20.8mpg. In the 1950s, throughout Germany, Austria and Yugoslavia, the most common car in the campsites was the omnipotent Volkswagen Beetle, and I couldn't help noticing the marked contrast between the chuntering clattering noise of their air-cooled engines and the smooth purr of our 6-cylinder Vauxhall engine.

When the delivery driver came to the office to collect the Friary, I warned him about the state of the rear wheel, but he knew all about it. I had sent a report to Vauxhall as soon as we were back, and he said: 'Don't worry, I've been told not to exceed 30mph.' At least he didn't have far to go, from our London office back to Luton.

LAND ROVER AND ASTON MARTIN DBIII CONVERTIBLE

The van coming the other way was probably doing about 60mph, so we had a closing speed of around 180mph

'Are they trying to pull the wool over our eyes?' asked Michael Brown, associate editor of The Autocar.

'No, I don't think so,' I replied. 'If it really happens, it's going to be extremely good. We're going to have a dual-carriageway road restricted to motor vehicles, running all the way from just north of London to Yorkshire, with limited access at flyover junctions and two lanes on each carriageway.' The date was Tuesday 20 September 1955, and Michael had sent me to cover a Ministry of Transport Press conference at which the minister, Harold Watkinson, announced the route for the first part of the proposed London–Yorkshire motorway, and I had certainly been impressed. Little did I know that even before it was opened, I would come within a few feet of being killed on it, in what would have been a spectacular accident.

The prospect of an end, eventually, to the agonies of that awful A5 journey, was encouraging. Almost every time I made my journey home – about every five or six weeks – to see my parents at Coventry there would be an appalling accident somewhere on the A5, so I had a strong personal interest in the plans. The new road would start south of St Albans, and would finish temporarily near Dunchurch.

A Land Rover long-wheelbase coped well with the often-deep ruts during our unofficial motorway reconnaissance trip while the first section of M1 was being built.

This section was estimated to cost £15,000,000. You wouldn't get a mile of motorway for that money these days.

I was tremendously interested in the provision of new roads and was always writing about them, especially when news came of developments on the Continent, to try to reveal how Britain, with one of the most antiquated road networks in Europe, was being left behind. One of the pieces I wrote, entitled 'Roads for France', gave details of construction of what was to become the world's most famous underpass – beneath the Place de l'Alma in Paris, where the fatal accident killing Diana, Princess of Wales and Dodi Fayed occurred in 1997. It was published in the news pages of *The Autocar* in the 2 March 1956 issue and clearly visible in the accompanying picture was one of the supporting pillars which was to cause so much damage to the Mercedes-Benz. The question that never seems to have been raised in all the endless inquests into the accident is why there was no protective Armco around the pillars. If such a safety barrier had been in place to deflect any out-of-control vehicles, the accident would have been a grazing side impact instead of a frontal one, and the likelihood is that no one would have been injured.

But back to the London–Yorkshire motorway as it was called at that stage, with the M numbering system still to be devised. Mr Watkinson declared later that it was hoped to begin land acquisition for the first part, including the spur from Dunchurch to link up with the existing A45 to Coventry, before the end of 1957. It was also announced later that to cope with future traffic growth there would be three lanes on each carriageway, except for the Watford and Dunchurch spurs which would have two lanes.

Early in 1958 it was declared that contractors submitting tenders for construction had been asked to quote for completion by October 1959 or October 1960, and it was revealed that John Laing and Son Ltd and Tarmac Civil Engineering – the two successful tenderers – had chosen the earlier date. They were going to do the whole job, totalling some 72 miles, in eighteen months. It would involve excavation of some 10,000,000 cubic yards – we didn't have metres then – of earth, and surfacing 2,400,000 square yards of road. Apart from the spurs at each end, the main carriageways would be 36ft wide, allowing three lanes with a grass shoulder for any broken-down vehicles.

From time to time early in 1959, colleagues from *Flight* magazine would come in with pictures and declared excitedly that the new road was sending a white scar across the earth visible in an aircraft from miles away. I was also excited about the progress, and asked if I could be flown over it with a photographer to record progress.

It was soon arranged, and I was taken up in the twin-engine Miles Gemini aircraft owned by *Flight* magazine and piloted by staff member Mark Lambert, with a photographer. This trip resulted in a fascinating batch of aerial pictures. But Mark made violent changes of direction from left to right and back again for the benefit of the photographer, all the time with the warning hooter blaring away to remind

Before the M1 was opened I set up my camera on a tripod and took this time exposure showing readers how it would seem in the dark. The car is an Austin-Healey Sprite.

us that we were very low with the landing gear still up, and it was the only time I was ever sick in an aircraft. Suddenly Mark noticed that the door on one side was not properly fastened, and we had to make an unscheduled landing at Elstree to close it properly, after which he had to go through all the pre-take-off cockpit drill again. After this enforced rest I felt much better.

My appetite for a ground 'recce' was all the stronger after seeing it from the air, and application was made to the Ministry, but we were told that to avoid risk of interrupting the progress of work no press-facility trips would be allowed but that we would be invited to the opening ceremony. I was disappointed and decided to have a go at just driving along it uninvited and see what happened. The worst possible outcome was that I might be prosecuted for trespass. The editor liked the idea, but said he could not give it his official sanction. A suitable vehicle was needed, and Rover provided a long-wheelbase Land Rover. My colleague John Davey volunteered to come with me, and we chose the 1959 May bank holiday, when we knew there would be no construction work going on. On Davey's suggestion we wore suits and ties with wellington boots as our disguise, and if asked what we were doing we were going to say that we were compiling a progress report. A millboard with a Ministry of Transport press release on the top completed the picture. The 'disguise' was so effective that when we stopped at a pub on the A5 on the return after a very exhausting day, a man approached us and asked if there was any chance of giving him a job on the new motorway. I had to disappoint him by saying that we were nothing to do with the new motorway, and I added, 'We're just a couple of spies!'

Progress in the Land Rover was slow, because although at times the road would seem to be almost finished, with the top tarmac surface wanting only its cat's eyes and lane markings, suddenly it would end, plunge down 3ft and we would be bounding over rutted soil and following the rough tracks of the contractors' huge earth-moving vehicles. Sometimes the ruts were terribly deep and of course the Land Rover couldn't straddle them, so we would be bouncing along with the wheels on one side about 2ft higher than the other. There would also be unfinished bridges, calling for a long detour. But at least the ground was dry and hard after a long dry spell.

As hoped, we didn't see anyone throughout our exploration and we had a lovely sunny day for the trip. John Davey had arranged a picnic, which we enjoyed, sitting on the grass above the Luton junction. Nearby was a huge steel girder crossing the carriageway as the first stage in bridge construction, and on it a notice: 'This end to arrive pointing to Luton.' We wondered if we ought to tell someone, because it was clearly pointing the other way.

It all took a long time, and dusk was falling when we arrived on the final section bypassing Dunchurch, so I didn't spot the single strand of barbed wire across the road. The Land Rover took it across the bottom of the windscreen and snapped it with hardly a mark on the vehicle, but any motorcyclist having an unofficial burn-up on the new road could well have been killed by it. In those days, of course, if the notice said 'Road Closed – Keep Out' everyone except Bladon observed it!

The project was well received in the office, the editor regarding it as something of a scoop, since nothing had appeared in the national press about it, and, as expected, there was tremendous reader interest. Six pages were allocated for the article, and the issue in which it appeared (5 June 1959) sold out.

After finding how easy it was just to drive on the new motorway without seeking permission, I came to use parts of it quite frequently on my journeys to the Midlands, keeping up to date with progress, and my last article before the opening ceremony, scheduled for 2 November, appeared in the 30 October 1959 issue. The heading picture was a time exposure, which I took at night with the camera on a tripod, showing the road lit up by the headlights of an Austin-Healey Sprite on which I was doing the road test. It gave a good impression of the motorway by night with the cat's eyes curving away into the distance and one of the reflective signs showing '½m to Northampton A45'. I don't think one could get away with doing that now! The article gave advice on motorway driving, with the recommendation to increase tyre pressures by 4–6psi if high speeds were to be sustained, and the important warning, 'If you see a knot of vehicles in the distance which may mean that there has been an accident, reduce speed at once and be prepared to stop.'

Maurice Smith received the official invitation from the Ministry of Transport to witness the opening ceremony on Monday 2 November 1959, and declared that he was keen to attend and wanted me to go along as well. Mike Clayton also regarded it as a great occasion, and said that he would like to be included in the party.

We arranged to meet at Radlett, where Maurice's mother still lived in the fine house called Pembury. In earlier times when Maurice's father, Iliffe director Geoffrey Smith, was alive new staff would say excitedly: 'I've been invited to tea on Sunday at Mr Smith's house, Pembury in Radlett.' Those in the know would smile and say: 'Take your gardening clothes!'

Perhaps the opening ceremony had generated a lot of extra traffic out of London, because I had a terribly slow journey and arrived about ten minutes late to find Mike Clayton's Ford Consul II parked half on the pavement in Radlett, and Maurice looking very impatient beside his Aston Martin DBIII Convertible. It was a magnificent car, which I had driven many times since Maurice was always very generous in allowing staff to borrow it. I presume it was company owned, though it was always spoken of as his private property. Immediately he jumped in and we set off up to Pembury, parked my Triumph TR3A and Clayton's Consul on the spacious drive in front of the house, then Mike climbed into the back of the Aston. I went in the front armed with the information from the Ministry about the opening, the windscreen sticker, which I still have, giving access to the ceremony, and the file of maps and data that I had accumulated about the new road. At the south end of the M10 police saw the

This windscreen sticker gave admission to the motorway for the short M1 opening ceremony under the new Minister of Transport Ernest Marples.

pass on the windscreen and waved us past the barrier; we were soon zooming up the M10 at 80mph. The extension of the M1 south to join the Watford bypass at Berrygrove was not scheduled for completion until later in the year.

As we joined the new three-lane carriageway after the M10 and cruised along in the Aston, I read to Maurice the instructions given by the Ministry that no southbound traffic from the Luton junction would be allowed until after the opening ceremony. Both carriageways were to be used for northbound traffic, and we saw several cars, including an Armstrong Siddeley Sapphire with mayoral crest on the roof, travelling north on the southbound carriageway. We were on the northbound carriageway. The opening ceremony was to be at the A6 junction near Luton, where the contracts of Laing and Tarmac Civil Engineering joined, and there is – or used to be – a plaque on the bridge wall marking the event. It may have disappeared following the major reconstruction work to widen the carriageways.

Maurice was quite carried away with the excitement of the occasion, and once we had taken the slip road from the M10 onto the M1, he said: 'I had no idea it was going to be so wide and extensive,' and proceeded to open up the Aston.

On the day of opening, M1 bridges were thronged with spectators.

Suddenly, just as we neared the top of the gradient near the A5 junction, a small contractor's van appeared heading south on our carriageway. The Aston was in the middle lane, its speedometer showing 120mph, and overtaking another car heading to the opening ceremony. The van coming the other way was probably doing about 60mph, so we had a closing speed of around 180mph. If we had collided it would have been a phenomenal accident in which all four of us would have been killed, but fortunately the van stayed in its lane (on our right) and we in ours. It happened so suddenly that there would have been little time for any evasive action, but contractors were familiar with using the carriageways in either direction as single roads before completion, and keeping to the left.

Somewhat surprised, Maurice gave one of his favourite comments: 'Oh! There's a thing!' For a fleeting instant the three vehicles filled all three lanes, the car we were passing on the left and the Aston in the centre, both heading north, and the contractor's van in the third lane heading south. Only later did I fully appreciate how close we had been to becoming the motorway's first traffic fatalities. If Maurice had been in the third lane there could have been a horrendous head-on collision.

After that, he eased up a little, and we duly parked on the Luton slip road and joined the crowd at the marquee. Brief speeches were made, with Sir Owen Williams, head of the engineering consultants that had overseen the project, telling us how the motorway was being handed over on the very day contracted eighteen months earlier and within the budget of £24,000,000. Then Ernest Marples snipped the tape, and used a radio-telephone at one of the Ford Zephyr police cars ordering removal of the barriers. I was a bit disappointed that Harold Watkinson had not performed the opening ceremony, since he was the minister who had done more than anyone else to get the motorway programme under way. But Ernest Marples was to prove equally vigorous in developing the network.

We hurried back to the Aston and drove north at speeds varying between 90 and 120mph, with Maurice all the time pointing out 'suitable straights for a max', as he envisaged that the M1 would be used for maximum speed testing of fast cars in future for the journal, as a cheaper alternative to taking them abroad.

We were soon at the front, waving to crowds on the bridges, but after every access point there would always be a small gaggle of traffic newly allowed on to the motorway. At Crick, where this first section of M1 ended near Rugby, we stopped briefly to put the Aston's hood down, then circled round and headed back south. It was soon very cold, but not enough to dampen our spirits.

By now there was quite a lot of traffic scattered along the motorway, but most drivers responded promptly to a flash of the Aston's headlamps. The DBIII, I recall, had an overdrive, and Maurice commented that the new M1 would increase the demand for overdrives. Indeed, within a year I had become fed up with my TR3A's engine revving at 4,000rpm at a mere 80mph, and forked out heavily to have a Laycock de Normanville overdrive fitted.

All too soon, it seemed, the great event was over. We went back to Radlett for a drink with Maurice's mother, and then drove individually back to the office.

Marples was reported to have commented later, 'I was appalled at the speeds I saw on the M1,' but then anything over about 60mph looked fast to those who had never been abroad or visited a race meeting. A number of drivers, unaccustomed to cruising at over 60mph, found themselves still going far too fast when they arrived at the two service areas.

In the next few years, tyre failures became the chief problem, with cars often leaving heavy black lines where they had burst a tyre and dry-skidded right across the centre strip and on to the opposite carriageway. There was no centre barrier in those early years, but with so little traffic the chances of not hitting anything on the other carriageway were quite good. The other problem was that the hard shoulder was anything but hard, and lorries that stopped there on breaking down often became stuck in the soft grass.

But the real disaster-causer was fog, as people just followed the cat's eyes and hoped it would be clear. After a particularly bad pile-up just before Christmas 1965, the new Transport Minister Hugh Fraser suddenly declared that there would be flashing amber warning lights, which would be switched on in fog to indicate an advisory 30mph speed limit, and that – shock and horror – there would be a mandatory upper speed limit of 70mph.

'Never mind,' everyone said, 'it's only for an experimental period of four months.'

T W E N T Y - F O U R

Austin Westminster A99

≡ I had changed the rule of the road six times in two weeks

'Perhaps you should take one of these new big BMC 3-litre cars,' suggested the editor, Maurice Smith, when he heard I was planning a holiday trip to Scandinavia. The loan of an Austin A99 was arranged with the press office of BMC. It was still called the Austin Westminster, though this name was tending to be dropped in favour of A99. It was launched with the Wolseley version, called 6/99, in August 1959 as the first of the 1960 range, so it was still a relatively new model when I set off with three companions and a rather poor borrowed tent, for a two-week tour of Scandinavia.

Just before departure a phone call from BMC told me that the car with manual four-speed transmission and BorgWarner overdrive had been involved in an accident, so did I mind taking an automatic instead. Reckoning that fuel consumption would be much heavier, and knowing that the BorgWarner automatic was a very stodgy and unresponsive transmission, I wasn't too pleased about the change, but gracefully and gratefully accepted.

We drove up to Newcastle and took the night ferry to Bergen, and the ferry cost – even at the much higher value of currency then – was very reasonable at £10 for the car and the same amount per passenger. On the quay at Bergen we met a British party waiting for the return boat, with the identical car, another Austin Westminster automatic. They warned us that although the scenery in Norway was wonderful, we wouldn't be able to cover much more than 20 miles every hour.

This seemed highly pessimistic, perhaps to be taken with large amounts of salt, but we were soon to learn that they weren't far out in their estimate. It wasn't the surface of the roads in Norway that was the problem but their narrow and winding nature. No doubt they are much better now.

All the time the surfaces were in water-bound gravel, adopted because of the resistance to frost damage, and in fact providing surprisingly good grip. Traffic densities were also very light, and one would often drive for nearly half an hour without meeting another vehicle, but when one did arrive, usually on a corner, very prompt braking was required, and it was often necessary almost to stop and squeeze past each other.

In these conditions I soon adopted the technique of left-foot braking. Approaching a corner I would have my left foot poised over the brake pedal and the reaction time was considerably reduced. After this journey with the A99 automatic it became second nature always to use the left foot on the brake if the car had automatic transmission. One year, in the 1990s, a stand at the Frankfurt Show was running a brake reaction test on a simulator. I wasn't going to have to drive again that day, so had consumed quite a lot of champagne at various stands, yet my times were consistently breaking 0.25sec, which is verging on Stirling Moss territory. Suddenly, the man running the test said: 'Oh, you're using your left foot on the brake. You're not allowed to do that – it's cheating.'

'Nonsense,' I replied, 'I always use my left foot on the brake when there's no clutch pedal.' I then had to be tested again using my right foot, and immediately the reaction times lengthened to nearly 0.4sec. I had long since established that this technique was much safer once one has mastered the need for proper control of the left foot in an action that is very different from that of pushing down a clutch pedal.

The weather in Norway was disappointing, with endless rain, so the unfortunate Austin was soon plastered with dirt from the untarred roads. Perhaps Sweden will be better, we thought, so we crossed into Sweden south of Trondheim and I drove hard right across Sweden to the east coast, 200 miles north of Stockholm, but still we could not shake off the rain and were glad of the two-speed wipers, a fairly novel

Norway provides fine scenery, but the gravel roads in 1960 made for slow progress.

feature in the Austin. They were almost continually on fast speed. Camping also was not very pleasant, with the tent always having to be packed away saturated.

Sweden at that time was the only country in Europe that drove on the left but had direct land connection with other countries that drove on the right. Iceland and

Great Britain, of course, also drove on the left but were surrounded by water so that the ferry made easy transition. How would we know when to change over, I wondered, but when we reached the border to Sweden we were told by an official in good English, 'Drive on the right for three kilometres.' At the end of this distance we came to a centre island with the international 'keep right' arrows, and 50 yards farther along another barrier had the arrows pointing the other way. Vehicles in the 'no-man's-land' between them had to take it in turns, and from then on I had to remember to drive on the left as was much more familiar.

Although the roads in Sweden were much better, and we were able to cruise fast, the scenery was much less interesting. We seemed to go for miles seeing only endless pine forests, and although the occasional lake would come into view in the distance we seldom were able to get near the water and find somewhere attractive to pitch the tent.

What I did notice with interest, and commented about in the articles I wrote later, was that nearly all cars in Sweden had left-hand drive, and as they were driving on the left it made overtaking difficult – an experience familiar to the British driver on the Continent. I learned that this was in anticipation that Sweden would one day change the rule of the road and start to drive on the right. On this holiday I had changed the rule of the road six times and instilled into my head the need always to think when starting the engine, especially when driving abroad or newly back in Britain, about which side of the road to drive om.

Also noticed, and regarded with some amusement, was the Swedish driver's meticulous observance of speed limits. Every time a town or village was approached, the brake lights all came on, and the speed of every car was down to or below the limit speed by the time the restriction sign was reached.

After passing through Stockholm we went to the west, crossing the border again briefly into Norway, before heading down to take the ferry to Denmark and return via Germany, Belgium and the Ostend–Dover ferry.

The Austin Westminster, with its rather unattractive square shape designed by Pininfarina, had served us very well. It had a 6-cylinder 3-litre pushrod engine, and despite an all-up weight not far short of 2 tons it performed well and proved capable of cruising at 90mph, with occasional spurts to an indicated 100mph. The highest mileage covered in the day was 541, and in a single hour, on German *Autobahnen*, 79. Fuel consumption varied from 17.2mpg in the Norwegian mountains, to 21.2mpg in Denmark. Overall, for the whole distance of 3,128 miles it averaged 19.5mpg.

When the time came to hand the car back, I had resumed work at the Coventry office, which I was running following Charles Haywood's despatch to London. Over the years I have met hundreds of car delivery drivers, but will always remember the one who came to the Coventry office of *The Autocar* to collect the Westminster. It was the time of the sex scandal involving government minister John Profumo and

Changeover point at the border: going from Norway to Sweden one had to pass the first arrow on the right, and the next one on the left, and from then on drive on the left in Sweden. Now, of course, Sweden also drives on the right.

Christine Keeler, and this very overweight delivery driver chatted away as we walked to the car, and asked me: 'Have you driven the Jaguar Mark X?' Then without waiting for the reply he hurried on: 'Cor, that's a marvellous car. I'll tell you what – I'd like to get that Christine Keeler in the back of a Mark X! Cor, she must be a passionate bloody woman.'

I laughed, but the laughter ended abruptly as we approached the Austin, parked in an official bay in the middle of Coventry's Corporation Street, and saw that a back tyre was completely flat. It had been alright when I drove up from London in the morning.

'Don't you worry,' said the driver, 'I'll fix it.' But I insisted on helping, so while he was jacking the car up, I started winding down the spare wheel, which was carried on a cradle beneath the boot. It didn't move at first, but then came down with a thump and spilt a mass of grit, dust and mud on to the road.

'That's Norway's dirt roads for you,' I said.

'Cor,' replied the driver, 'you didn't need to bring them all back with you!'

TWENTY-FIVE

SUNBEAM ALPINE AND LOTUS SUPER SEVEN

I asked him to get me to a hospital in Athens; if he had done that I would not have survived

What is the common factor between a Sunbeam Alpine and a Lotus Super Seven? is a question that may well be asked. Well, they are both two-seater sports cars, but the really significant linking factor came when both of these cars in the same year were involved in very bad accidents with near-fatal results for two members of the staff. The first happened early in 1961.

An offer came from Helpa, the Greek National Tourist Office. They were very anxious to increase tourism to Greece, and would reimburse the travel costs for a journalist and photographer from *Autocar* to drive out to Greece in May, showing that the road journey was now good, and at the same time to cover the international Greek car rally called the Acropolis. I was asked by the editor to take on the task. The photographer would be Bill, and it was suggested that Rootes would provide an example of the new Sunbeam Alpine for the journey. In those days the photographers were still using bulky plate cameras, and a huge case of glass photographic plates had to be accommodated, so the little Alpine two-seater was hard-pressed to provide space for it all. But there was quite a lot of room behind the front seats for our luggage while most of the lockable boot space was taken by the expensive and valuable photographic equipment.

The journey started off well as we traversed Belgium and Germany, where we called briefly to look up my brother who was stationed in the army near the Dutch border at Venlo. We fell into the habit of changing drivers every time we stopped for fuel. Only occasionally after this ill-fated journey did I ever again allow one of the photographers to drive the test car.

Studying the map as we drove in Austria, I noticed a possible shortcut that would save a lot of mileage, so we decided to try it. The road crossed the mountains and became unsurfaced, but we were making good progress when suddenly I smelt oil, and noticed that the oil pressure gauge had dropped to zero. I cut the engine at once, and freewheeled to a stop. Sure enough, there was a long oil slick along the centre of the single-track road, and the sump plug was missing. Walking back to the start of the oil slick we saw a mark in the centre of the road where the sump plug had obviously hit the ground and been spun out.

'It will have gone a long way,' said Bill, and picking up a stone he threw it along the road. Almost like magic, there was the sump plug only a few feet from where the stone came to rest. We obviously couldn't use the engine, but the road at this stage was a long downhill slope, and near the bottom we could see some houses, so we coasted up to the first of these that had a telephone line.

This was one of the occasions that persuaded me later to learn German, but at that stage I knew nothing of the language, and nor did the lady who answered the door know any English. Eventually we put the message across with 'Wagen kaput', and the lady telephoned to a garage where they found someone who spoke English. It took a lot of persuading to convince him that all we needed was oil, and that there was nothing else wrong with the car. How much oil did we want? I took a flyer and thought a gallon would be enough, and I knew that meant about 5 litres.

We settled down to wait, and the good Austrian lady offered us some food, but unfortunately we had no Austrian currency. The offer of a quite high-value German *deutschmark* note left her baffled, but then she rang a friend and a long discussion followed as she described the note she had been offered, and then suddenly her eyes lit up on hearing its equivalent value in Austria. A good meal followed, and eventually the mechanic arrived with the oil. He had no difficulty understanding the value of another German note we provided.

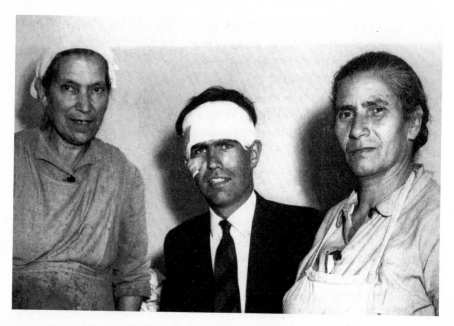

Bandaged and ready for the flight back to England after three days in a Greek hospital following the accident in which the photographer put me head first through the windscreen. I think my female companions here are cleaners, not nurses! (Bill Banks)

Yugoslavia was terrible. As we drove along the *autoput* towards Belgrade, it poured with rain, and whenever the brakes had to be used they would pull to one side or the other as the pads bit through the film of water. On catching up with the occasional lorries throwing up torrents of spray it was difficult to see if it was clear to overtake, and most of the time there would be nothing coming the other way, but when there was, and the brakes had to be used, there was always this uncertainty as to which way the steering would pull. It reminded me of my dreadful Hillman 10, though of course the Alpine had a completely different braking system with discs at the front. The *autoput* in those days had only one twin-lane carriageway.

We eventually reached Belgrade and found one of the few good-quality hotels there, and set off next day feeling refreshed and in much better weather, but it was a nasty change to find that our map, showing the *autoput* unfinished after Nis, was correct. Our cruising speed dropped from 60–80mph in overdrive to as little as 20 or 30mph, and the little Alpine didn't like it a bit. The bonnet kept coming open, and the cover behind the seats at the front of the compartment where the hood was stowed constantly flopped forward. Eventually we put one of Bill's camera bags there to jam it closed. The engine also didn't like the low-octane Yugopetrol, which was all that was available, and pinked whenever the throttle was opened. On one of the really bad stretches of unmade road I said to Bill: 'You realise we've got to do all this again getting back to civilisation after we've finished covering the rally?' But it was not to be.

Stretches of good newly laid concrete alternated with stones, gravel and dust. Twice we met a British car going the other way, and both stopped to chat and exchange notes about the state of the road behind and ahead. We passed through Skopje and were glad we didn't stay there as the following year it suffered a devastating earthquake. It was sheer joy to arrive at the border, cross into Greece and see Mobil and Shell fuel stations where we could treat the Alpine to some better – but far more expensive – petrol, and enjoy consistently good roads, albeit subject to tolls. The weather was now sunny and very hot. When we saw the sign in Greek and English by the roadside reading 'Spring of Diana' we enjoyed stopping and having a cooling drink of clear fresh water.

It's a long way – some 400 miles – from the Yugoslav border to Athens, and after checking in at the rally control it was very disheartening to study the route book and find that the rally immediately went right back up to the north, exactly where we had come from. We had already done 2,000 miles since leaving London, and now we were on to the rally route and rally schedules, so there was not much time for such luxuries as sleep and meals.

Over the next few days we worked hard and long, chasing the rally, taking shortcuts wherever possible and with Bill taking pictures while I grabbed every opportunity to talk to competitors and find out what was happening. But I had become increasingly concerned about Bill's driving: he was jerky, impetuous and very bad on judgement. When the Alpine arrived from Rootes before our long journey I transferred to it some triple-trumpet Nanucci air horns that had been on my Triumph TR3A, and on one occasion when we caught up a lorry, which was more to the left of the road than the right, he blasted away with the Nanuccis. Then, to my horror, as the lorry trundled on hogging the crown of the road, he proceeded to overtake it on the inside. If it had suddenly pulled over to the right we would have been knocked clean off the road and into a ravine.

Finally the rally was finished. We were both pretty tired and it was dark, but the car needed fuel. We saw a Mobil garage and pulled in, then, as we had done throughout, changed drivers. Bill swept out of the garage and through the little village, then needlessly fast down a long hill. At the bottom of the hill were the lights of a vehicle coming towards us. Suddenly Bill realised that the main road went round to the left, and that the vehicle approaching was only coming along a track, and he swerved to the left to go in front of the oncoming vehicle, which would probably have stopped anyway before joining the main road, but then he made a fatal last second change of mind and swerved back to the right.

We hit the vehicle pretty well head on, and it turned out to be a big army lorry with a huge steel bumper. The Alpine took most of the shock on my side and the back wheels lifted off the ground as the tail swung to the right then stopped its lateral movement abruptly as the wheels came down on to the ground. There was a tremendous bang like a rifle shot, which was the noise of my head smashing the laminated windscreen, and then as the car made this violent jerk to the right I was flung sideways against the broken glass. The other noise was the prolonged wail of those strident Nanucci air horns going full blast as a result of a short circuit.

I leapt out of the car, put my hand to my face and realised I was bleeding hard. Bill went back into the car and turned off the ignition, which stopped the noise of those fearsome air horns, and it was only then that I heard the noise of my blood clattering on to the ground like large drops of rain at the beginning of a storm. I yelled to Bill that I must have something to stop the bleeding. Had I only been able to think rationally I would have remembered that I had a towel in my case, which could have served as a bandage, but Bill simply replied: 'I'm hurt, too.' In fact he had knocked his nose against the steering wheel but was not bleeding. This was 1961, when seat belts were being talked about, and I had fitted some in my car, but there were none in the Alpine. Had belts been fitted I would certainly have been wearing them and would not have been injured at all.

Men from the lorry took me round to the back and lifted me into it. I was then aware of being driven a short distance and then carried into an unlit building. It must have been some kind of nunnery, and my state was not much improved by various of these old women coming along almost in turn carrying burning tapers to have a look, then gasping, throwing their hands up in the air, and spilling taper wax everywhere.

Suddenly there was a voice speaking English: 'What do you want us to do?'

'Please tell them to get me to a hospital in Athens,' I replied. If they had done that I probably would not have survived the journey. Instead, they put me lying down in the back of a taxi with Bill in the front and we were driven very fast to a hospital in Thivai, the nearest town. There was an awful lot of sounding of horns, and I heard later that the taxi driver went up the wrong side of the road with his hand on the horn, forcing the oncoming traffic to move over, and thus avoiding any delay for the left turn into the hospital. Bill said he thought it was going to be his turn to go through the windscreen.

In Thivai hospital they saved my life. The doctor stopped the bleeding then started the agonising business of stitching the wounds. I had a massive compression cut across the forehead, another above the right cheek bone, but the greatest loss of blood had been from the sliced cut across the right ear, caused when I was flung sideways against the jagged edge of the windscreen.

The doctor spoke no English, but he could write it, so I was given messages like: 'Do you have headache?' What would have been good would have been if he had written: 'Do you know your blood group?' I could have written straight away B Rh+, but instead they had sent a sample over the mountains to Athens. I learned later that three donors of the likely blood groups were waiting, and when the message eventually came from Athens the two not needed were sent home, and the compatible one gave direct transfusion to me.

The next few days in Thivai hospital were pretty dreadful, and I was appalled when they brought me a mirror to see the state of my face during renewal of the bandages. Bill came to see me and the small sticking plaster on his nose showed how well he had got away with the accident, being braced against the brake pedal and the steering wheel. But with fresh blood in my veins I soon started to feel a lot better and I saw no reason to make the disaster worse than it was by losing the rally report. So Bill brought me my notes and a wad of paper and I wrote the 1,500-word rally report with a pencil lying in the bed, and told Bill to advise the editor to expect the copy with his pictures on the first available plane. I heard later that the editor, Maurice Smith, enjoyed showing off his classical knowledge by writing in Cyrillic characters the names of some of the Greek drivers who had done well in the rally. The printers must really have enjoyed that!

The next three days were pretty agonising, as I found that the bed I was on had a thin mattress over a steel lattice with no springing at all. Every three hours the nurse came in to give the penicillin injection in my backside, which was also pretty painful. The teacher I had spoken to after the accident came in several times, glad to practise his English, and he taught me some basic Greek phrases. I was able to surprise the nurse by saying in Greek: 'Is it time for the injection again already?' She replied in the affirmative before suddenly realising I had spoken to her in Greek. But although unpleasant, those penicillin injections ensured that the dreadful wounds healed up without infection. My father, a doctor, said later: 'If you're giving the patient penicillin you could spit in the wound and it wouldn't matter.' Helpa, the Greek travel office, were marvellous and paid all the hospital expenses.

Eventually the time came to say goodbye to the hospital that had saved me, thank them profusely, and be taken with Bill by taxi to the airport and a BEA flight on a Viscount aircraft back to London. On arrival at the airport I was very grateful to see that the editor, Maurice Smith, had come out to meet me, with the firm's nurse and an ambulance, which I didn't need – I would much more happily have travelled in a car, and I vowed later to write a piece about the appalling discomfort of travelling in London's Daimler ambulances.

Before we set off I had chance for a few quick words with Maurice Smith, and I said: 'It was an absolutely stupid bit of driving.'

'On the part of the other vehicle?' he replied.

'No,' I said. 'Bill's terrible erratic driving.' It was only then that I learned that in all the conversations Bill had been having with the London office he had never once mentioned that he had been at the wheel, and it had been presumed that I had been driving.

I was taken to St Thomas's hospital but discharged next day after some routine tests, and went back to my flat in Hampstead. I returned to the office to resume work only two days later.

Twenty years later, when the scars of the accident had long since disappeared, I was troubled by a slight itch on my forehead, and ran my finger across it. There was blood on the finger, but none on my forehead. Then carefully working away at it I removed a small fragment of glass, which had been lodged in my forehead all that time and had caused a small cut on my finger. I wrapped it in cotton wool and sent it back to John Rowe, who had been the Rootes press officer at the time, with apologies for retaining part of his test car for so long. In fact, after about three months there had been a call to say that the 'remains' of the Sunbeam Alpine, with the distinctive registration number ALP 10, had arrived back at the Rootes repair depot at Ladbrooke Grove in London. It had been worth the cost of shipping it back to avoid paying the enormous Greek import duty, though when I went to Greece again later the details of the car were still in my passport as a tourist temporary import. I had a lot of difficulty convincing the authorities that the car had been wrecked in an accident and later shipped back to Britain.

I went over with two colleagues in the lunch hour to see it, but it was in an appalling state. It had come back as deck cargo and there were rusty streaks across the crumpled bonnet and the boot lid where steel cables had been lashed across to secure it. All sorts of things had been stolen – the radio, of course, but also the gear-lever knob, the pedal rubbers and the window handles. There was the ominous left half of the laminated glass windscreen missing where my head had broken it, but structurally it was not too bad. I realised that if it had been fitted with seat belts and I had been uninjured, we could have driven it back!

My father's sister, Aunt Gynny, taught me to drive, starting when I was 7.

Sent to cover the formation of the Institute of Advanced Motorists in 1957, I passed the test, and passed again fifty years later. Here I am with examiner Steve Mead.

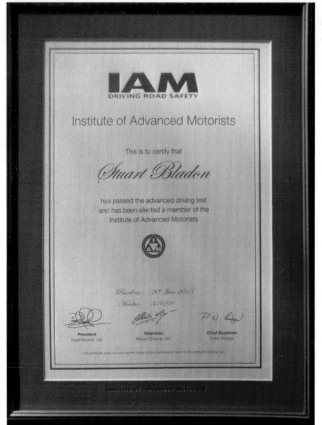

I said I would take it again on reaching 80, which I did, and passed for the third time in 2013, here with chief examiner Peter Rodger.

After three IAM passes I was given lunch and this fine framed certificate.

Just before leaving *Autocar* I enjoyed taking this Rolls-Royce Corniche convertible to North Wales in 1981.

No speed limit in Hungary: we had a special dispensation for the launch of the Bentley Turbo R in June 1987. The driver here is the late Lord Strathcarron, with the speedometer 'off the clock' at 150mph.

As well as the Bentley Turbo R, we were able to drive the new Rolls-Royce Silver Spirit with fuel injection for its 6,750cc engine.

On the Col des Diablerets in Switzerland, the four-wheel-drive Jensen FF showed its remarkable capabilities.

To the amazement of skiers, we even took the Jensen on to the piste; here young children showed great interest in the funny car that goes on the snow.

Lotus Elise in 1996 was a most exciting test with its fabulous handling, but I would not like to live with its rather basic interior.

My friend Clive Jacobs, well-known broadcaster and motoring journalist, kindly provided his magnificent 1924 American-built Rolls-Royce Silver Ghost for my son's wedding in June 1994. Clive, here sitting on the bumper, sadly died in 2014.

Arranged by the Press Officer Michael Schimpke, there were many memorable Porsche launches in the 1990s. Here we are at Schloß Lerbach near Cologne with the new Porsche Boxster in September 1996.

Almost as a ritual each spring I competed in the annual Economy Run, usually partnered with my brother Hugh, seen here at the wheel. After beating the Marina for two years in succession, we decided to drive the Marina for a change in 1976 and turned the tables by beating the Triumph Dolomite.

Each year for six years I was commissioned by Auto-Sleepers to take their latest motor caravan on ever more demanding European test tours. In 1999 Jennetta and I took this Auto-Sleeper Pollenza, based on the Peugeot 1.9 TD, over the St Gotthard, Gavia and Stelvio mountain passes.

In August 1994 this Jaguar XJS convertible provided magnificent transport to drive out to Paris for the launch of the revised Volkswagen Polo and then on to Stuttgart for the Porsche Carrera 4.

After the Polo, the new Porsche Carrera 4 was most exciting and featured Porsche's new four-wheel-drive system using a compact differential unit, a boxed sample of which I was given to take home; we still have it in the loo!

For our daughter's wedding in August 1996 I was able to borrow from the Jaguar Museum the Mark VII, which had been the Queen Mother's car for many years; and at the same time I had on test very conveniently the beautiful Daimler Century.

After the wedding was all over, Jennetta and I took the magnificent Daimler Century to Cliveden in Berkshire for an extravagant celebratory lunch. The luxury model of the Jaguar range, the Daimler Century had a V12 6-litre engine and 4-speed automatic.

A new concept in convertibles – for Europe, at least – came with the November 1996 launch of the Mercedes-Benz SLK, which neatly takes off its own roof and stows it away in the boot and then closes the lid. Other makes followed a similar concept.

First of many Jaguar launches in France in February 1993 was the magnificent Jaguar XJ12, based at the Hotel du Palais at Biarritz. Although the Jaguar was superb, I thought the Daimler even better.

Daihatsu's little Compagno saloon was the first Japanese car to be imported to Britain, and I carried out the road test on it in 1965. It was later found, restored and I was invited to drive it on the 1993 Norwich Union Classic Cars rally.

After the Audi 100 had finally run out of fuel after 1,338.1 miles, setting a new record for longest distance without refuelling, the RAC observer Bob Proctor broke the seals and poured in fuel from the emergency can to get us back to the Auchen Castle Hotel.

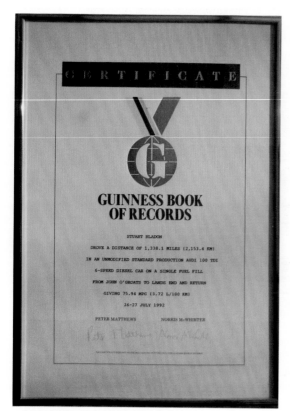

Hard-earned certificate: after the Audi had been nursed along all the way from John o' Groats to Lands End, and back to Scotland, I was rewarded with this certificate from the *Guinness book of Records*; the red ink signatures have almost faded away.

CERTIFICATE

GUINNESS BOOK OF RECORDS

STUART BLADON

DROVE A DISTANCE OF 1,338.1 MILES (2,153.4 KM)

IN AN UNMODIFIED STANDARD PRODUCTION AUDI 100 TDI

6-SPEED DIESEL CAR ON A SINGLE FUEL FILL

FROM JOHN O'GROATS TO LANDS END AND RETURN

GIVING 75.94 MPG (3.72 L/100 KM)

26-27 JULY 1992

PETER MATTHEWS   NORRIS McWHIRTER

In 1967 I went to Abingdon for the first time, and covered the launch of the MGC, which was effectively the B with a 6-cylinder 3-litre engine derived from that of the Austin-Healey. This drive came much later in a beautifully restored example. (Maurice Rowe)

Peugeot used the long straight and traffic-free roads of Egypt for a number of their international launches. Here we are in a Peugeot 607 V6 in February 2000 on the way to Jordan. A policeman stopped us and I feared trouble, but he just wanted a lift, and was quite happy sitting in the back of the Peugeot at 120mph!

Understandably, in view of their high cost and limited production, Aston Martin is rather restrictive over the loan of test cars, but in 1998 I was able to get hold of this V8 for a day of photographing, as here at Woburn Abbey.

Of all the MGs I have driven over the years, I thought this MGR V8 was quite the best, offering high performance and with a very attractive interior. I even measured up the seats to see if they would fit in my Triumph TR7!

Segrave Trophy 1989

The Ford Commendation for

Contributions to the Environment

STUART BLADON

World Fuel Economy Record for Production Vehicles and

previous successes in this field.

Ford

Ford's managing director Roger Humm kindly nominated me for a special environmental award for economy driving as part of the Segrave Trophy for 1989, which is sponsored by Ford. The presentation took place at the RAC's headquarters in Pall Mall, London.

In 1988 I was asked by Ford to make an economy drive to Berlin in this Fiesta 1.6 diesel, which it did at 89.1mpg, on £8 worth of fuel. This was before the Berlin wall came down, and the car is shown here after the finish with all the graffiti still evident.

Another commission from Ford came in May 1991 when I was asked to organise an economy run for eight Ford Escort diesels, from Westminster Bridge to Red Square in Moscow. I went first in a Sierra Estate car with two mechanics to plot the route, and then on the event, run in conjunction with Saga, to drive one of the Escorts.

After seeing this 1979 Rolls-Royce Corniche Convertible at Beaulieu Garage, I just could not resist it. I decided to buy it in 2009 and have enjoyed many classic events in it as seen here with my wife Jennetta on a rally in 2010. (Reg Burnard)

Purchased in 1993, this Triumph TR7 gave wonderful service and many miles of fun motoring, but was sold in March 2015 to make way for another lovely open car, the Audi A3 Cabriolet 1.4 TFSI, seen here alongside

The second disaster in that fateful year, 1961, came in November with a Lotus Super Seven, which for some reason was being tested by the sports editor, Peter Garnier. As he was a great friend of Lotus originator and owner Colin Chapman, it wasn't really desirable for Garnier to be testing one of his cars. Moreover, he was not one of the main road-test team, but in the outcome it made little difference as he never did write the test.

Accompanied by colleague Martin Lewis, Garnier drove up to the MIRA proving ground on a very cold and foggy morning for performance testing. The freezing fog should have convinced them that testing was out of the question, and on arrival at MIRA they were not surprised to be told that the proving ground was closed. Could they just, they asked the manager, Mr Dalby, do a few quick check figures?

Rather reluctantly he agreed, warning them to be careful because although the No. 2 straight, which we always used for acceleration testing, was only about 100 yards from the old war-time control tower, which was the headquarters office, it couldn't be seen through the murk.

They made their way to the No. 2 straight, which was only just over half a mile long, and ran through a quick blast through the gears. When the solitary horizontal pole which marked the end of the straight loomed up out of the fog, they stopped while Martin wrote down the acceleration times, then turned round and had another go. It was always road-test procedure to measure times in both directions to neutralise the effect of any wind, and the published figure was always the average of the best run each way.

If Garnier had been a more frequent road-tester he would have known that there wasn't sufficient distance, even with a very quick car like the Super Seven, to do two sets of acceleration runs in the same direction. But once Martin had written the figures down, Peter set off again to attempt a further set. With its ample power and low weight, the Super Seven was very quick – it reached 80mph from rest in only 14.3sec – but it wasn't quick enough to do this twice in 0.6 miles. Martin dropped the stopwatch, and bent down to retrieve it – an act that might well have saved his life.

At the opposite end of the No. 2 straight there were two cables like huge steel hawsers draped across at heights of about 1ft and 3ft above the ground. The intention was to stop any car that over-ran, because across the end of the straight was the inner high-speed circuit. The cables were intended to stop a conventional car, but they weren't designed for the little Super Seven, whose height from the top of the scuttle to the ground was only 2ft 4in.

When the cables suddenly loomed up out of the fog, Peter Garnier hit the brakes, but there was no chance of stopping in time. Both cables whipped over the front wheels, ripped off both headlamps and flattened the little windscreen, before hitting Garnier in the face. The car ran on under the cables, crossed the inner high speed circuit, and came to rest in the parking area about 100 yards farther on. Poor Garnier was a mess – bleeding heavily and knocked unconscious.

Nearby some engineers from Girling, who were doing some static work on a test car, heard the horrendous noise of the crash and saw what had happened. They drove rapidly across, hurled a wad of cleaning materials across to Martin, and roared off to the control tower to report the disaster and call up an ambulance. Martin did what he could for Garnier with the cleaning rags, but it took half an hour for the ambulance to grope its way through the fog to the proving ground. Garnier was still unconscious when he was taken off to Nuneaton Hospital.

Two days later, in good weather, I had to go to MIRA for a road test, and inspected the scene of the accident. Heavy black lines from the locked wheels passed unbroken under the cables, finishing about 10ft on the other side. Some of Martin Lewis's blond hairs were caught in the lower cable, which showed what a lucky escape he had experienced. I went to see Peter in the hospital where he was already beginning to recover though he could hardly talk through his smashed teeth. He was astonished to learn that both of those sturdy hawsers had come over the top of the bonnet and hit him in the face.

Everyone said afterwards that a man less strongly built than Peter Garnier might not have survived, but he did and returned to work some weeks later. Subsequently he underwent further cosmetic surgery and a lot of dental work to repair his teeth. Over time, the scars diminished so that latterly he showed no disfigurement from the accident, which had so nearly cost him his life. He introduced me to the surgeon who had done a lot of the remedial work on his face, and in a short visit to the London Clinic the same surgeon opened up my damaged ear, which had been stitched up out of line, and put it straight.

A few weeks later, the Lotus Super Seven came back, repaired, for the test that never happened earlier. Garnier wasn't going to drive it again, and this time the technical editor, Harry Mundy, opted to tackle it. I was to be his assistant on the test, and I don't think he trusted it, and asked me to drive in convoy with him in his Jaguar 3.4 Mk 2, which I was very happy to do. It was just as well, since before reaching the Watford Gap service area on the M1, the Lotus ran out of petrol. Its fuel tank held only 5 gallons (22 litres), and the consumption was only 22mpg. After stopping behind him on the hard shoulder there was no choice but to drive on in the Jaguar, get some petrol in a can and come tearing back at 110mph to the first flyover where I could turn round and come to Harry's rescue.

Although it was again very cold weather in December, Harry had the hood down, and as he drove along at 90mph I saw his little knot of hair blowing wildly in the slipstream and almost feared that it would blow right off! We completed the test without incident, recording acceleration to 90mph in 20.5sec, and a top speed of 103mph. Harry then jumped into his Jaguar and I was left to drive the little Lotus back to London, a journey that I greatly enjoyed despite the discomfort.

TWENTY-SIX

SIMCA 1000

She did a kind of forward roll over the top of the seat and landed on the back seat as an untidy bundle with her best Sunday hat all askew

During the war, in 1941, I had been evacuated from Coventry to escape the bombing, and lived for six months with my paternal grandmother and aunt at the family home in Llanbedr, North Wales, and formed an affectionate relationship. When the sad news came that my grandmother had died aged 82 in May 1962 it was inevitable that I should make the 240-mile journey from London to be present for the funeral. My father phoned and told me that it was to be held at 12 p.m. on the following Saturday, and asked if I could pick up Uncle Fred and Auntie Ida on the way through, as they were staying at a guest house in Barmouth. He gave me the house number and added 'don't be late'. Ida Hall was my late grandmother's sister and her husband Fred had been a keen motorist before the war. But now they were both in their 80s and he had been obliged to sell his beloved Riley 1½-litre and replace it with a little Austin 10. Evidently he regarded the long journey from their home in South Devon as too much for them so they had gone up by public transport.

My next test car, the new Simca 1000, had arrived on the Friday, only the day before the funeral, and as soon as I had finished work I went down to the car park, flung my case into the boot, which was at the front of the rear-engined car, and drove round to the local garage to fill the tank and start the fuel record card, which was always the first thing to be done at the start of any road test. Time was short, as I had arranged to break the journey at my fiancée's house conveniently on the way, near Hinckley, and I was already running late. There was no time to examine the Simca – that would be done later.

Instead, I took stock of the new test car as I drove along, and realised that it wasn't a very good car to use for such a long journey. The Simca had a 944cc engine mounted at the back, and a four-speed gearbox. Power output, I discovered later, was a modest 45bhp, and the speed on the M1 varied between 65 and 80mph according to whether the gradient was uphill or down. It also lacked directional stability and needed constant steering correction to keep in lane. To save time next day I filled the tank again at the Jet garage on the A5, and was a bit shocked to realise it had barely managed 35mpg, but I had been pushing it rather hard, which explained the poor economy.

At my fiancée's home I was given a warm welcome and a fine dinner, and next day I was getting ready to leave when the call came 'breakfast's ready'. I knew I ought to get going but the magnificent spread of bacon, eggs, mushrooms and fried bread was too tempting to resist, so it was nearly 9 a.m. when I set off with 140 miles to cover, about an hour later than I had intended.

I was soon appalled by the traffic on a sunny May weekend heading to Wales, and at each of the seemingly endless series of roundabouts on the old Shrewsbury bypass there was a tiresome traffic queue. It became a little better after I had turned off to take the A458 to Welshpool, but there were frequent columns of traffic, always with a 35mph dawdler at the front and the drivers behind either unable or unwilling to overtake. When I tested the Simca later, it took over 26 seconds to accelerate from rest to 60mph, and it just didn't have the performance necessary to go steaming past the column whenever an opportunity presented itself.

Eventually I was at Welshpool with its annoying traffic lights and the main road jammed with parked cars, and then it was on as fast as possible to Dolgellau, later to be blessed with a much-needed bypass. At last I reached Barmouth where the pedestrians always seemed to regard the road as a kind of shopping precinct rather than a through route, and going out of the town I tried anxiously to see some of the house numbers, all on the right-hand side of the road. As I rounded a bend, there the Halls were, standing by the gate of their guest house and looking very forlorn.

As soon as I had stopped I leapt out and apologised for being late, then hurried round to the passenger side to tip the seat forward for access to the rear, but I couldn't find the release catch. I could make the front passenger seat slide to and fro, but couldn't make it tip.

Looking anxiously at his watch, Uncle Fred said: 'Don't bother, Stuart; Ida can get over there. Go on, Ida.' A small and always very slim lady, she obliged, and with an unseemly display of petticoats, stockings and a shoe coming off she did a kind of forward roll over the top of the seat and landed on the back seat as an untidy bundle with her best Sunday hat all askew.

I dashed round to the driving seat and we scurried off at peak revs in each gear while I apologised again for being so late and explained about the horrendous traffic, but I added that I thought we would get to the church in time. We hit 70mph – which turned out later to have been nearly the car's maximum speed – on the long straight after Dyffryn Ardudwy and entering Llanbedr nearly took off at the humpback bridge over the River Artro.

The funeral was at Llanbedr church, where Sir John Black, former head of Standard-Triumph is buried. The hearse had just arrived as we skidded to a halt, and they were busy unloading the coffin. Auntie Ida made a more dignified exit, managing to squeeze her small legs through the narrow gap between the seats, and the three of us walked together up the short path to the church.

When it was all over I stood at the top of the path and saw the sun glinting on the little Simca. Suddenly, like the flash of brilliance bringing the solution to an astute problem, I realised why I hadn't been able to tip the seat forward: the damn thing had four doors!

TWENTY-SEVEN

TRIUMPH HERALD 12/50

The Leica had disappeared. 'It's that bloody lorry driver,' I exclaimed. 'He must have nicked it.'

When the phone rang and woke me up in my Hampstead flat, I looked at my watch and saw that it was 4 a.m. It must be bad news, I thought, for someone to be ringing at that hour; and it was – but not the sort of bad news I was expecting. 'I've found your car,' said the voice, which I recognised as that of the junior press officer at Standard-Triumph.

I was absolutely furious. That weekend I was due to cross the Channel and drive out to France and meet the photographer Ron Easton, and together we were to cover the 1962 Alpine Rally. Covering international rallies was an assignment I enjoyed tremendously, meaning lots of exciting motoring in exotic locations, as well as admiring the skills of professional rally drivers. I had suddenly realised late on Friday afternoon that the car that had been arranged for me by the editor to use for the Rally, a Triumph Herald 12/50, hadn't turned up. I thought it a totally unsuitable car in which to go charging about France and Italy in pursuit of an international rally, and when I told the editor that the Herald hadn't arrived and suggested that I should take my own Triumph TR3A, he gave a resigned 'Oh, very well.' With about 3,500 miles in prospect I was looking forward to a lovely bucketful of mileage allowance. But now they had found the Herald!

'The only problem is,' said the press officer in the middle of the night, 'there's no gearbox in it.' Hopes raised again; perhaps I would be able to take my TR3A after all. But then he droned on: 'Don't worry, we'll get it fixed as soon as the works opens tomorrow – sorry, today – and have the car down to you on Sunday.'

Ron Easton was already in France covering the Monaco GP, and we were due to meet out there on the Tuesday ready for the start of the rally at Marseilles. The little Triumph was duly delivered to my Hampstead flat on Sunday afternoon, and once I started driving it on Monday morning I was happier with it than I had expected. It buzzed along very well at 70–75mph, and I appreciated the accuracy of the steering – something not many cars could match in 1962. Although there were no autoroutes in France then, I managed to drive from London to Lydd, fly with the car to Le Touquet, and drive all the way to Grenoble in the day – over 600 miles single-handed, and with no radio, not to mention the in-car cassette player, which had yet to be invented!

The Herald 12/50 had the twin-carb engine, and featured Girling disc brakes. The engine proved acceptably quiet even in hard driving, but the limited fuel range was a nuisance. With consumption around 31mpg it meant a fuel stop every 130 miles or so. If it was left too late it meant I had to get out to turn the fuel tap on the top of the little tank to the reserve position, and hope to find a filling station in about the next 20 miles.

Ron Easton came into the hotel we had agreed on as our meeting point, and we loaded his gear into the little car and went to the start of the Rally. We then pursued it as well as possible on its traverse of northern Italy, taking short cuts to get ahead of the competitors and take pictures as they came past. In those carefree days of international rallying, the roads were still open to the public as the cars came hurtling over the Italian mountain passes.

We had parked the little Triumph as far off the road as possible on a hairpin bend of the Passo del Vivione with its rough, stony surface, when an Italian lorry loaded with building rubble came trundling down the pass and pulled in to take refuge from the rally cars at the same hairpin bend. The driver climbed out and sat on the ground next to the Herald, watching the rally cars.

There was great excitement when the leading Austin-Healey of Seigle-Morris and Ambrose skidded on the ball-bearing surface and clouted a rock, puncturing a tyre and damaging the jacking point so that even if they were prepared to lose time changing the wheel, it was impossible to do so. They pressed on with the tyre flat, shedding first the inner tube, then the tyre itself; they clattered past us on the wheel rim.

Soon the spokes separated from the wheel rim, which broke free and went bowling down the road just as another Austin-Healey, driven by the Morley brothers, was overtaking. They completed the stage on three wheels and the rear brake disc.

As soon as it was safe to go we jumped into the Herald and set off in pursuit, and caught up with them after a couple of miles at the time control. Ron jumped out to take pictures of the emergency repairs on the Austin-Healey but exclaimed: 'Where's my camera?' He had two cameras, and his favourite one, the Leica, was missing. When a rapid search of the car failed to reveal it, I exclaimed: 'It's that bloody lorry driver; he was sitting next to the car, and he must have nicked it.' We had walked some way up and down the pass in search of different viewpoints, and the car had been left unattended much of the time. 'Come on,' I said, 'we'll catch him. He can't go very fast.'

We went zinging back up the Vivione, and I was cursing the Herald's too-low second gear, when we met the lorry coming down the hill towards us. I did a rapid turn-round and gave credit to the Herald's excellent tight turning circle. A suitable opportunity enabled us to roar past and then force the lorry to stop.

We spoke no Italian, but the word 'camera' was fairly international. The lorry driver at first didn't comprehend what we were meaning, but when we started rummaging about in his cab he soon realised what was afoot, and started to get very angry. Was it bluster to prevent us from finding it, or genuine indignation?

The Triumph Herald 12/50 coped remarkably well on the hard battle of covering the 1962 Alpine Rally. (Ron Easton)

We didn't know, and, there being no sign of the missing camera, we had no choice but to let him go and keep our dark suspicions to ourselves. Ron was resigned to the loss, saying the firm's insurance would have to replace it, and fortunately he had changed the film not long before so not many of his rally pictures were lost, and he still had his back-up camera.

With the Alpine eventually finished, Ron flew back from Nice with his pictures and my rally report. I had enjoyed writing it, because the Morley brothers had won the rally – 'we could have done without our teammates throwing a bloody wheel rim at us' they joked later – and Pat Moss in another Austin-Healey won the ladies' prize and was third overall. I was now faced with another solo drive in the long-suffering Herald, from Nice back to the London office.

A few weeks later I wrote an article about the use of the Herald 12/50 to cover the Alpine Rally, and ordered up some more prints to illustrate the piece. One of them, which Ron had taken looking down on the hairpin bend showed the Herald, the lorry, the lorry driver and me; and there, plain to see, was the Leica lying on the boot of the Herald. The unfortunate lorry driver had been completely innocent after all! I often wondered what happened to that expensive camera after it flew off the back of the car on the first bend, and whether any deserving Italian subsequently found it.

TWENTY-EIGHT

Austin-Healey 3000

≡ Suddenly the lights went out. We had visions of our mechanic working away
under the Healey and being suddenly plunged into darkness

For those of us on the staff of *The Autocar,* and for me in particular, the year 1962 was one of momentous changes. Our company, Associated Iliffe Press, had been taken over by the *Daily Mirror* in 1960, and an early move was to send over two directors from the new parent company. Their names were Basil de Launay and 'Don' Ryder, quickly given the nicknames De Launay Belleville (after the ancient car of that name) and Ryder Haggard (after the famous author of, among other books, *King Solomon's Mines*). An unwelcome indicator of how things would go under our new owners was the cancellation of the traditional Christmas bonus, because it was 'not *Mirror* policy'.

Interference and reorganisation followed, and several subsidiary companies were set up, *The Autocar* being grouped among similar journals such as *Flight* and *Bus and Coach* as part of Iliffe Transport Publications. The definite article was dropped, the traditional name *The Autocar* being changed to plain *Autocar*. Then in 1962 came the plan for the Transport group to be relocated close to their respective industries, in the Midlands. As a former Coventry man, I didn't mind the idea at all, but for directors and senior management the idea was anathema.

My personal change in 1962 was a friend's wedding near Coventry in March, at which I met my future wife, and only five months later we were married. The honeymoon at the end of August and into September would be a three-week holiday in Portugal, and I approached BMC, as they were then known, to see if I could borrow one of the new MGBs for the trip. It was just about to be announced, but they said they couldn't spare one of the press cars for such a long time, and offered an Austin-Healey 3000 instead.

My new wife was soon to learn about my characteristic fussiness where cars are concerned, when I declared that the engine was running far too rich, and she would have to be patient while I re-tuned the three SU carburettors. I claim to have made not too bad a job of it, because afterwards the fuel consumption improved from 18mpg to 21–22mpg, and instead of being black as soot as they had been, the insides of the twin exhaust tail pipes were more the colour they should be, light brown. I also thought the engine pulled better on its leaner mixture. The only drawback was that it made the engine difficult to start from cold, but where we were heading the temperatures were not going to be low.

We had a good fast run to Paris, where we spent a night and explored the Eiffel Tower in the morning, before cruising on at an effortless 90mph towards Biarritz and the Spanish border. Our initial destination was booked at Figueira da Foz on the Atlantic coast, and we were running well behind schedule, but the night porter was not at all put out by our arrival at 3 a.m. We were the only English visitors in the hotel, and seemed to be regarded as something of a novelty to such extent that the porters and staff at the reception desk always stood up and bowed as we passed through the entrance hall – a little gesture that made us feel very grand. After a week there we became disappointed with the way a lovely sunny morning would suddenly change to being quite chill and misty as an Atlantic fog rolled in, so we packed up and headed south to an area that had looked most attractive in the brochures, Praia da Rocha.

Farther down the coast, we stopped at a hotel at Praia da Santa Cruz, and could hardly believe it when we heard that the charge for a night was only £1 5s to include

Many of the roads in Portugal were unsurfaced, and clouds of dust followed the car at speed, but the Austin-Healey 3000 suffered it all very well.

dinner and as much wine as we wanted. Even with the much higher value of sterling, this was a real bargain. The hotel room was plain but clean, and the meal very good.

As we drove on south next day, we certainly shook off the cold misty weather, and instead it became quite insufferably hot. The Healey didn't have much insulation on the engine bulkhead, and heat poured in, roasting us even with the hood down. We even tried putting the hood up for a bit, which kept the sun off but made it even hotter. By the time we reached Praia my new wife was suffering from mild sunstroke, and we gratefully accepted the only available room at the sole hotel there, although it was right up in the attic. Later, we were told, we would be moved down to a better room, but when the offer came we preferred to stay where we were and enjoyed the benefit of its specially low cost. The only other cars there, apart from Spanish ones, were from Gibraltar with the telltale GBZ plate on the back, and it was delightfully peaceful and uncrowded. But then we heard 'they are going to build an airport at Faro' and we felt it unlikely that the area would stay so unspoilt. The resulting transformation when I visited twenty years later confirmed our fears, with high-rise hotels all along the coast.

Every day the weather remained beautiful, roasting hot, so that we spent a lot of the time splashing about in the warm sea, until the time came with just the last few days of our three weeks available for the return trip, to start the journey back into Spain. A final swim was enjoyed at Cacela before taking the ferry to cross the Rio Guadiana. While waiting for the ferry we spoke to a very smart lady with a Mini, who introduced herself as Lady … (the surname long since forgotten), this being the first British-registered car we had seen for two weeks. Looking over from the ferry deck we saw a huge jellyfish – the menacing Portuguese Man of War – and were glad not to have met it when swimming in the sea only a few miles away.

We hadn't gone very far in Spain when an ominous chinging noise revealed that the rear exhaust bracket had broken and the exhaust was trailing along on the road. Fortunately, although space was at a premium, I had taken my toolkit with us, and was able to nick some wire from a nearby fence and wire the exhaust up to the chassis.

We spent a night of suffocating heat in a hotel at Seville – there was no air conditioning in those days – and in the morning located the official BMC agent. I was surprised to find that they had in stock the strange bonded rubber mountings used to locate the exhaust system, and fitted them for the equivalent of about £1, but within a couple of hours they had failed again. As before, the bonding had survived, but the rubber between the two metal surfaces had simply sheared with the heat. It was back to another fence, and another wiring-up job.

Spanish roads were notoriously badly surfaced in 1962, and I realised what a good job that Humber Super Snipe had made of absorbing the bumps and roughness the year before. While we were cruising along at about 85mph I noticed that the handling seemed to have gone wrong, and stopped to find a rear tyre had punctured. There was enough air pressure left to trundle very slowly about 100 yards to where a solitary tree provided some shade for the task of changing the wheel.

The Healey had 'knock-on' wire wheels with a central hub nut to be hit with a copper hammer, but when I took the jack out and started screwing it up I was shocked to find that it was broken. There was supposed to be a second spiral, which would come out when the outer spiral reached its limit, but it didn't work and I had only about 1½in of lift. There weren't many bricks and rocks about, but what could be scrounged was piled up under the back axle, the jack wound down and then screwed up again from a slightly higher position. At the fourth try the wheel was high enough to be taken off and the spare fitted. The hub nut was carefully screwed back on, but at the first hit with the copper hammer the improvised column of bricks, stones and pieces of wood fell apart, reminding me of the near disastrous collapse of my Hillman 10 nearly ten years earlier. But it

In 1962 the only way to get to the Algarve was to drive, so we had the beautiful beach at Praia da Rocha very much to ourselves.

didn't matter – I certainly wouldn't have risked being under such a precariously mounted car. The hub nut was sufficiently far on to finish the hammering process with the wheel on the ground.

Kept until the job was finished, we enjoyed a delicious melon as the late afternoon sun blazed down, but our troubles were still far from over: on a fast left-hand bend my eye caught the movement of the oil pressure gauge down to zero, but it came back up again as soon as the road straightened. A stop and inspection revealed no oil on the dipstick, and it was dripping from a place where the sump had obviously hit the ground on one of the rough sections of road. We motored on, keeping a careful eye on the oil pressure, and arrived at a small village which boasted a *mechanizien*. It was just one of a row of terraced houses, but the ground floor had been turned into a garage. The mechanic said he could repair the sump, and directed us to where we could get a meal while he was working on the car.

We were sitting at the table awaiting our dinner when suddenly the lights went out. It was nearly dark outside, and the loss of all lights in the village showed that it was a general power cut. We had visions of our mechanic working away under the Healey and being suddenly plunged into darkness. After about twenty minutes, the lights came on again; our meal arrived and was very good, after which we walked back to our friendly little garage to find the Austin-Healey sitting outside with a neat brazing job done on the sump and the oil topped up to the mark. The charge for all this came to just over £1, and the mechanic was delighted with a generous tip, which left the total cost still under £2.

We were now rather weary and Madrid was still some way away, but we roared on through the darkness and promised ourselves that at the first hotel we reached we would turn in for the night. In spite of the delays we had done quite well, having left Seville and motored half the distance across Spain to reach Madrid. Suddenly I spotted the word 'Motel' to the right behind the trees in large fluorescent letters and we turned in. At the reception we received a slightly odd look on requesting a room for the night, and were handed a huge key with a number on. Following the signs we found the numbered room, attached to an enormous garage. The key unlocked the great twin doors, the Healey was duly driven in looking slightly ridiculous in a space that was obviously intended for a big lorry, and we spent the night in a not very clean or comfortable bedroom.

The reward came next morning when we were given a good breakfast over in the reception area, and the bill for accommodation and breakfast came to about 12s. I was quite relieved at the low cost, as funds were running low – I hadn't budgeted for the new experience of going away and having to pay for two people instead of one! As we drove out, the full lettering, which had been hidden by the trees, was plain to see: *'Motel di Camione'* (motel for lorries).

Still enjoying lovely weather, we motored on next day and were well on our way across France when another ominous zinging noise from the back brought us to a stop. I had twice more wired up the exhaust pipe, but this time I found it was the number plate, 699 DON, that was trailing on the ground. 'Well, we don't need that,' I said, and chucked it in the boot. As we neared Calais various British motorists whom we overtook spotted the deficiency – a car with no GB plate and no number plate – and made frantic gestures to make us aware of it. When we made it plain that we knew and didn't care, their anxiety changed to fury as we waved, laughed and accelerated away.

On arrival at the Calais port we still had some Portuguese money and a little Spanish, but we were down to our last few francs of French. At a little self-service *friterie* we showed what we had left, and it proved enough to buy a glass of white wine and a bag of chips, which we shared to tide us over until we were on the boat and could cash a cheque. It had all been a great adventure, a most memorable start to our married life, and in spite of the problems suffered we have fond memories of the Austin-Healey 3000.

TWENTY-NINE

MORRIS 1100 AND HILLMAN SUPER MINX PERKINS DIESEL

The catalogue of problems experienced with the 1100 and the poor way in which they were dealt with were typical of the unhelpful attitude of BMC at that time

After searching all over London to find a house that we could afford, my fiancée and I finally settled on a small property at South Mimms in Hertfordshire. At least it was on the right side of London, since most journeys were to the north, especially to the Midlands where both our parents lived, and to MIRA at Nuneaton where road tests were carried out. One journey to East Grinstead had been enough to put us off moving south. But shortly before we were due to get married, a major bombshell upset all our plans. It appeared that our new ex-*Mirror* directors, Don Ryder and Basil De Launay had cobbled up a plan to ease the overcrowding in our London office. The magazines involved with the transport industry, including obviously *Autocar, Motor Transport* and others would be relocated to the Midlands.

On hearing that I was about to buy a house in Hertfordshire, our new managing director by the name of Priaulx warned me about the proposed change, and suggested that instead I should look for a house in the Midlands with a view to working from our Coventry office until the main move took place. I thought that he was being considerate and only later did I realise that he might have been trying to avoid possible moving expenses.

There was no time to do much about it, except cancel the proposed purchase at South Mimms, and try to find a flat we could rent on our return from honeymoon. This also proved pretty well impossible as everyone letting a flat wanted immediate occupancy and was not prepared to wait three weeks. I still had my shared flat at Hampstead where my possessions could be left while we were away, and we reckoned we would have no difficulty finding somewhere at short notice on our return.

When we came back from our delightful tour of Spain and Portugal, another dramatic piece of news awaited: the firm had decided to offer me a company car. It meant I could sell the Triumph TR3A, which would help towards the deposit on a house, but the downside was that the car offered was the newly announced Morris 1100. We were both torn over the decision, but the Triumph was still costing little to run and producing useful cash through the still quite generous mileage allowance, so we decided to decline *Autocar's* offer of a company car.

The director was taken aback: no one had ever refused a company car before. So the pressure was put on, and I was obliged to take up the offer. My new bride found herself deprived of two of the things she had looked forward to – my job in London, and my likeable little sports car – but if it was any compensation, she still had me!

By bullying local estate agents, her father found us a very desirable house we could just afford at Dorridge, near Solihull, and at least we had a firm footing on the property market, which was already beginning to take off. When we arrived at our new house after all the legal arrangements had gone through, the new neighbours asked when our removals van would be arriving, and were rather surprised to learn that everything we owned was in the road-test Vauxhall Victor estate car parked outside. But the bed and a cooker would be arriving soon.

After taking over the Morris 1100 and driving it back up the M1 to our new home I was very depressed by it. There was little performance, taking 26 seconds to get from rest to 60mph, and the engine whirred and whined its way along in a far-too-low top gear, but worse was to come. I was convinced that all the research in development of the 1100 had concentrated on its novel Hydrolastic suspension, with rubber spring units at each end connected by water under pressure. The faults became an endless series of irritations, but I do admit that a lot of the problems derived from the severe 1962–63 winter with spells of prolonged snow and ice.

Quite unnecessarily, in my view, the 1100 had its radiator at the side, so that its cooling fan could be driven by belt straight off the front of the engine. This gave rise to a lot of the noise that beset the car, but the worse result was that all the salt spray from other vehicles came straight through the open grille and saturated the engine.

The catalogue of problems experienced with the 1100 and the poor way in which they were dealt with were typical of the general attitude of BMC at that time, which

Nearing the end of its troublesome two years, the Morris 1100 in January 1964 was much improved by a modest engine conversion.

led eventually to the company's downfall. In the second month we had to have a new clutch, after which the gear change was stiff and unpleasant to use. I had exhaust fumes being sucked in through a poorly sealed boot lid, the wiper blades were wrongly mounted on their splines so that one day they collided and jammed, burning out the motor, and there were endless problems with corrosion.

This put paid to the horns, which had to be replaced, and difficult starting was eventually traced to corrosion of the engine earth strap, which was revealed when it was found that the cable for the heater control was nearly red-hot because it had been serving as the earth during a prolonged battle to get the engine started. Another difficulty of having the engine exposed to the icy blast without any radiator in front of it was that the screen-washer bottle, even heavily laden with meths, was perpetually frozen solid, and the one thing that was vital in that bitter winter was to be able to spray liquid on to the windscreen to get rid of the salt thrown up by other vehicles.

I made a lot of modifications to try to improve things. The washer bottle was relocated close to the radiator so that it would get a little heat at low speeds. A much higher-setting thermostat was fitted, which kept the engine at a more reasonable temperature close to the 90°C, which is normal these days, and an aluminium plate fixed behind the grille kept much of the salt spray off the engine. The higher running temperature made the heater more effective, but the warmed air was wrongly directed, blowing up instead of down on to the feet. This was improved by blocking off the side outlets from the heater box and cutting new ones underneath. By reversing the seat mountings I was able to get 2in more of rearward travel, which made the driving position rather more comfortable.

One weekend we set off from Coventry on a long journey down to Devon to cover the Exeter trial, and left a Vauxhall, which could have been used for the trip, in the Coventry multistorey car park, because the aim was always to get as many miles as possible on the long-term-test 1100. After not many miles the 1100 suddenly stopped and it was found that fuel was not getting through. A wallop on the electric fuel pump, which was stupidly mounted below the boot, got it going again, only for it to stop once more a few miles farther on. I hit it once more, managed to get the engine running and turned round to head back to Coventry and get the Vauxhall, but the 1100 then seemed to be behaving well enough so we stopped, turned round and continued west again. It was almost as if the car didn't want to go on this journey, and it stopped again. So a final decision was made to get it back to Coventry and take the Vauxhall, which proved far more comfortable and totally reliable.

This problem was reported to Alec Issigonis, who had by then been promoted to engineering director at BMC, but he kept insisting that the electric fuel pump was a sealed unit and there was no reason why it should not keep working while covered in mud, salt and damp. It wasn't until they had a mountain of failed fuel pumps that had caused the same problems for other owners that he had to relent and have it mounted in a more protected position at the back of the boot.

The editor, Maurice Smith, had been provided with an 1100 on long loan from BMC, so when my report about the unhappy experiences with this awful car was published in November 1963, the criticisms were watered down by praise for his 1100 which had given much better service.

There was only one time when I was pleased to have the 1100 in place of a test car, and this was at the very depths of the 1963 winter when it was so cold that the water froze in the upstairs toilet of our house, which had no central heating, and I was testing a Hillman Super Minx with diesel engine conversion by Perkins of Peterborough. I had gone over to Peterborough to collect it, and left the 1100 there, but next morning the diesel engine started, ran for a few seconds, and then stopped. I knew what the problem was, because we had read about the difficulty many lorry drivers were experiencing with diesel fuel 'waxing' in the fuel pipe and stopping the engine. The outside thermometer was registering 2°F (−16°C).

The papers had been full of pictures of lorry drivers lighting a bonfire of newspapers under their vehicles to get them going, and if they could do it, perhaps I could as well. Our neighbours probably already thought we were a bit weird, but when they saw my newspapers burning furiously in the snow under the Hillman Super Minx their worst fears about us were evidently confirmed. But it didn't work – I learned later that much more heat than you could reasonably generate in this way was necessary to thaw out the waxed fuel. The Perkins engineers came over with my 1100 on a low-loader and took the Super Minx away.

This was an unhappy introduction to diesel motoring, but of course later improvements in fuel technology and engine design have made the enormous strides that have led to diesels being now more popular than petrol. In that early Super Minx, and in an Austin A60 tried later with BMC's own diesel engine, one experienced appalling engine roughness and noise, clouds of smoke on start-up and

A Perkins diesel engine conversion was fitted to this Hillman Super Minx, but early diesels didn't take kindly to the severe cold weather of 1963.

on the overrun, and a long wait for the 'glow plugs' to warm up in the morning. The Super Minx with Perkins engine took 33.8 seconds to reach 60mph, against 21.9 seconds with the standard petrol engine of the same 1.6-litre capacity. The big benefit, relatively unimportant with petrol at less than £1 for 18 litres, was the improved fuel economy at 37.5mpg instead of 23.9.

My love-hate relationship with the Morris 1100 soldiered on for a second year, during which many of the problems were overcome, and a modest performance conversion by a Hungarian engineer, Les Ronson, made it much more acceptable, but it was still a great joy when it was eventually replaced and I was asked to run one of the new Vauxhall Vivas as my next staff car.

THIRTY

MGB

I thought a picture of this shambolic set-up would be good but declined on being threatened with a gun and told that it was a military establishment

It had not been possible to borrow the newly announced MGB for our honeymoon trip to Portugal in 1962, but in 1963 BMC were keen to have publicity for their new sports car, and there was the added advantage that in January it had become available with overdrive working on third and top gears. I explained that I had in mind a grand tour – out to Greece by way of Yugoslavia (as it was called then), and returning on the Adriatic ferry to Italy.

My wife was fast asleep when we came to the division of the *Autobahn* and unwittingly I took the wrong turn, heading east towards Nuremberg instead of south for Stuttgart and Munich. But it turned out to be a lucky choice. What is often not realised now is that in the 1960s and early 1970s motorway driving in Germany was very hazardous, with too much traffic crammed into only two lanes, resulting in frequent traffic jams and accidents. The turn-off towards Wurzburg and Nuremberg, by contrast, was blissfully uncrowded and we were able to bowl along at 90mph until suddenly and unexpectedly the *Ende der Autobahn* sign loomed up and we were back on the ordinary non-motorway road. After sixty quite quick miles, though, a new section of *Autobahn* resumed, taking us all the way to Nuremberg and then south to Munich – a much better and less-crowded route, which I used many times later, noting the steady closing of the gap between the two sections.

On a tight budget, a three-week holiday in hotels with all that travelling was out of the question, so we were camping, and it was most impressive how the MGB, aided by a luggage grid on the boot, took all our camping gear including a large frame tent. Despite the bulk sticking up in the slipstream behind us, the MGB still had a good turn of speed, and there was brisk performance to allow overtaking on the rare opportunities that presented themselves in Austria. Not only did we have to contend with meandering, heavily congested roads, all too often descending into a morass of roadworks but a torrential downpour lasted nearly all the way to the Yugoslav border.

We were then on to the rough stone-covered roads of inland Yugoslavia, and although the MGB took it all very well to the accompaniment of the fusillade of stones thrown up into the wings and underneath, it also suffered from the shocking so-called 'super' Yugopetrol. It caused pinking on any sudden opening of the throttle, as well as violent running-on when the engine was switched off. I found the best technique was to give a stab of full throttle in neutral, then switch off and let the engine die, while being ready to snatch first gear and stall it to stop the engine shake. The combination of the running-on and the rough roads resulted in the same trouble we had experienced with the Austin-Healey 3000 the previous year – shearing of the bonded rubber brackets holding the exhaust system. I had to get underneath and use my well-practised technique of tying it up with wire.

Conditions improved when we reached the *autoput* running from Zagreb to Belgrade, and the weather became much better as well, changing to scorching sunshine as we enjoyed a delightful run to what was then the capital. On the run south-east to Nis we caught up with and overtook an ancient single-decker bus belching exhaust smoke, with GB plate and the legend 'Oman or bust' on the back. At Nis we had set up our tent in the pleasantly shaded campsite when the roar of a diesel engine, headlights and much shouting and activity announced the arrival of the bus. It turned out to be crewed by London Bible College students who had bought the bus for £150 and were hoping to complete the journey without having to buy any tyres. They said they were 'still on schedule but getting later and later'. The next morning their engine thundered into life and they were away while we were having a leisurely 9 a.m. breakfast. Later we overtook them again but never saw them after that and often wondered if they made it alright.

The helpful Yugoslav tourist office map showed fuel stations, and with the MGB running fairly low we turned off down a dusty track in search of the mythical petrol station, but couldn't see any sign of it. The track ended at some neglected looking buildings but there was no sign of the petrol station that the map had promised. I was giving up, and turning the car round, when a shabbily dressed soldier emerged and asked if we wanted *benzin*. He went off and returned with some jerrycans clearly marked 'US Army', sloshed it into the MGB spilling it everywhere, and then held us to ransom over the price, including charging for the half of one jerrycan that the tank couldn't take. I thought a picture of this shambolic set-up would be good, but declined on being threatened with a gun and told that it was a military establishment.

We motored on through Skopje, a city that within a fortnight would be largely destroyed by a massive earthquake. If we had made the expedition the other way round, out through Italy and back through Yugoslavia, we could well have been camping there on earthquake night. I might have got a scoop!

Arrival at Greece with its better roads was a welcome change, and we found a delightful campsite by the sea with only one other party there – Austrians with a caravan and large awning. We started putting up our tent, only to be asked: 'Please don't camp there, that is where we have our dinner when the sun is going down.' We obligingly moved to the other side, only to be asked not to be there either, because that was where they had their breakfast!

As we motored south next day I diverted to the scene of the fateful accident where the photographer had put me head first through the windscreen of the Sunbeam Alpine in 1961, and in daylight it was even more obvious how crazy the accident had been. We were on the main road, which curved to the left at the bottom of the hill, and the lorry into which the photographer managed to crash was simply at the end of a military track and not on the road at all. We then went on to the hospital where they had saved my life, and I met again the doctor who had stitched me up that night. We had another written conversation, because he could write English but not speak it, so he wrote: 'Are you now well?' and I wrote 'yes, thank you for saving me!'

We had a lovely tour of Greece in the MGB and found a secluded site by an inland lake open to the sea called Loutraki, where the only other occupants – apart from huge insects, which kept crashing into the tent while we had the light on – were a few people camped around a little café, illuminated from a generator. Now, of course, Loutraki has been developed into a huge holiday complex with hotels and apartments. From there we made a fascinating excursion into Athens and climbed the Acropolis. A large American lady sat on a rock at the bottom, perspiring in the heat, and said: 'I'll tell the folks back home that I did it!'

A visit to the Greek Touring and Automobile Club, to thank them for kindly paying the enormous hospital costs after my accident, resulted in an invitation to join them for dinner, but unfortunately it would have to be next day. Our campsite at Loutraki was 70 miles away but no matter, we motored in to Athens again next day and had a pleasant dinner on the roof of the Automobile Club building, and were invited to come out again next year to cover the Acropolis Rally, which was going to be made into a much bigger event. They offered to cover the expenses. It was an interesting proposition, but I would have to find a way to interest the editor in the idea.

We crossed to the vast island that forms the southern part of Greece, and then made our way on the ferry, which was then a tank landing craft, back to the mainland heading north-west to Igoumenitsa with the objective of taking the ferry

Two small boys show interest in the MGB where we stopped for a quick shopping visit while in Greece. A luggage grid on the boot took our huge load of camping gear.

across to Brindisi in Italy. At one time the road became very lonely, and when we had seen no other vehicle on it for about an hour I became very anxious that perhaps I had missed the turn and we were on the road to Albania, where they were known to shoot at tourists. But a check of map and compass showed that all was well, and soon the ferry terminal came into view. It was quite a long crossing, taking from 7 a.m. to 5 p.m., and cost just under £9.

In lovely sunshine we had a gorgeous run over the mountains to Rome and arrived in good time to find the site and set up our camp, but Rome was to prove unkind to us. The first disaster came next day when I wanted to track down the editor's former secretary, Liz Hussey, who had been the first person I met when I joined *The Autocar* eight years earlier. She had left the magazine and was now working for UNESCO in Rome. We found where she lived but as she was not yet back from work we went off to get a drink, leaving the MGB parked just round the corner. While waiting, I thought I would quickly change the film round in my cine camera and walked back to the car only to find the tonneau cover partly pulled back. Clearly someone had interfered with it, so I got in and drove it round the corner in front of the café where we were having our drinks. At first, nothing seemed to have been taken, and I thought I had returned just in time to thwart the thieves, but then we found Jennetta's small case of toiletries and make-up had gone, as had my shaver and the jacket in which was our emergency cash of £10.

Next day we went to explore the Vatican and climbed up on to the roof from whence the magnificent view over Rome revealed the heavy black clouds of an approaching storm. Stupidly we stayed there watching it come nearer, and when it arrived the rain was absolutely torrential. It was about a quarter of an hour before we could even rush from the place where we had found a bit of shelter to get to the exit door. The MGB had a lake of water on the tonneau cover, and when we returned to the tent it was to find everything soaked. There had been a similar downpour on our site in Athens, but on that occasion the rain soon ended and everything dried out quickly with the return of scorching sunshine – but not in Rome, where it stayed dull with intermittent rain, giving us a most uncomfortable night.

In better weather next day we set off, and wanting petrol we passed the first two or three filling stations at which cars were queuing up, and pulled into the fourth one where the staff just stood and laughed at us. Only then did we discover that there was a strike of forecourt staff. We were now very concerned, being down to a quarter on the fuel gauge, as well as low on paraffin for the Primus cooker. We decided to head for the coast and try to find a campsite, but on the way i noticed a small shop with a solitary pump outside. We were down to our last half gallon, with the fuel gauge no longer moving from the E mark on corners. The owner was clearly very anxious about serving us, but responded to our hard luck story that we had to get back to England, and gave us a fill-up for which we were most grateful and tipped him generously.

By keeping the speed down to 60mph and driving gently, I managed to raise the normal consumption figure from 28mpg to 36.8, and we reached Pisa in the dark where a queue of unlit cars revealed a strike-breaking filling station being run by the manager in complete darkness. We were just being served when someone came running and shouting a warning and the operation stopped, but we had been just in time, and had a full tank again – the last to be served. After this we knew we had enough fuel to get out of Italy if we took the shortest route along the coast instead of the inland *autostrada* to Milan.

Five days after taking the ferry from Greece we were back in England where, only a few miles from home a sudden downpour was so heavy that we had to stop and put the hood up for the first time since leaving Rome, because the splashing on to the inside of the windscreen was making it difficult to see where we were going. The MGB had provided delightful transport, and apart from the broken exhaust bracket there were no problems of any kind. Fuel consumption for the whole trip was 28.8mpg, and only 3 litres of oil were needed in the total distance of just under 4,000 miles. Mileage out through Yugoslavia was 1,986, almost exactly the same as the 1,961 return journey through Italy.

The very next day I was back to work, but with an interesting job to do – driving north in our long-suffering MGB to attend the opening ceremony of a long stretch of M6 including the Thelwall viaduct and the Charnock Richard service area. After the ceremony was over, with a very interesting speech by Transport Minister Ernest Marples, I drove the MGB across to the pumps to fill the tank. A tall, robust gentleman came across and said: 'You are the first person to fill up at our new service area, so it will be our pleasure to let you have the petrol free of charge.' I thanked him profusely, though what I really wanted to say was: 'Actually, I'm on expenses, but if I could have a receipt that would be really helpful!' I told the girl on the till that the gentleman over there had kindly said I could have the petrol free of charge. 'Yes,' she replied, 'that is Mr Charles Forte.'

THIRTY-ONE

LAND ROVER CARAWAGON

≡ Suddenly we ran into a particularly deep drift, and the snow came right over
≡ the bonnet

In the 1950s a new kind of vehicle emerged, destined soon to become immensely successful. It was the conversion of a van into a motorhome, providing sleeping accommodation and facilities for cooking, washing, toiletry and so on. At first, they were very crude but inevitably improved and became much more sophisticated with the original idea of basing them on a van being replaced by a coach-built body mounted on the van chassis. No one else on the staff of *The Autocar* wanted to be involved with these new vehicles, although it was agreed that we should cover them, and the editor was always keen to borrow one for his annual holiday in France, so I added them to my increasing list of responsibilities.

Finding a name for them was difficult, and we wanted it to be something using the word 'auto' rather than our rival's 'motor', but finished up resigned to calling them first of all 'motorised caravans', later abbreviated to 'motor caravans' or 'motorhomes'.

Encouraged by the fact that – for some completely illogical reason – they escaped purchase tax, they soon became popular and the number of small manufacturers doing the conversions also increased rapidly. Often, the van converted into a motor caravan cost little more than the equivalent car saddled with purchase tax.

New ideas evolved and were put into production, and in early 1963 I was intrigued by the design offered by R.J. Searle Ltd for a conversion of the long-wheelbase Land Rover, which Searle called the Carawagon. Mains current boosted from the 12-volt battery supply to power electric blankets, a water heater using engine heat, and a tent extension at the rear were among the novelties. A test vehicle was supplied, and my wife, still fairly new to the demands of weekend motor caravan testing, came with me as we set off in the Carawagon to the West Country.

It was February 1963 – one of the coldest winters of the century – and we soon came to experience the shortcomings of a design that hadn't been thoroughly researched by the firm building it. Fortunately the Land Rover had a heater, though it was only a crude recirculating unit fitted as an extra at £13 15s and barely able to cope with the bitter cold. The 230-volt AC power converter produced only 3 amps, so not much heat came out of the electric blankets, and they would only work while the engine was running. An auxiliary 70-amp-hour battery was fitted, but charging was limited to the output of the dynamo. Some years were still to pass before the arrival of the alternator with its much higher output.

The hot water system used a heat exchanger built into the bypass circuit of the Land Rover's cooling system. Again, the engine had to be kept ticking over, and then it worked well, but its usefulness was limited by the small size of the water container, holding only 6 gallons.

There were many shortcomings, one being the stretcher-type bunks, nowhere near as comfortable as the upholstered beds adapted by folding down the seats as provided in most motor caravans, and when the time came to retire for the night we were shocked to discover that there were no curtains. Due to the lack of insulation in the vehicle, and the recirculatory heater, the windows were streaming with condensation and we found that sheets of newspaper stayed in place against the wet glass, serving as a poor substitute for the curtains that every other motor caravan manufacturer supplied as standard.

We tested the tent extension on pull-out framework, which was quite effective and a clever way to do it, but there was no question of leaving this in use with the prevailing ice-cold weather. We needed doors and windows to be closed, and the heater going full chat.

After a pretty uncomfortable night, we decided to make tracks for home, but in the afternoon the snow started. Councils weren't very effective at gritting and salting the roads back in 1963, and the surface was soon quite treacherous, so it was good to have four-wheel drive. There was very little traffic about – in those days the very mention of snow made most drivers leave their cars at home – but after a while we caught up with a bus. After following it for some miles there came an opportunity to overtake safely and we then made good progress until rounding a corner we found a lorry that had skidded off the road, and the driver, red in the face, was frantically digging to try to get the snow away from the back wheels.

Lots of clever ideas but not very well executed in Searle's Carawagon conversion of a long-wheelbase Land Rover. With no proper heating, it was a very cold test in 1963.

I stopped and asked if he had a tow rope, but he hadn't. However, I noticed that the bumper of the lorry was about the same height as that of the Land Rover, and offered to give him a bumper-to-bumper push. He responded eagerly, climbed back into the cab, and I was most impressed to find how readily that wonderfully versatile Land Rover in first gear with low range selected pushed the lorry back on to the road. Just as we started moving, the bus appeared and had to stop as the back end of the lorry was protruding across the road. I expect the passengers thought that we had collided. We gave a wave and continued on our way, with a feeling of camaraderie at having helped someone in the exacting conditions.

With darkness came the wind and much heavier snow. Feeling great confidence in the abilities of the Land Rover I saw no reason not to take to the high ground south of Broadway on the little road from the village appropriately named Snowshill to Chipping Campden. The sight lit up by the headlamps on that high road across the Broadway hills was quite amazing: there would be a length of road often as much as 100 yards completely clear of snow, with the cat's eyes visible, but then the snow would be piled up in drifts forming beautiful curving shapes like a stormy sea without the movement.

We ploughed into it with confidence, presuming that the road went straight, but I became increasingly anxious as the headlamps revealed nothing of the road beyond and I realised that we could very easily be steering off the road altogether. Suddenly we ran into a particularly deep drift, and the snow came right over the bonnet. I took this as a warning sign that it was silly to continue. The snow was still driving past the headlamps, and the windows on the right hand side of the vehicle were completely opaque with their thick covering. We reversed back through that terribly high drift and had an alarming moment when the Land Rover stopped, with all wheels churning away in the snow, but a little shunting to and fro soon had it back on firmer ground, and in one of the clear areas where the snow was just blowing across and not settling, we were able to turn round and make our way back down the hill and pick up the main A44 road which was still reasonably clear.

It had been quite a terrifying experience up there on that lonely road where we might have become bogged down and trapped for days on end, and it was with some relief that we arrived back at the home we were living in then, at Dorridge near Solihull – albeit a house with no central heating. The Land Rover had certainly proved its worth in the most demanding conditions. It had a 2¼-litre 4-cylinder petrol engine, basically that of the then discontinued Rover 80, and with all the low-gear work and long spells spent with the engine ticking over, its overall fuel consumption worked out at a shattering 12.2mpg. In more normal conditions, it was good for 20mpg.

T H I R T Y - T W O

ROVER 3-LITRE

≡ 'I thought you'd be back,' said the policeman, with typical Welsh lilt to his
≡ voice, 'that road doesn't lead anywhere!'

'Why don't we,' asked my colleague Howard Vyse in 1960, 'talk the editor into letting us put in a proper *Autocar* entry for this economy run?' I had driven in the press section of the Mobil Economy Run, and produced a report of the event, which had interested Howard. He was in charge of layout and production at the magazine, and I was on the road-test and general staff. Maurice agreed to the idea of letting the journal submit an entry for the 1961 Run, and it started for me a lifelong interest in the fascinating business of squeezing the maximum mpg out of cars.

After looking at the regulations for the 1961 event, we decided to enter the big car class for engines over 2 litres, and asked Rover if they were interested in supplying a car for us to drive in the economy run. They were, and a 3-litre saloon with overdrive was provided, coming wonderfully well prepared. It had been on long loan to thequeen, and had a filled hole on the bonnet where the flagstaff had been. Numerous requests came when we presented the car at scrutineering: 'May I sit in your car?' We always responded with: 'Yes, of course, I suppose you want to try the back seat, where the queen used to sit?'

The late Peter Wilks, then engineering director of Rover, drew up a list of all the special preparations to be done to it. There was nothing contrary to the regulations, of course, but such things as introducing some end float on the wheel bearings to ensure that the brake pads would be pushed clear and not rubbing, slackening off the rear drum brakes, fitting a new fully charged battery with the dynamo set to the low limit of charge, and running on Avon tyres that were nearly bald to reduce rolling resistance, were among the clever wheezes introduced by Peter. In subsequent years there was a new rule in the regulations to the effect that tyres had to have sufficient tread to last, in the opinion of the organisers, the full distance of the event.

Could we have beaten the wizard George Kendrick, who obtained 37.2mpg out of an Austin A99, which had the asset of a BorgWarner overdrive with built-in freewheel? Well, we certainly had a marvellous advantage over him on the first day. The route went from Coventry up to Holme Moss, over the Snake Pass, and past Castle Howard on a sunny Sunday in April. 'It'll be crawling with slow traffic up there,' said Howard, so we agreed to get time in hand in anticipation. We arrived so early at the Coventry route check that, being car number two, they weren't ready for us, but we were soon on our way again and the minutes in hand were marvellous, enabling us to take it all gently, and then smile knowingly later when people told us how hard they'd had to drive to get in on time after all the traffic delays.

But we were very much novices at the Mobil Economy Run, and hadn't spent the time we should have done studying the regulations, nor did I pay sufficient attention during the pre-run briefing. The result was that we drifted happily along through North Wales on the second day, running about half an hour late but gradually catching up, and thinking we had all afternoon to get back on schedule. We hadn't realised that soon after lunch the first stage ended with a time control.

Suddenly, the horror of it hit me when I turned the page of the route instructions and read: TIME CONTROL! I was navigating, and colleague Howard Vyse was driving. I yelled out the shocking news, and in a panic Vyse asked: 'How far have we got to go?' 'How many minutes left?' 'What are the time allowances?'

We were running along the side of Lake Vyrnwy, and I told Howard to step on it, softly but swiftly, while I worked out the figures. A pocket calculator would have been invaluable for doing the calculations based on the required average speed of 30mph. In those days competitors were allowed all time delays, even for a one-minute hold-up at a roadworks traffic light, so these needed to be added on when working out our scheduled arrival time. Later, they restricted these allowances to the amount by which any single delay exceeded five minutes. I was deeply immersed in

On our first attempt at the Mobil Economy Run, the Rover 3-litre formerly used by HM the Queen, is seen here tackling a favourite economy run road, over the moors at Blubberhouses, in the 1961 event.

the figures and trying to work out how bad the situation was, when Howard called out: 'Which way?'

I looked down quickly at the route instructions and saw *At end of lake, L at J*, and called out: 'Left!'

I knew it was a mistake straight away, as the road went steeply uphill and began to get narrower, soon showing signs of petering out. We hadn't reached the end of the lake, and had left the main road too early. We had to turn round at the only place that gave any chance of doing so, and the Rover 3-litre was a big car. 'I'll have to zoom it,' said Howard, and after about four to-and-fro shunts reversing up the bank he was able to head back down the hill.

At the junction with the main road there was a policeman – a rather rare sight in that part of North Wales before they were all given cars – and as we prepared to rejoin the road, he held up his hand. 'Now what?' said Howard, winding down the window as the policeman ambled over.

'I thought you'd be back,' said the Welsh policeman, 'that road doesn't lead anywhere!'

We were away at last, back on the correct road but now even later. We still had 35 miles to cover in only forty-five minutes. Knowing the road better than Howard, I took over and punched the Rover along as hard as I dared. Fortunately some fast stretches of road opened up, and the precious minutes came trickling back. The observer in the back seemed to be enjoying it, and of course there was no 60mph speed limit in those days. We weren't late at the time control, but it was a close thing, and it had wrecked the economy. Lateness was always penalised at the rate of 0.5mpg deduction from the final result per whole minute late, so it was always worth almost any amount of hard driving to avoid a lateness penalty.

We knew precisely how much fuel we had used because I was going to write an article analysing the fuel consumption of the Rover 3-litre on the economy run afterwards, and had fitted a fuel consumption meter in the boot. At every route check one of us jumped out and read the meter, so that we could plot economy over every stage. The Rover 3-litre had been giving over 30mpg, but that section in Wales took its toll, at 21.7mpg. Entitled A Time and Petrol Study, the article appeared in *The Autocar*, 5 May 1961.

There had been a little upset about the fuel meter at scrutineering. 'What's all this?' we were asked. 'A fuel consumption meter,' I replied. 'It was declared on the entry form under "modifications to the car".'

'Oh,' came the reply, 'I'll have to ask Holly about this.' Holland Birkett, the clerk of the course, later killed in a tragic light-aircraft accident, was suitably embarrassed, as the declaration on the form hadn't been noticed. So it was announced to competitors at the briefing, and when he pointed out that we had introduced six points of possible fuel leakage into the system, no one objected. The reason for the extra connections was because those early fuel meters were notoriously unreliable, so we had to have a by-pass system to be able to turn two taps and carry on if the meter packed up. In fact, it performed perfectly throughout the event, giving a final reading of 29.7mpg, fairly close to the official figure of 29.1mpg determined by the usual meticulously accurate defuelling process. How the Hants & Berks Motor Club officials checked the fuel economy of each competing car was to drain the tanks by suction at the beginning of the event, and repeat this process at the end. All fuel taken on was recorded, and the final amount drawn out at the end was measured by weighing, and credited against the total supply.

Our fuel meter was fitted in the boot so that no one could say we had a forbidden economy 'aid' in the car. In fact, so quiet was the Rover that you could hear it clicking away, but it didn't help much to hear it going like mad when the engine was hauling the 2-ton Rover up a mountain pass in Wales.

Even without the mistakes we made as novices, I don't think the Rover would ever have beaten the amazing achievement of the ace economy driving team of George Kendrick and Mike Bloodworth with the Austin A99, but with a little more experience, forethought and planning we would certainly have been in the prize money. Only 0.83mpg better would have been enough. We drove back from the finish at Harrogate disappointed, but determined to have another go the following year.

THIRTY-THREE

JAGUAR E-TYPE

≡ Did it really do 150mph, as published in the road test?

Maurice Smith, editor of *Autocar*, came into my office one morning in July 1965 and said: 'I'm going to see Charles; do you want to come?'

I was terribly busy, with a road test going to press next day, but I knew Charles Haywood was very ill in a hospital in Amersham and I owed it to him to go along and try to cheer him up. Charles had been Midlands editor of the journal when I joined in 1955, had introduced me to road-testing, and had taken me as 'assistant' on a number of Continental road-test trips. The work would have to wait, and I would have to catch up later.

Maurice and I went down to the car park together, and as it was a beautiful day we quickly put the hood down on his Jaguar E-Type and set off. We were burbling quietly through Hampstead Garden Suburb – the back-double which those in the know take to avoid Golders Green – and two girls were walking towards us on the other side of the road. Ever the showman, Maurice changed down into second and floored the accelerator. The Jaguar's exhaust changed from a gentle burble to a purposeful roar, and the car rocketed away. The girls stopped and gawped at us in unconcealed admiration. In no time we had leapt up to 60mph.

When they were out of sight and the car had settled back to a normal speed, Maurice commented: 'Nothing like a bit of sunshine for bringing the tits out.'

'Maurice!' I exclaimed. 'I'm quite shocked.'

'Oh, did you not see them? The blue tits up there in the tree?'

'Ah, of course, I knew that was what you meant,' I said with a chuckle. 'I think I was looking the wrong way.'

We enjoyed a pleasant drive to Amersham, chatting and joking, but there was no humour when we parked the E-Type at Amersham Hospital and found the private ward where Charles Haywood was languishing. He was suffering from stomach cancer and was clearly desperately ill.

'Ironic, isn't it, Stuart,' he said, 'when you think what we went through with those Jaguars in Belgium, and now for me to finish up like this?' I had never felt at the time that we were in danger doing those two XK150 road tests, but on reflection, remembering the number of times we had been doing 120mph, and the frequency with which we had stopped and then made a U-turn through the bit of scrub on the centre strip of the dual carriageway to go back and time acceleration in the opposite direction, I realised that it would only have needed one mistake to finish us. I had put my trust completely in Charles, and was nearly all the time looking down at the electric speedometer or writing down the figures on the road-test cards.

Maurice invited me to drive on the journey back to the office, and I remember a lovely run, relishing the exhilarating speed and response of the E-Type, with its ability to zoom past a whole column of traffic and then tuck in waiting for the next

In November 1963 I was able to borrow this E-Type Coupé for a preview inspection of an unopened stretch of the M6 in the north, before going on to cover the RAC Rally.

opportunity. We were back in the office in time for a late lunch, and only a few weeks later we were attending Charles's funeral.

My involvement with the E-Type had started at its initial launch, when the technical editor, Harry Mundy, decided to take me with him to help cover the 1961 Geneva Motor Show. On the second press day we left the show and drove along the north side of Lake Leman to the magnificent restaurant called Eaux Vivres, for what was then the traditional press lunch given by Mercedes-Benz. After the lunch we went out into the large open space at the back of the restaurant and joined a crowd of waiting journalists. Among the many people there I recognised Sir William Lyons, founder and head of Jaguar. Suddenly there was a great stir and this magnificent, fabulously low and long sports car arrived. At the wheel was the Jaguar press officer, Bob Berry. Sir William was a bit harsh on him, asking 'Where the blazes have you been?' not knowing that the car had been passed out late by the factory, that Bob had driven it through the night, and was just back from having it washed at the Jaguar dealership.

There was the inevitable scrum to take turns to sit in it, and when I was able to climb in I found it hard to imagine driving this car, with its slatted cooling outlets in the top of the bonnet, and the bonnet itself disappearing from view, making it hard to tell where the front of the car would be. I was absolutely enthralled by it, and delighted when only a few days later, back in England, I was asked by the assistant editor, Ron 'Steady' Barker, if I would like to accompany him to do the road-test figures at MIRA.

They hadn't extended the M1 in those days – it ended near Watford – and I parked my Triumph TR3A on the grass near the M1 terminal roundabout and joined Steady Barker in the E-Type. I don't think one would park a car in such a casual way nowadays, and leave it there for the day!

The E-Type was the same left-hand drive model in gunmetal grey, registration 9600 HP, that I had seen first at Geneva. The journey to the MIRA proving ground gave exciting glimpses of its staggering performance, and when we fitted the fifth wheel and I had the electric speedometer on my lap, I was amazed at the acceleration. We did timed runs to 130mph on the 1-mile straight at MIRA, reached in only 33 seconds from rest, and then fitted the fuel meter and measured fuel consumption round the banked circuit at constant speeds right up to 110mph. It was still returning 19mpg at constant 100mph – not bad for a car with four-speed gearbox and no overdrive.

It was never within our remit to measure the maximum speed. Although legal, it would not have been possible on the M1 except perhaps with an early start on a Sunday morning, and the editor had taken on the responsibility to do this in Belgium on our traditional Jabbeke straight of the Ostend–Brussels autoroute.

Did it really do 150mph, as published in the road test? It was fitted with the optional Dunlop R5 Racing tyres for the maximum speed tests, and Maurice much later wrote an article in *Classic Cars* in which he related what had happened. He had gone

Everyone is familiar with the external view of an E-Type, but here is an impression of the driver's view, showing the M6 still under construction south of Preston.

out with a colleague who didn't stay long on the staff, and they were obviously hoping that the magic 150mph would be achieved. The electric speedometer wasn't calibrated above 140mph, so they were checking the speed by timing over a quarter of a mile.

After a number of runs they stopped on the grass, and Maurice recalled the smell of the hot oil, the machinery all clicking away as the engine and exhaust cooled off. The calculations of time taken for the quarter-mile showed that it hadn't quite made it. Then this assistant went off alone, and did two more runs, returning to say that it had made it, with a best one-way speed of 151.7mph, which gave it a mean two-way figure of 150.4. It was quite wrong for this test to be done with only one person on board – tests were always 'two up' – as well as being unsafe for the driver to be trying to concentrate on timing.

My own view was that it was also wrong to set out on a road-test trying to obtain a predicted figure, just as we had when trying to get 100mph out of the Rover 105S in 1957. Also, it seemed to be no more than a talking point. The undoubted fact of the matter was that the E-Type was an amazingly fast car and, at its launch in 1961, one of the fastest road cars in the world.

As soon as it had been launched, the company's managing director by the name of Priaulx decided that he wanted one, and although he was running a policy of extraordinary meanness against the staff, holding back salaries and moaning about expenses, his E-Type convertible arrived in October 1961.

A matter for great amusement came shortly after my return from honeymoon in 1962, when Priaulx was very keen to try a car on which I was doing the road test. The loan was arranged, but oh dear, what would he do with the E-Type? Couldn't leave it in the firm's open car park at Waterloo – it might get vandalised. 'Perhaps you'd better take it home, Stuart.' I didn't need a second invitation, and drove it for the first time. What Priaulx didn't know was that we were 'between houses' and living in a rented flat in the New Cross area of South London. The E-Type spent the night parked at the kerb in this not-very-salubrious area, and there were frequent occasions for leaping out of bed and looking down from the window to check that the E-Type was not being molested.

After a couple of years, including a long holiday trip to the south of Italy, Priaulx began to tire of the unsuitability of the E-Type for his wearying commute to and from home in Beckenham, and passed it on to Maurice Smith for the second half of the five years' service as one of the journal's staff cars, and this was when we made that 1965 trip to Amersham. On a number of other occasions I was able to borrow it, and driving it was always a special delight.

During what was to prove my temporary assignment to the Coventry office, I was asked to share coverage of the RAC Rally in November 1963. Rally reporting was always great fun, and this one was going to involve enormous mileage so I was delighted when Bob Berry agreed to lend me an E-Type fixed-head to use in covering the rally. We went right up to Scotland, back through Wales, and down to the finish at Bournemouth – over 2,000 miles in a few days – but all did not go well.

The appalling weather was the worst problem, with torrential rain in Wales resulting in many flooded roads. Perhaps we shouldn't have driven through the floods, but we had a job to do, and there were few possible detours to avoid them. At one time my photographer, the late Ron Easton, let out a cry that his camera was sitting in a lake of water on the back floor! I had asked for seat belts to be fitted, and I suspect that the water was coming in through the bolted lower mountings. When we trickled through the floods, steam always came up through the bonnet vents from the hot exhaust manifolds, and streamed over the windscreen as quite a good indication of the smooth air flow over the car.

The other problem was on the undulating roads in Scotland, when the exhaust pipes would frequently ground. I was told later that this was due to weak rear suspension dampers, which were being changed, but I always felt the ground clearance a little marginal. I handed the car back and apologised to Bob Berry about the soaked carpets, but he took it very affably and was setting off the same evening on a Jaguar Owners' Club Rally.

I had many other E-Type adventures, including assisting Maurice Smith on the road test of the new model with 4.2-litre engine, when Jaguar engineers were shocked to see that we were testing the car with one of the headlamp cowlings broken. It had been hit by a stone, but Maurice wasn't going to let that spoil his day of testing. 'It's ruined the aerodynamics,' complained the Jaguar people.

Another test that went smoothly was when I accompanied the newly appointed technical editor, Geoff Howard, on the test of the 2+2 model. Carvair flights to distant locations on the Continent were proving popular, and we had a 'contra' deal – a free advertisement in *Autocar* in return for a free flight with the test car to Basle. We did the test figures on the Basle *Autobahn*, but the high roof 2+2 was considerably slower than the two-seater, and never looked as sleek.

Shortly before the editor's E-Type was sold off in January 1966, we were having a discussion over lunch at the Jaguar factory in Coventry about this amazing car and its probable successor, the XJS. Always prone to exaggerate, Maurice said to Bob Berry: 'The next E-Type I have will need to be at least 3ft shorter at the front; I can't cope with that great unprotected nose sticking out at the front.'

'That's all right, Maurice,' replied Berry, 'we'll do you a special one with no front wheels!'

THIRTY-FOUR

Vauxhall Velox PB

We were absolutely scuppered, with the tank empty, and our spare fuel cans and toolkit trapped in a boot that could not be opened

With today's proliferation of motorways, especially on the Continent, one may presume that long-distance motoring is much faster now than was ever possible nearly fifty years ago, and I was quite surprised to look back at the records and recall how far I had driven in 1963 when covering the famous Spa–Sofia–Liège Rally for *Autocar*. I had a fairly humble car for the journey – a Vauxhall Velox Mk III saloon, known as the PB series, with 2¾-litre 6-cylinder engine – and covered 3,213 miles in six days. It was quite a punishing schedule, made possible by using the Yugoslavian *autoput* on which, with care, one could cruise at 85–90mph. Of course, speed limits in those days were hardly known.

Accompanied by Mike Barnes as the photographer for the job, we drove out to Liège and arrived in the dark, looking for the hotel and somewhere to park when I heard the sound of English voices and recognised some of the rally drivers and crew relaxing at a table on the pavement in the warm August evening, and drew alongside for friendly greetings, still sitting in the car. The request: 'Two glasses of wine, please' produced immediate response. Two glasses were passed through the open window, and after a few sips in the car I pulled the Velox over to the kerb and we joined them. Entertaining competitors was a chargeable expense.

We watched scrutineering next day, and then set off ahead of the start, down to Munich, and the following day took the all-too-short stretch of *Autobahn* to Salzburg and then across Austria in torrential rain. One of the problems of going to Yugoslavia in those days was the difficulty of getting money, since British banks would not issue dinars, so whenever we saw a likely-looking bank in Austria I went in to change currency, but with the strict limits in force I had amassed only £6 in *dinaron* by the time we reached the border.

We didn't have much in the way of equipment, and the Velox was completely standard, but I took the precaution of carrying a gallon tin of oil and three jerrycans for petrol to supplement the Velox's inadequate 10½-gallon fuel tank. This took the total supply to 22 gallons (100 litres), and although it was much cheaper in Yugoslavia (3.7p per litre!) I made sure that everything was full as we left Austria. Also in the boot was a comprehensive toolkit in the hope of being able to cope with any mechanical emergencies. The bench front seat didn't give much in the way of lateral location when cornering, but most of our journey was to be at speed on motorways or bouncing our way over very rough tracks in Yugoslavia.

We hoped to cut across to the fearsome Col du Moistrocca, which was the first of the rally special stages, but there was so much traffic waiting to enter Yugoslavia at the frontier that we turned round, went back 8 miles and took instead the Wurzen pass, which had given me a terrifying time with brake-fade in an earlier Vauxhall. This Velox, fourteen years later, took it very well though still with only a three-speed gearbox with column-mounted change, but now with the advantage of disc front brakes. By the time we reached the Moistrocca pass dusk was falling, and only the tail-enders were going through. We pursued the rally, which was taking the direct route from Ljubljana to Zagreb and Belgrade.

I was pleased that I had insisted on a Velox equipped with the optional Laycock de Normanville overdrive, which enabled it to cruise effortlessly at 80–90mph, but halfway to Belgrade there was a sudden momentary dimming of the headlamps, as the overdrive switch burnt out, followed by a change in engine note, and I knew at once what had happened. 'Oh, oh,' I said to Mike, 'we've lost the overdrive.' We pulled in and I used a piece of wire to bypass the overdrive switch, which put it back into action for 100 miles, then it suddenly failed again. We had to continue without it, and the Velox still cruised impressively well at 85mph in direct top gear, but the petrol now started going through rapidly. The car had been doing about 22mpg, but now the figure dropped to 18.

With the fuel gauge at the bottom of its scale I pulled into a rough parking area to swill in another 10 gallons from the tins, but when I pressed the boot release the whole tumbler fell out, complete with its chromed release button. All attempts to open the boot were defeated. We were absolutely scuppered, with the tank empty, and our spare fuel cans and toolkit trapped in a boot that could not be opened.

Nearby three burly Yugoslav lorry drivers were working on the engine of their lorry by the light of an inspection lamp, and they were impressively quick to understand our problem. They came over to the car, but even with all five of us trying to pull the lid up, the boot remained resolutely closed. Then one of them returned to the lorry and came back with a huge screwdriver. One sharp jerk with this made the lid spring open. I couldn't spare any dinars, but they were all very glad to receive a few German marks each as thanks for their help.

We motored on through the night, arriving at Belgrade at what we thought was 4.30 a.m., surprised to find the rush-hour in full swing with trams, bicycles and people hurrying everywhere, until we realised that the time zone had changed and it was actually 6.30 a.m. We followed the rally to Nis, stopping to talk to competitors, but didn't attempt to follow the rally's diversion into Bulgaria, and went in search of money again. The solitary bank in Leskovac was open, and after a lot of persuasion some travellers' cheques were exchanged for bundles of dinars.

Could you imagine that in these days they would take an international car rally through a town that, only a month earlier, had been struck by a devastating earthquake? Well, this was 1963, and the plans for the Spa-Sofia-Liège rally were not going to be affected by a little matter of an earthquake, so the rally still passed through Skopje. After our return to Britain, people who had read about the earthquake asked me: 'Was it flattened?' The answer was that it was not utterly devastated but more like a town that had been severely bombed, and reminded me of Coventry after the blitz. Many buildings were still standing, but most had cracks all over the walls to tell of the tremor, while some had lost the whole of one face exposing the floors and furnishings like some weird sectioned model. In other parts, the poorer and older houses were reduced to a sea of bricks and rubble. I admired the trust of the Yugoslavs in the way that furniture and possessions were stacked on the pavements, while frontless shops were still open and doing business.

The road from Skopje south towards Titograd was quite terrible, and although we took it carefully in bottom gear, the Velox lurched and plunged on its suspension. We had no sump guard or underbody protection like the rally cars, but we only bottomed badly once, striking the front suspension cross member without doing any structural damage.

We stopped at a time control where the official was seated at a desk in the open with the schedule form in front of him, and as the second hand on his big timekeeping watches passed each minute he put his ruler over the time entry and drew a line across it. About forty minutes had passed when the first competitor arrived; it was Eric Böhringer in his very efficient-looking Mercedes-Benz 230SL. It was obvious that the rally cars were suffering as a result of trying to go too fast to keep on schedule, and by evening the hotel at Titograd was full of rally crews who had retired.

Well stacked with pictures and rally stories, we left the competitors at Titograd and bounced our way back to Skopje where we were able to join the new *autoput* back to Belgrade. Night was falling as we checked into the Hotel Metropol for 'dinner and a room with bath – but for only two hours'. We were both pretty weary, having had no real rest for forty-eight hours other than brief shut-eye on the back seat. I had relaxed my rule never again to let the photographer drive, and Mike Barnes had proved a good driver. We felt much better after our brief halt, for which the bill was only just over £2 each including dinner and wine. Yugoslavia was unbelievably cheap in those days. We were then back in our long-suffering Velox pounding along the single-carriageway *autoput* back to Zagreb and Ljubljana. Even with the straightness of the Yugoslav motorway it was no time to relax, especially as the rain was now pouring down again. Yugoslav lorry drivers were always late to dip their lamps, and as they dazzled you a conscious effort had to be made to slow down sufficiently to see in time the many hazards, such as unlit cars and roadworks with no advance warning.

After Ljubljana we rejoined the rally route, which now crossed the frontier into Italy, and as we drove into the service and control point at Gorizia I was just in time to see a Hillman Minx with a banner on the side showing the magic words 'Laycock overdrive service' and dashed across to ask if they could help bring our unit on the Velox back into action. Although anxious to hurry on to the next control, they quickly jacked the Velox up and worked like demons on their backs in the dust and soon fitted a new solenoid, and replaced the control switch. It was great to have the overdrive working again. It operated on second gear as well as top, which was often useful for overtaking.

Mike Barnes had to travel on by rail to do the pictures for a GP, so I left him at Trieste station, and headed off alone across Austria. During the afternoon I made excellent progress until I arrived in darkness at a sign warning 'Halt in 1km'. Surely this wasn't the German border already, I wondered, and stopped to study the map. Only then did I notice something I hadn't spotted when quickly plotting the route: the words *Gr Glockner*. I pressed on to the toll barrier, only to learn that the pass was closed because there was a blizzard raging higher up, although it was still August. The choice explained to me was to retrace my route 50 miles in the hope of catching the last train under the Tauern tunnel, or try to find a room at the little village of Heiligenblut. This seemed the better option, and so it proved. I had an excellent dinner and the first real night's rest for three days. Next morning I woke to a blue sky, and brilliant sunshine, and the drive over the Gross Glockner pass with its first covering of snow was breathtakingly beautiful.

I made good progress until nearing Stuttgart, where there had obviously been an accident, and in an hour we covered only half a mile, until a genius in a car some way in front found a way off. Gingerly, we all followed, slithering and scraping down a 1-in-3 slope off the *Autobahn*, through an orchard, round the edge of a field, then down a dusty track and eventually by minor roads to Stuttgart. I don't think they allow that sort of diversion these days!

At Liège I called at rally headquarters and caught up with final news and collected the results sheets. Before heading back to London with the pictures, I walked round the *parc fermé* and examined all the finishers. There were only twenty of them, and I made notes of the body condition of each one, which were included in the results list at the end of my 2,000-word story of the rally. Only ten of them had no visible body damage. It had been one of the most demanding rallies ever, with over 100 cars scattered about in various stages of destruction in the wilds of Yugoslavia. The German crew Böhringer and Kaiser won the rally in their Mercedes-Benz 230SL, and Erik Carlsson and co-driver Palm were second in a Saab 841, which was also one of the few cars with no evident body damage. Three Citroën DS saloons survived, finishing third, fifth and seventh, to win the constructors' cup.

The Velox had served very well indeed, covering 3,213 miles in six days of hard driving over often-terrible roads. There were still 2 pints of oil left in the tin, which meant that it had done 4,000mpg on oil, which was good for the 1960s, unlike today when no one ever bothers to check oil level, and the overall fuel consumption was 19.6mpg. On the return trip with the overdrive back in action the economy had improved to 22.5mpg. The most exacting part of the journey had been the long flog from Jesenice all the way to Skopje and Titograd, then back to Ljubljana – more or less non-stop, covering 1,223 miles in twenty-four hours. Although I had been impressed by the comfort, quietness and road performance of the Velox, I was appalled at the sloppy, vague steering. This is one aspect of ordinary family cars that has improved enormously over the years, and I hope that my report to Vauxhall played some small part in persuading them of the need for steering to be more precise.

THIRTY-FIVE

TRIUMPH 2000

The fuel-gauge needle tumbled rapidly down to the half mark, and I knew
we had lost the cap, which had no retaining wire, along with at least
5 gallons of fuel

When we called at the headquarters of the Greek Automobile Club in 1963, there was a clear promise that if I would go out to Greece the following year and cover the Acropolis Rally in *Autocar*, they would pay reasonable expenses and provide accommodation in Athens at the end of the Rally. They were very keen to build up interest in the Acropolis Rally, and said they were impressed with the coverage I had given it in 1961, in spite of the accident that had put me in hospital for five days. It was an offer not to be wasted, but I was determined to make rather more of it than just a drive to Greece and coverage of the Rally. I put forward to the editor the idea for a special project – a 5,000-mile journey, going to Greece via the Iron Curtain countries.

'Well I can't spare two staff men to be away for as long as that,' said the editor, Maurice Smith. It was rather what I was hoping he would say, as my wife, Jennetta was keen to come with me. In Greece we would cover the Acropolis Rally, I would take all the pictures and I had to take much of the time as holiday. We would go out through East Germany, Czechoslovakia, Austria, Hungary and Yugoslavia, returning by the more direct route through Yugoslavia and Germany. He liked the project, and asked what car I planned to take.

One of the star attractions at the 1963 Earls Court Motor Show, the previous year, was the new five-seater saloon from Triumph, the 2000; at the same time, Rover launched its rival, also called 2000. I liked both these new models, but of the two I preferred the Triumph, which I thought handled better, and certainly gave a more comfortable ride, having independent rear suspension instead of the Rover's odd De Dion layout. Its 6-cylinder engine was also quieter and smoother than the Rover's 4-cylinder. So it was the Triumph that I picked.

The Triumph press office responded enthusiastically to the idea, and loan of an overdrive model was arranged.

An awful lot of boring preparatory work was necessary, getting visas, booking and paying in advance for hotels in Prague and Budapest. It's difficult for today's young traveller to visualise what a caper it was in those days, with the bolshy restrictions of Eastern European countries and having to take with you all the money you would need, there being no credit cards.

In Hungary quite a lot of the transport was horse-drawn. Of the four countries in the Soviet bloc in 1964, Hungary was quite the friendliest and most welcoming.

Eventually the planning was over, and the feeling of excitement started when we arrived at the Helmstedt checkpoint that marked the entry to East Germany. US Army signs on the *Autobahn* warned all Allied personnel: 'You are now leaving the West. Park on the centre strip and report to control.' We then went through a routine of being passed from office to office, filling forms and getting rubber stamps on them, and when I finally thought we had suffered enough bureaucracy, we set off only to be stopped within 200 yards and sent back by an East German guard. A British serviceman explained: 'You haven't paid the 20 marks for road tax.'

'I've paid 10 marks,' I said, and he replied: 'Ah, that was for the visa. You now have to pay 20 marks for road tax and insurance.' We were finally away, but under strict instructions not to leave the *Autobahn*, and to report to police as soon as possible if we had a breakdown. A specific time was shown by which we had to be out of East Germany, and we were warned that if we arrived suspiciously early they'd be working out how fast we had been travelling.

At the slower pace of 60mph – a big contrast from the steady 85–90 I had been holding most of the way from the Hook of Holland – there was time to settle down and take stock of the Triumph, and I was well pleased with the choice. We were comfortably seated, the car cruised confidently and quietly, and the fuel was lasting well: 26mpg was very good by the standards of 1964, and the 2000 had a generously big 14-gallon tank. Not knowing how easily we would be able to get fuel, I had stowed a 4½-gallon jerrycan in the capacious boot, giving nearly 500 miles' fuel range.

Traffic became worryingly light after we passed the last turn-off to Berlin, and about the only other vehicles on the *Autobahn* were motorcycles, most of them with a large *Frau* on the pillion. There was another control point where papers were inspected to see why we were still heading towards Poland and Russia. We were allowed to continue, and it was a relief to see the car compass swing round to south-east as we took the Dresden exit.

Nineteen years had passed since the flattening of Dresden during the war, yet rebuilding was still in progress everywhere. Not knowing whether we were allowed to stop we trickled quietly through the city following the odd sign here and there pointing to Prag (its German name) and the rest of the time putting faith in the compass. We were soon at the Czech border with its ominous barbed wire barricade, for more checking of paperwork and the opening of every car's boot. The driver of a Bulgarian Renault Dauphine smilingly opened the lid, revealing its rear-mounted engine, but the guard had a 'we are not amused' expression, and this was clearly no place for humour.

With darkness falling we were through at last, and a mere 60 miles took us to the capital (here called Praha). It was quite the gloomiest city arrival I have ever experienced – no neon lights, hardly any street lights, and very few people about at 8 p.m. – one might have thought it was two in the morning. We managed to find some people to point us in the right direction to our pre-booked and paid-for hotel, which had something of the pseudo grandeur seen in films of Russia before the revolution, but it did provide a good meal, to the accompaniment of a quartet playing Western pop tunes of ten years earlier, and we were amused to hear the song *London Bridge is falling down*.

Prague is now reported to be magnificent, but some fifty years ago it was grim, and the atmosphere was not enhanced by a two-hour delay getting the pre-paid hotel voucher accepted and cashed, but we couldn't complain about the cost – £2 2s each for dinner, bed and breakfast was cheap even by 1964 standards.

Taking Czech crowns out of the country was forbidden, but after wandering round looking at shops displaying the sort of shoddy goods one might have seen in England ten years earlier, we located a glass shop and disposed of our Czech money by buying a fine decanter and set of six beautiful crystal glasses. We had been able to park the Triumph right outside the hotel, and when we were finally able to go we had to nudge through a small crowd of admirers examining it.

A guard on duty in national dress greeted our arrival in Greece.

Petrol at only 2s 7d a gallon was another of Czechoslovakia's few attractions. Although of poor quality and foul smelling, it didn't seem to impair the Triumph's performance, and at that price, who cares?

After the delayed start we continued south-east through Bohemia and Moravia on pleasant, undulating and tree-lined roads, arriving at the frontier to Austria at Haugsdorf only to find it closed for lunch. After a further hour's delay in which we sat in the car confronted by the barbed wire barrier stretching from horizon to horizon, and hearing the barking of the patrol dogs, we were finally inspected and allowed to proceed. What a difference 50 miles made, as the Triumph arrived in cheerful Vienna with its colourful neon signs and atmosphere of bustling prosperity!

Leaving Vienna next day, we took the new six-lane *Autobahn* for 30 miles although heading south-east instead of north-east, then turned east to Pottsching and the Hungarian border, where the guards seemed amazed to see a car, let alone a British one. As well as opening the boot, we had to display the 6-cylinder engine, which came in for careful examination, more from interest, I suspect, than any question of security.

The road soon became little more than a track across the fields, and I began to wonder how much of this we would have to suffer, but it turned out to be just a lengthy diversion from which we soon emerged on to fine metalled roads carrying little traffic as we ran along the west side of Lake Balaton. One of the longest in Europe, Balaton is 48 miles in length and only 10ft average depth.

Of the four countries then in the Soviet bloc, sampled on this trip, Hungary proved quite the easiest and friendliest, and we enjoyed a couple of days there exploring Budapest, including time to sample one of the 117 thermal springs all over the city, all having different temperature, composition and effect for treating such ailments as rheumatism.

After a late start from Budapest we enjoyed good roads all the way to Belgrade, drove through the city and south for 6 miles to Avala where I knew from earlier visits to Yugoslavia that there was a good motel. On the way I made a bad mistake when I stopped to fill the tank, paid, but didn't check that the fuel cap had been replaced. Unfortunately on the first left-hand bend I saw the fuel gauge needle tumble rapidly down to the half mark, and I knew we had lost the cap, which had no retaining wire, along with at least 5 gallons of fuel. We returned to the garage but there was no sign of it, and a time-wasting search next day failed to reveal it.

After pursuing the Acropolis Rally for 615 miles, the fly-spattered front of the Triumph 2000 looked more like one of the rally cars.

We were now on the good, lightly trafficked single carriageway *autoput* heading south-east from Belgrade to Nis, where more time was wasted visiting various garages trying to find a replacement fuel cap. For the rest of the journey we had to keep the tank never more than half full, and use the best of the caps we had purchased, packed with plastic to stop most of the leakage. Fuel consumption for the first 1,750 miles to Belgrade had been 28.3mpg; after that, I couldn't measure it reliably because of the wastage.

Skopje was still showing ample evidence of the devastating earthquake the previous year (1963), but rebuilding was going on apace, and the northern bypass was nearing completion. Rapid progress continued with the Triumph singing along in overdrive for mile after mile on the nearly deserted ribbon of concrete to Titov Veles, and then through a succession of tunnels and bridges to the Greek border at Gevgelija. We then enjoyed the good roads of northern Greece, and a final long section of toll motorway to Athens, where we arrived in good time to get the atmosphere for the forthcoming Acropolis Rally.

Covering the Rally we travelled 615 miles round Greece, taking in many of the shocking road surfaces included in the route. Over these, the car made excellent time, demonstrating its impressive independent rear suspension. It coped well even when we gave lifts, first to a vast Greek policeman, and later to the giant Swedish rally driver Toivonen with his co-driver after their Volkswagen 1500S had run its bearings.

With the rally report and films safely on an aircraft heading back to the office, we were able to enjoy a couple of days' holiday as guests of the Greek Touring Club before starting the long trail homeward. By the end of the rally the Triumph had covered over 3,000 miles, and the only attention needed was topping up the battery on three occasions, and the addition of 3 pints of oil to the sump. Our return trip by the more direct route was covered in five days, with night stops at Katerini (in northern Greece), Belgrade and Bled in Yugoslavia, Kufstein (on the Austro-German border) and Cologne, at an average of 470 miles per day. All told, we had been away just under three weeks,

On the way back through Yugoslavia, with Jennetta driving, I thought I detected slight roughness of the engine and asked her to pull over. On opening the bonnet I saw the trouble straight away: number one plug lead had come adrift and was hanging loose. It took only a moment to tighten the fastening and put it firmly back on, and this was the only problem experienced with the 2000 in the entire 5,167-mile round trip, a remarkable tribute to the reliability of a car that had been launched as a completely new model only eight months earlier.

THIRTY-SIX

Austin 1800

The final indignity for Howard and me was to find that the Triumph 2000 that we had pushed much of the way over the Hirnant Pass just pipped us to fourth place in the class

After the first attempt at the annual Mobil Economy Run, my colleague Howard Vyse and I entered the event again each year, but success always eluded us. Beat the bogey – that was always the big challenge. The industrious organisers at the Hants & Berks Motor Club had devised a formula taking account of overall gearing, engine capacity and weight, designed to put all cars on an equal footing. Each car was given its 'bogey' figure at the start, and the one achieving the greatest percentage improvement was the overall winner, rewarded by holding for a year the magnificent silver rose bowl that had been presented in memory of the late Holland Birkett, former organiser of the event, after his tragic death in an air crash.

Howard and I had noted that the Austin 1800 always seemed to do well against its formula target, and decided to enter one for the 1965 Mobil Run. The Austin 1800 wasn't an efficient design with its square shape, which earned it the name 'Landcrab', because it looked as it if would as happily go sideways as forwards, and its low overall gearing and relatively high weight earned it a low 'bogey' figure, which in theory could easily be beaten. But it didn't work out like that.

On previous events we had always been impressed at how well whatever car we had entered would run after the thorough pre-run scrutiny in which ignition and carburation would be set absolutely spot-on, but this time it was a disaster. We never found out what went wrong, but although the car started off very well and was consistently on the right side of 40mpg, it started to become increasingly sluggish and unresponsive after a few hundred miles, and towards the end, we were barely getting 30mpg out of it.

The final result of 35.3mpg was most disappointing and gave it only fifth in the class. It was also very sad to find that we didn't need a lot more to have won the overall award. As it was, we were second behind a Riley Elf, which had achieved a remarkable 54.4mpg.

We also, I think, had more than our share of bad luck. It was the year of the snow, which fell steadily all day on the Saturday during scrutineering at Harrogate, and all night as well. The first task before the start was to clear several inches of snow off the Austin 1800, and although it was very wet and slushy at the start, it meant that many of the higher sections of the route, including the Hardknott and Wrynose passes in the Lake District, had to be cancelled. Our bad luck came when the decision was taken to scrub the Hirnant pass in North Wales, and the diversion sign put up was missed by about half the field – including us.

The Austin climbed very well over the rutted snow. With its weight concentrated over the driving wheels it had remarkable traction, but we soon caught up with a Triumph 2000 making very heavy weather of it with its rear-wheel drive, and when it became bogged down we had to get out and help manhandle it up the steeper parts of the climb. We were given a time allowance for this, of course, but there was no compensation for the fuel wasted on the Hirnant, and I still remember the discomfort of trying to drive economically with shoes full of water! We cursed ourselves for not spotting the diversion sign.

The next bit of bad luck came on the way to the Oulton Park race circuit for the first of two one-hour sessions at 50mph. We were rather short of time on the approach to Oulton when we arrived at a level crossing and the red lights started flashing. There was plenty of time to have nipped across, and it would have been perfectly safe as the lights had only just come on and the gates hadn't started to close, but I did the proper thing and stopped. There was then an infuriating wait of nearly a quarter of an hour for the train to come, and although we were allowed

A snowy start to the 1965 Mobil Economy Run, but it was an unlucky event for us.

In search of more realistic economy figures, all competitors had to complete an hour's running at average 50mph on the Oulton Park and Mallory Park race circuits.

all of these except the first five minutes it meant a frantic flat-out drive for the last few miles to Oulton.

The snow gave way to torrential rain, and one crew arrived at the Bamford supper stop looking like drowned rats after bravely continuing with a broken windscreen on their Ford Anglia, but they were rewarded with fourth in the class at 42.5mpg.

Mobil, the sponsors of the event, had been campaigning for some time that they wanted mpg figures that were a bit more credible to the ordinary motorist, and after the rotten weather plus two race-track sessions at 50mph, at Oulton Park and Mallory Park, the consumption figures certainly seemed more down to earth than they had been in earlier years.

The big car class required entries to have automatic transmission, and was won by a Ford Zephyr 6, and another Ford, a Cortina Super, won the 1,401-2,000cc class at 40.0mpg. A Vauxhall Viva won the 1,001-1,400cc class at 47.1mpg.

The final indignity for Howard and me was to find that the Triumph 2000 that we had pushed much of the way over the Hirnant pass just pipped us to fourth place in the class by getting 35.34mpg, a mere 0.02mpg ahead of our 35.32mpg. One doesn't often miss a class prize as closely as that!

So 1965 was not a great economy run year for us, though that of course did not prevent us from enjoying it enormously and vowing to be there again next year. The Austin had proved comfortable and very easy to handle over the often tricky minor roads included in the route, and it was a pity that something had gone wrong with the ignition – perhaps the points had closed up or the timing slipped. If it had continued running as well as it was at the beginning, the huge silver bowl would have been ours.

THIRTY - SEVEN

FORD CORTINA LOTUS

There was suddenly an enormous noise, like an aircraft overhead at
low level, and rising to a crescendo

When I heard that I could use a Ford Cortina Lotus test car for my share of the great annual effort of covering the Monte Carlo Rally I was quite excited at the prospect. Despite Ford's insistence on their name in the title of the car, everyone called it simply a Cortina Lotus. This Monte Carlo Rally was in 1965, when the great adventure of entries starting all over Europe and converging at St Claude in France was all part of the glamour of what was then the foremost rally of the year.

My humble share of the coverage was to see the London start, cross with the British contingent and a photographer, Bill Banks, to France, and try to get sufficient action pictures back to the office in time for the press schedule. It was unfortunate that the issue's publication date was after the rally had ended and yet only 'first day' pictures could be included.

Traditionally, the Monte for British entries had always started at Glasgow, but this was abandoned for the first time in 1965, and the start was at Chelsea. The authorities grossly underestimated the keenness of motorsport followers, who turned out in their thousands although the first car was not due away until 3.26 a.m. on a Saturday morning.

The result was a shambles, with police desperately trying to keep space clear for the departing cars to leave Chelsea Barracks. In the scrum, I became separated from the Cortina Lotus, which I had parked inside the start arena well before the crowds arrived, and was jostled out into the street only to find that, without any passes (as they were in the car) I was trapped on the wrong side of an obstinate policeman who wouldn't let me back in. I wondered what to do, as we had to leave promptly to get on the *Lord Warden* at Dover before the competitors, but I soon found the window where everyone was climbing in and dropping to the ground, and was able to join the queue and get back in to rejoin the photographer.

'We must go,' I said, after seeing the first few competitors flagged away. We drove south through a rather bleak windswept London, and made our way to the M2.

On the motorway I became rather disenchanted with the Cortina Lotus. It was very noisy – both wind and mechanical roar – and it was not very comfortable. I was struck by how much harsher the ride was than in a standard Cortina. As part of the Lotus modifications, the rear suspension had been converted to a different layout and general toughening of the ride was part of the procedure to make the car more sporting and better suited for competition driving. It still had a live rear axle, but location was by an A-bracket with radius arms, and coil springs were used instead of the standard leaf springs.

The important change of the Lotus version of this popular family car was, of course, the conversion of the engine to a twin-OHC layout, allowing the output of the 1,558cc unit to be increased to 105bhp. Most of the design work for the top end of the engine was done by our technical editor, the late Harry Mundy, in the days when it was intended only for use in the very small-scale production Lotus sports cars. Adoption of the engine for Ford's Cortina opened the way to far greater sales, and Harry complained bitterly to me that he had not shared any of the vastly increased profits that resulted. Colin Chapman had offered Harry the choice of a one-off fee of £250, or a royalty. Had he taken the royalty, he would have received thousands of pounds, but Harry was always short of cash and went for the immediate option of £250, which was quite a lot of money in those days; however, he was very bitter when Chapman did not offer anything more after the deal with Ford opened the way for much greater sales. I discussed all this with the photographer, Bill Banks, who was accompanying me.

It had been a windy night in London, and now on the exposed M2 a gale was blowing and the Cortina Lotus was wandering about badly, making me more aware of its woolly steering.

We were about 5 miles from the end of the M2 when disaster struck. There was suddenly an enormous noise, like an aircraft overhead at low level, and rising to a crescendo. Wondering what on earth was happening I pulled on to the hard shoulder. As the speed came down, the noise at last diminished and become more identifiable as a harsh, groaning rumble from the back end. We both knew what it was, and I said: 'It's the diff.' At exactly the same moment, Bill said: 'Back axle's gone.'

By chance, Bill Banks lived at Faversham, close to the M2 motorway, and we were, he said, only a few miles from his home. His company car was there. I visualised his grubby, tired old Hillman Minx, but it would be better than nothing, if the Cortina Lotus could get us there.

The axle hadn't broken, but it was near to seizure. I had heard about the problem of the modified suspension causing the back axle to shed its oil, and I guessed that this was what had happened.

In second gear we trundled along the hard shoulder to the accompaniment of the most dreadful noises from behind, punctuated by the occasional shockingly loud bang as something became chewed up in the final drive gear wheels. But at last we crunched on to the drive at Banks Towers, and we had made it. I have memories of Mrs Banks leaning out of the upper window and throwing down keys, of a hurried cup of coffee in the kitchen, and then setting off in a Hillman Minx that had over 50,000 miles on the clock and was even worse than I had anticipated.

On the way to Dover I suddenly realised that we had no green card insurance for the Hillman. In those days before EEC rules made insurance obligatory in all member countries, you had to obtain the green card from your insurer and take it with you. Fortunately, I had with me the one that had been issued for the Cortina Lotus. In the queue at Dover, I crossed out the Lotus details and boldly entered in all the particulars for the Hillman. To make it look official, I initialled every entry. I was under no delusions that it gave us insurance – my road-tester's all-embracing policy would cover that – but I thought it might convince a bleary *douanier* when the *Lord Warden* docked at Boulogne at 8 a.m., and it did.

The Hillman behaved well enough, and although desperately slow, it was notably more comfortable than the Cortina Lotus. We were able to get our rally pictures and put together some kind of story, although at this early stage of the rally there was little to report. That would be covered by other members of the team already out in southern France. The job was done, and two days later I was back in the office arranging removal of the Cortina Lotus from the Banks premises.

We were persuaded to get the car back to our London office, so I set off for Faversham with a mechanic and the firm's appropriately named 'wrecker' – a Standard Ensign towing a close-coupled four-wheel drop-ramp trailer, which had a mind of its own as to which way it wanted to go at any speed above about 35mph.

Apparently it towed best with a vehicle on it – so what it must have been like solo I dreaded to imagine. The long-suffering Hillman was loaded up, but as we headed through south London it started snowing quite heavily. On the final long climb before the M2 lorries were getting stuck and then, as though under the orders of some unseen marshal, taking it in turns for a flying run at the hill.

When our turn came, we failed lower down the hill than even the most heavily laden artic. In the driving snow we had to unload the Hillman and, with a tow rope attached, Hillman Minx and Standard Ensign, with wheels spinning all the way, just managed to drag the empty trailer to the top of the hill. From then on we drove separately and very slowly to Faversham, where we parked the Minx.

There was no winch for the trailer, so with the snow and the state of the back axle making the most appalling noises whenever not running straight as we manoeuvred it, getting the Cortina Lotus on to the trailer was quite a frightening performance. One final bang as something serious broke inside the chewed up back axle gears and that would be it. And now what would we do if the Standard Ensign became stuck in the snow, we wondered? We could only hope for the best, but by the time we returned it had all been gritted and salted.

A few days later, the Cortina Lotus was removed and we never saw it again. Later that year, the unsound back axle location by A-frame with coil springs was abandoned in favour of conventional leaf springs. It had been a Chapman folly that offered little merit and gave enormous problems.

THIRTY-EIGHT

DAIHATSU COMPAGNO BERLINA

≡ After the test was published, the importers realised that they were on a
≡ no-hoper with the little Daihatsu, and beat a hasty retreat

In an earlier chapter I recorded that one of my few achievements was to be issued with the first parking ticket ever issued in London. Perhaps another less dubious claim to fame may be made: that I was the first British motoring writer to test a Japanese car. It happened in 1965, when the Daihatsu Compagno Berlina became the first Japanese car to be offered for sale on the British market, and it was allocated to me to carry out and write the road test. The importers were a firm called Dufay (Birmingham) Ltd, with offices in Great Portland Street, London, and they thought that a road test in *Autocar* would be a good sales fillip.

It was approached with enthusiasm, in the expectation of great things from the up-and-coming Japanese motor industry, but, as I felt obliged to write in the first paragraph of the test, it emerged as a car that was well made but technically retrograde. It had a two-door, four-seater body built on a separate chassis, but in the design of its engine, transmission, suspension and brakes it followed all that was conventional on British cars some ten years previously.

The suspension was by wishbones and torsion bars at the front, with a live axle on semi-elliptic leaf springs at the rear, and the damping was quite inadequate. The result was a very lively and bouncy ride, while on corners there was a lot of howl from the Yokohama tyres. Even with only the driver on board, the Compagno oversteered badly. Over-responsive brakes were all too inclined to lock the back wheels. Yokohama nowadays produce excellent tyres, but those on the Daihatsu in 1965 were appallingly lacking in wet-road grip.

Although bad in so many ways, the Compagno had many redeeming features, and it was clearly very well built with good body fits, doors that closed neatly without a slam, and in particular a very smooth and quiet 4-cylinder engine. Its gear change also had a slick, light movement, and all the controls worked well with positive action. A clever feature was a little window on the side of the carburettor, so one could see at a glance that fuel was getting through if there was any problem with the engine. On cars of that era, fuel supply was often the cause of many breakdowns, but this feature made it possible to check this straight away.

There were many amusing mistakes in the handbook, which had obviously been translated from Japanese, and the headlamps flasher switch – itself a feature unfamiliar on cars of the early 1960s – was charmingly described as the 'light hooter'.

In comparison with its rivals, the Compagno made a poor showing, being slower, using more fuel and costing a lot more to buy. Its acceleration from rest to 60mph was too slow to be timed, and instead we quoted the time of 21.2 seconds to get to 50mph, compared with 14 seconds for a Hillman Imp costing about two thirds of the price set for the Compagno. The importers had grossly overpriced it.

After the test was published, the importers realised that they were on a no-hoper with the little Daihatsu, and beat a hasty retreat. It was not until some two years later that Nissan, under its then current name Datsun, and Toyota, started to make the massive inroads into the British market, which scared the home producers into demanding import quotas to keep the Japanese at bay, and forced them to take a major reappraisal of their own prices and quality control. For years people were saying that nothing ever went wrong with Japanese cars, while British-made cars, suffering poor workmanship by employees more often on strike than working, were giving constant trouble and bringing the whole industry into disrepute.

Some forty years later, International Motors were doing very well importing the latest very competitive Daihatsus, and they came across that original test car, bought it and restored it. As the person who had written that original road test in 1965, I was invited to drive the little Compagno, still with the same registration CGH 8B, on the Norwich Union classic cars rally. It was horrible weather, and the wipers went wrong, with the left one being hit by the one on the right, so I had to remove it and drive with just one wiper, but otherwise it went well and brought back many memories. More recently, the industrious former public relations director of International Motors, Arthur Fairley, drove the little Compagno on various classic car rallies, although on one of these occasions the little car let him down with ignition trouble, and he arrived late for the dinner that he was hosting.

Looking back at my road-test experiences of the Compagno, I remember in particular a journey from London to my home with my wife's grandmother on board. Our first child had just been born, and in her new role as Great-Granny, she had come down to London to 'inspect' the new baby. As I had done several times before, I arranged to meet her at the Waldorf Hotel in Aldwych and take her home. On such occasions I would always try to have a suitably luxurious car in which to collect her, and I would always find her sitting in the Waldorf looking for all the world like a dowager duchess, examining every new arrival with interest. But on this occasion, because of road-test commitments, she would have to make do with the little Daihatsu.

I led her out to the car, which was parked at a meter bay in Aldwych off the Strand, and noted her slight look of disapproval as I opened the door to let her in. We set off with Great-Granny looking decidedly uncomfortable as she bounced about on the rather topply and not very well shaped passenger seat.

After a while, she said in her high-pitched voice: 'The last time you kindly came to meet me in London, I remember that you had a Rolls-Royce,' pronouncing it as two separate words. She was too polite to say anything about the bouncy little Daihatsu, but her thoughts were clear when she added: 'I *did* enjoy that Rolls-Royce.'

THIRTY-NINE

DAIMLER 2½-LITRE

'Look out,' exclaimed the marshal at the top of the Hardknott Pass in the Lake District, 'you're on fire.'

By the time of the 1967 Mobil Economy Run I had competed in this event six times with colleague Howard Vyse, who was *Autocar's* art editor, and as the closing date for entries approached we were very flattered to receive a letter from Mobil's press officers Alec Moseley and Peter Bedwell, saying 'a Mobil run without Bladon and Vyse would be like a wedding without the bride!' We had been pondering what car to enter for the event, and decided to have a crack at the over-2-litre automatic class with a Daimler 2½-litre. After Jaguar took over the Daimler concern at Coventry, they adopted Daimler's unusually small and compact V8 engine, and installed it in the Jaguar Mk II saloon, with BorgWarner automatic transmission as standard. Daimler's traditional radiator grille with fluted top completed the transformation.

Under the ill-fated and misguided Ryder plan, instigated by Lord Ryder, Jaguar was engulfed in the horrendous British Motor Holdings fiasco. Jaguar was losing its identity, and renamed 'Large car assembly plant No. 1'. But in spite of this there was still great enthusiasm and loyalty to Jaguar, and they responded warmly to the idea of running one of their Daimlers in the economy run. They prepared the car superbly, and even removed the power steering to reduce engine power losses. The car ran and handled beautifully, its small V8 engine as smooth and quiet as an electric motor. Looking back on that 1967 economy run, I recall it as one of the most enjoyable of all. But we did have our problems.

'Look out,' exclaimed the marshal at the top of the Hardknott Pass in the Lake District, 'you're on fire.'

It certainly must have looked like it, as clouds of black smoke belched out from underneath when we stopped at the Route Check control, but I was aware of the problem and reassured him: 'It'll cool off as we go down the pass – it's leaking transmission fluid.'

At scrutineering the sharp-eyed team of organisers from the Hants & Berks Motor Club had spotted a leak from the automatic transmission and told us about it, but it was too late to get it fixed at that stage. All we could do was check the level at every possible opportunity and keep it topped up. At each refuelling control we asked the marshal to phone the next one and make sure they had ATF (automatic transmission fluid) for us, and it worked like magic. Often we had the can thrust at us even before we had checked in.

Not so good was that measuring the fluid level in the power steering reservoir could be done only with the engine running, wasting precious petrol, and the other problem revealed on the Hardknott was that on a steep gradient the leaking fluid ran out on to the hot exhaust pipe, vaporising into dense black smoke.

I used to say that any success we achieved in the Mobil Economy Run was owed to meticulous pre-event planning with the maps laid out on the floor of the hotel bedroom, and in doing so we determined a strategy for the tough third day. The start had been at Edinburgh, and two easy days on Scotland's quiet and fairly straight and undemanding roads gave the impression that this would be a relatively easy economy run. But the sting was in the tail, with a third day starting at Carlisle, down through the Lake District and then on a long and very hilly route over the Pennines to a time control just outside Newcastle-upon-Tyne.

The Lake District section took us over the Wrynose and Hardknott passes heading west, and although extra time was allowed we knew we would be running as much as half an hour late for much of the day, but we had planned also exactly how fast we would have to go, and where, to get back on schedule. It all worked out perfectly, and the car was absolutely delightful. Even with the power assistance deleted, the steering heaviness was noticeable only at low speeds.

When the pictures were produced after the run, there was a lovely shot of the Daimler taking the Devil's Elbow – the notorious double hairpin bend on the Cairnwell Pass in Scotland – in fine style with the offside front wheel squashed up into the wing and the Michelin X tyre leaving a gracious black line on the road all through the hairpin.

Our efforts were rewarded at the finish when we saw one of the organising team get into the Daimler after the final fuelling and drive it away to the secret enclave where they would carry out the post-run scrutineering reserved for class winners. They would work away during the night, removing cylinder heads, measuring cylinder bores, and even sometimes cutting fuel tanks in half to look for illicit reserve compartments.

During the run we had got through about 6 pints of ATF (litres were yet to be introduced in Britain), and we had two cans of the stuff to take us the 370-mile run back to London after the prize-giving next morning. We were not the only ones to have problems on this 13th Mobil Run: J.A. Turner and A.C. Hamer had to retire their Morris 1800 with collapsed Hydrolastic suspension, and M. Day and

Our Daimler 2½-litre climbs the Hardknott Pass in the Lake District, with the Wrynose Pass in the background.

C.N. Ramus had a stone fly up through the vents in the wing of their Austin 1800, which bent a fan blade and chewed a hole in the radiator. With admirable initiative, they obtained the observer's permission to break the bonnet seals and used some of the bungey plastic material that comprised the seals to plug the leak! They finished with 35.88mpg but were well down the batting list in their class, which was won by Mr and Mrs B.R. Greaves in a Hillman Hunter. They had no overdrive on this Hunter, yet managed to obtain 42.53mpg, nearly 2mpg better than the Hunter of B.D.L.R. Smith and A.P. Chambers, with overdrive. This impressive performance won for the Greaves the coveted Holland Birkett Memorial Trophy for best result on the formula of efficiency.

D.V. Burnside and J.B. Twort had their Triumph Herald excluded under the 'no body damage allowed' rule, after grazing the side on a rock while traversing the Hardknott, and the class went to the Morris Minor 1000 of T.W. Allison and D. Holliday with 50.19mpg. Best mpg figure of the run was set by economy veterans J.M. Readings and P.B. Davenport with 57.96 from an Austin Mini 850.

Our hopes were fulfilled when the results showed the Daimler first in its class at 26.64mpg, a clear 1mpg ahead of the Ford Zephyr V6 driven by G.M. Rood and R. Palethorpe. *Autocar* had been taken over by the *Daily Mirror* and salaries were being squeezed, so we were both jolly glad of the £100 cash prize, and 'over the moon' as we pointed the Daimler south for the return to London, but as we shook off the Edinburgh traffic and began to enjoy the lovely road over the moors, I became aware that all was not well. A misfire became evident when I took the Daimler over 90mph for the first time, and then it began misfiring at 80.

On opening the bonnet I noticed smoke coming from the distributor, and removing the cap showed the cause of the problem: there was no carbon brush to take the high-voltage current from the cap to the rotor arm. The Hants & Berks mechanic, working away in the night to remove one of the cylinder heads for bore measurement to confirm that all was standard, had allowed the carbon brush to fall out of the distributor. Where had it fallen? Into the engine, perhaps? Perish the thought!

We were nowhere near any garage, so could only press on more slowly, with thoughts of ringing the Jaguar Press Officer Bob Berry to meet us somewhere with an exchange car – the sort of thing they would do for us in those days. The Daimler became slower and slower until it could only manage about 55mph, but it didn't get any worse so we decided to keep going and hope for the best.

It was a tedious and tiring journey, and much less safe than if we could have cruised at normal speeds, but in the end I dropped Howard off at his Barnet home and arrived back at Radlett weary but doubly elated, having won and also managed to limp home with that lovely but very sick Daimler.

FORTY

NSU WANKEL SPIDER

The journey had to be made with great trepidation since vaporised petrol fumes were coming out of the cooling system overflow pipe

'Message from the managing director: please be sure to call him the moment you get back. He wants to hear it running.' This message was lying on my desk when I made my disgruntled return to the office. Everyone knew I was due to collect the NSU Spider with the world's first production rotary engine designed by Felix Wankel, and all wanted to know what it would be like. How would it sound? Would it be spectacularly different from the ordinary reciprocating piston engines we all knew so well?

It had been a long wait. NSU had shown the little two-seater Spider with its strange single-rotor Wankel engine at the Earls Court Show in October 1963, and a few weeks after theshow closed, Maurice Smith convinced the managing director that we ought to place a firm order for one. It was to be operated as an ordinary staff car, and I was informed that I would be running it, at least for the first year.

This news was delightful. All through the bitter winter of 1963 I had been running the most unreliable car I ever suffered – one of the first of the Morris 1100s – so the promise of replacing it with what looked like a jolly little two-seater sports car with convertible top was very exciting. But the date of the expected changeover kept fading into the future as the months passed. I had almost given up hope of it, when finally, in May 1964, a date for collection was named. So it was all the more disappointing when I returned to the office by Underground without it.

'What's the problem?' everyone wanted to know. 'Is the engine no good?' I had arrived at the NSU depot, which was then in London, and had actually seen the Spider but not been allowed to take it away. 'Why not?' I kept asking, but the service manager was adamant that he couldn't say what the trouble was. Five years were to pass before I found out.

A few days later, another call came saying that the car was ready, and I was finally able to hear it running, and to drive it for the first time. It was a slight anti-climax, because the engine – with a single rotor – was fairly noisy, lumpy at low speed, and developed little torque below about 2,000rpm.

One of its advantages – very rare in those days – was that the engine required no running-in, and I cruised it above 80mph a lot of the time even on the first long

With its extraordinary single-rotor Wankel engine mounted at the back, the Spider proved very capable on snow on the way to the Glasgow Motor Show.

trip, within its initial few hundred miles. The faster the car went, the better the engine became, and one had to watch the rev counter rather carefully since there was strict advice not to exceed 5,500rpm – which was just when it really seemed to be superbly smooth and unobtrusive.

In London traffic I would seldom be out of first and second gears because of the snatchiness of the engine at low speeds, and when coming to a halt I always used to slip into neutral otherwise there was a lot of jerkiness on the overrun like that of a two-stroke. It was all part of the different way of life with the Spider, which I enjoyed tremendously. NSU never built any right-hand-drive examples, but with such a small car the problem of driving from the left was not too much of a handicap.

It was also fascinating to be driving a car in which there was so much interest. People would see it, recognise it at once, and want to know all about it. I wished we could have had a counter fitted to record the number of times the engine cover had to be raised for people inquisitive to see inside.

In the first few months, too, it was amusing to be driving the only example on the road in Britain. There were two others at NSU, but these had not been registered and were mainly used for service training. When anyone said: 'I haven't seen one of these on the road before,' the cheeky reply used to be: 'I know, I haven't been here before!'

Various little problems concerning the car occurred, such as failure of the speedometer within the first 11km, but at first the engine seemed impressively reliable and unobtrusive, which was just as well. 'Bring it back to us if *anything at all* goes wrong,' I had been urged but then learned that NSU was to move from London to Shoreham near Worthing. The prospect of having to go all the way down there every time there was a problem was a little discouraging.

In November of the first year I felt confident enough in the Wankel engine to take the Spider up to Scotland to cover the Glasgow Motor Show, and a long run seemed to suit it much better than town work. The fuel consumption, which had been around 28mpg, improved to a more reasonable 33mpg. Oil supply was on the total loss principle, and consumption was consistent at around 150 miles per pint – not too excessive by the standards of the 1960s. On the way up we stopped at my favourite hotel, the Auchen Castle about 70 miles south of Glasgow, and in the night snow fell. Next day I was able to appreciate the good traction of having what little engine weight there was over the driving wheels at the back.

The engine was mounted at the rear in the Spider, giving quite good access once the floor of the boot had been opened, and cooling water was pumped to a radiator at the front. There was a little bit of space behind the seats, and when our first child was born, a year after we started running the Spider, I constructed a wooden platform so that the baby could ride there in his pram with the wheels removed. Both with hood up and down, he covered many miles behind us in this arrangement – no doubt contravening all today's rules about safety of children in cars.

There was another small luggage compartment at the front, but neither was really big enough to take a large suitcase. Somehow the photographer and I managed to stow away all our kit for the journey to Glasgow, but we came to dread the request, wherever we stopped, 'May I please see the engine?', which meant the removal of carefully stowed luggage and photographic equipment to be able to reveal it.

After some 4,000 miles the first problems with the engine developed. At first it suddenly conked out in the rain one night but then picked up again just as the spot to pull off the road had been chosen, and a few days later it refused to start. On removing the solitary sparking plug it was found that the insulation around its electrode was completely burnt away. The plug was a very special kind made for the Wankel engine by Beru, and fortunately a replacement had been ordered, and received from Shoreham just in time.

For a long while the engine then ran extremely reliably until it was just over a year old, and had covered some 11,200 miles, when severe smoking on the overrun was noticed, and this was followed by backfiring, as well as a big increase in fuel consumption. A date was fixed for a visit to Shoreham.

By the time I was due to go down there, the journey had to be made with great trepidation since vaporised petrol fumes were coming out of the cooling system overflow pipe. The Spider was clearly far from well, and I took the precaution of carrying a fire extinguisher with me for the journey down to the South Coast.

The engineers at NSU were as interested in the progress of the Spider as we were, and it was arranged that I could go back a few days later and watch the technical supervisor, Michael Hoppis, dismantle the engine to find out what had gone wrong.

I enjoyed assisting and watching Mike Hoppis at work; it was like seeing a surgeon doing a delicate operation, complete with immaculate white coat. In the meantime, the Spider had been fitted with a completely new engine assembly, ready for me to drive away at the end of our engineering session, and the old unit was on the bench in the NSU mechanics' training school.

Various components such as the clutch had to be removed, then twenty nuts were undone allowing the outer plate – equivalent to the cylinder head in a conventional engine – to be lifted off, revealing the trochoidal-shaped rotor. Everything was certainly impressively made and machined, and all showed little wear, but the cause of the trouble was revealed. It was a crack across the casing, both sides of the sparking plug hole.

As I had changed the sparking plug myself, I was fearful that I may have over-tightened it, but there was a reassuring report from Germany that this was a design weakness, and the casing had been modified to prevent it from occurring on future engines.

By the time we had stripped everything down to the last component, all neatly arranged on the bench, it had taken less than two hours, and I then drove away in the Spider with its completely new engine. The new unit was less prone to the

The NSU Spider was always more enjoyable with the hood down, as here on an unopened stretch of the M6 in 1964.

jerkiness on the overrun that had spoilt the first one, and oil consumption had been improved dramatically, from the original level of 150 miles per pint, to about 1,000.

There was no charge for that replacement engine. To reassure buyers, NSU had undertaken to provide all owners with the first engine change free of charge – and its cost of £550 was enormous in those pre-inflation days. To put it into proportion, the price of the car, excluding tax, had been 'only' £1,150. In contrast, I had needed a new spring clip for a window winder, and a few days later a bill arrived by post requesting 3*d* less 30 per cent trade discount, balance 2*d*!

The second engine proved less reliable than the first. It was often difficult to start, and sometimes it would suddenly cease running, then equally abruptly it would behave normally again. It was felt that we had learnt all that was to be gained from running the first Wankel car, so it was advertised and sold. I was sad to see it go; driving this little sports car had been fun, and it had always been fascinating to run a car which aroused interest wherever it was parked. Fitting this completely new type of engine in a charming little sports car had been a good idea of NSU, making it a thoroughly intriguing vehicle, and taking advantage of the compactness and low weight of the power unit. But more attention should have been paid to wind noise generated by the design of the hood. At speed, there was so much wind roar that it didn't matter whether the engine was quiet or not – you couldn't hear it anyway above the din – which was much worse with the hood up than when the car was open.

Some three years later, at a Volkswagen engineering conference, I met again the man who had been service manager at NSU before they moved out of London. 'I can reveal now,' he said, 'why you weren't able to take your Wankel Spider away that first time you called for it. They had completely missed out all the welds for the rear sub-frame. If you had driven it like that it would have been dangerously uncontrollable!'

FORTY-ONE

Audi Super 90

I yelled out from the back: 'Look out! You're going to hit a lorry.' Not a second too soon he did a wild swerve and just missed it

It couldn't have happened at a more appropriate time. After the return and sale of the little NSU Wankel Spider, which I had run for two years, I was allocated one of the new Vauxhall Vivas as my company car and I enjoyed it with its snazzy short-travel gear change and quite good handling and suspension, but rearing its ugly head was the government's imposition of a tax called 'Benefit in Kind' for all those enjoying provision of a company car. Initially the tax was fairly modest, as are all such imposts. But for me, with a young child and a salary being deliberately almost frozen by our particularly mean managing director, it was a disaster. So particularly welcome was the news that Mercedes-Benz wanted the journal to run one of the new Audi Super 90s on a long-term assessment, and the press officer, Erik Johnson, with whom I had struck up a long-lasting friendship, requested that I should be its allocated user-driver and write the subsequent long-term appraisal. I was able to inform the tax authorities that my company no longer provided me with a car. The fact that I had a semi-permanent test car did not affect the issue.

What was this car from a hitherto unknown maker called Audi? I was assured that it would have Mercedes-Benz quality, and it would feature front-wheel drive, which was gradually becoming more commonplace than rear drive. It looked good in the pictures, and I awaited eagerly its arrival in July 1967. But another change affecting motoring was on the way: the annual 'year letter' for registrations was causing a difficult situation for manufacturers and dealers, with huge demand for new cars to be first registered at the beginning of each year. Proud owners liked to show off their new possession on 1 January. So the decision was taken to move the year letter change to what was normally always the slackest month of the year, August. It would happen for the first time in August 1967, and with my new Audi

With elegant styling for its day, and bright finish with lots of chrome, the Audi Super 90 set the Ingolstadt company on the road to success.

due the month before, I asked for the hand-over to be delayed until August, so it came with the new year letter.

Brightwork on cars had gone out of fashion because it gave rise to corrosion problems, but the Audi was well protected against rust, and it was lavishly embellished with chrome strips around the wing edges and along the doors. I had chosen dark blue as the finish colour, and when I saw the car for the first time I was absolutely delighted by its appearance. I was very pleased also to see that it had a sunroof, operated by winding handle.

Wherever it was parked it aroused interested comment from people who wanted to know what it was and who had made it. 'Ordie,' they would say, 'never heard of that before. Is it Japanese?' Unaware that the year letter change had been brought forward five months, they also wanted to know how I had managed to get a registration with the 'F' year letter so soon.

A special feature of the Super 90 was its high-efficiency engine, which had been designed by Mercedes-Benz engineers. It had spiral tracts in the inlet manifold, which created great swirl in the cylinders allowing the unusually high compression ratio of 10.6-to-1 to be used. A similar technique was adopted much later by Jaguar to obtain better efficiency from their fuel-gobbling V12 engine.

I soon became very happy with the Super 90 and enjoyed driving it enormously, but it had some bad problems. One of these was the automatic choke, which gave excessively rich mixture until it had warmed up. I tried weakening it, but that made it more difficult to start from cold, so I had to become resigned to the erratic running and black exhaust smoke when the engine was cold. The tickover speed was always set too high, at about 1,200rpm, whenever the car went into Mercedes-Benz for service, and there was a favourite lay-by on the route back to the office where I would pull in, put the bonnet up, and reset the idling speed to a more reasonable 800rpm.

Another problem was the massive understeer. On a motorway – of which we still had precious few in 1967 – its stability made it a dream to drive, and it was obviously developed in Germany to make the best of their wonderful and rapidly expanding *Autobahn* network. But on corners, it always wanted to go straight on. In the wet, it was prone to do this whatever one did with the steering. A further result of having all the weight of the engine ahead of the front wheels was that front tyre wear was rapid. One weekend I was shocked to notice that the Metzeler tyres on the front wheels were nearly through the tread. Without further delay, I got the jack out and changed them over, since the rear tyres showed virtually no wear at all. At this stage it had done only 7,000 miles, but the timely tyre swap gave another 7,000 before these were worn out as well, and I was able to obtain a set of the then new Michelin XAS tyres, which gave much better grip as well as lasting better.

The Super 90 had a steering-column change for its four-speed gearbox – a feature widely despised although I didn't mind it and thought that having the gear lever close to the steering wheel was quite convenient. Some drivers, however, had great difficulty with it, and I was present when it nearly caused a terrible accident.

Striving all the time to promote the Audi marque, the Press Officer Erik Johnson arranged a visit to the Audi factory at Ingolstadt – a name into which many English writers liked to put two 'd's, spelling it Ingoldstadt. I was invited to represent the journal, and on arrival at Munich airport we found that some Super 90s were waiting for us to drive north to Ingolstadt, and I was teamed up to share one of them with the late Colin Dryden, who was then assistant motoring writer to John Langley of *The Daily Telegraph*. Erik pointed out that I knew the Super 90 well, and as there was another journalist in the party he suggested that Colin should drive, and I was relegated to the back seat, which I was quite glad to try for the first time.

Colin had trouble with the steering-column gear change right from the beginning, and simply couldn't remember the layout. On one of those rather steep *Autobahn* gradients, the engine was clearly labouring a bit with three of us and luggage on board, and Colin decided to change down to third. Then he got into a terrible mess, and inadvertently pulled the lever outward, which was the way to engage reverse. As he pulled the lever down he actually hit reverse while we were doing about 65mph. The unfortunate Audi made the most awful noise of gear crash, and Colin then looked down at the offending gear lever to try to sort it out. We were in the inside lane and rapidly catching up a lorry, but Colin wasn't looking where he was going. Just in time, I yelled out from the back: 'Look out! You're going to hit a lorry.' Not a second too soon he did a wild swerve to the left, missed the back end of the lorry by a fraction and then, thanks to prompt reaction and violent braking by a car that was just about to overtake us, an accident was avoided. But it was a close thing.

Reliability was a good feature with the Super 90, and so was the economy, so at the end of the test period there was not a lot to relate except for general satisfaction at the performance and behaviour after running one of the first Audis imported to Britain. Handing it back was a sad occasion but was alleviated by the knowledge that my next long-term loan car was to be a Jaguar.

A few months after the departure of the Super 90, the regulations arrived for the 1969 Mobil Economy Run, and on seeing the break points of the classes based on engine size, I realised that the Super 90, with its capacity of 1,760cc was just over the 1,750 limit for the Class, and had a very good chance of success. For this event one always wanted to have the smallest engine in the class. Mercedes were keen to lend me one of their press cars, but my former trusty navigator, Howard Vyse, who had guided me for 10,000 economy-run miles had left the staff and was no longer available.

After a lot of enquiries I learned that the late Tony Kyd, my opposite number on *Motor*, was keen to come along as co-driver, but his editor, Charles Bulmer, also now deceased, did not like the idea of this kind of collusion, which, he argued, tended to confirm in people's minds that the two journals were not rivals but were working together. In the end, I persuaded him, and had Tony as my navigator for the event.

The Super 90 confirmed its reputation for superior fuel economy, beating all the others in the class by a substantial margin. The organisers of the event, the industrious members of the Hants & Berks Motor Club, were concerned that the economy run was getting the reputation of being a low-speed doddle, with its required average speed of 30mph, which was the most the RAC allowed on non-motorway roads. Critics had no idea how hard it was to achieve that 30mph average on the demanding terrain of hilly and narrow roads. So they decided not only to

Aged 3, my son Bruce demonstrates the size of the Audi's boot by sitting in it in his Jaguar E-Type pedal car.

include a long motorway section in the route but also an hour of track test averaging 50mph on the Oulton Park race circuit.

To obtain further information about the effect of the race circuit on fuel consumption figures, they also arranged to defuel all the cars before and after the test, to determine the actual fuel consumption on the track.

In normal road running on the Mobil Economy Run, freewheeling was strictly forbidden, with an observer in every car to ensure that this rule was obeyed, but they weren't going to risk putting young students as observers in the cars for the track test. It was confirmed that freewheeling was allowed on the circuit, but they added: 'If you think you'll have time for it; don't forget you have to average 50mph.'

In fact, I found it very easy to do so, and actually spent more time with the gear lever in neutral and the engine switched off than I did using power, which was necessary only on three parts of the circuit, thanks to the free-running and eager acceleration of the Audi. Tony was in the pits giving very efficient and clear time signals, which enabled me to use almost the whole of the final minute of time allowance: you weren't late until you had passed your last minute by 60 seconds, and that additional 59 seconds made a useful contribution to the result.

After the Audi had been refuelled at Oulton, and the fuel consumed measured by the organisers, they knew its consumption from start to Oulton Park, as well as for the hour on the circuit. I overheard one of the Hants & Berks officials ask one of his colleagues: 'How's that Audi done? Is it as bad as it was on the first stage?'

'Even worse,' came the reply. They were joking, of course, and the car's overall fuel consumption at 40.4mpg for the 1,000 miles of the event not only won the class but would have been third even in the class below. It was a final wonderful experience with that very impressive Audi, and the start of a long and happy association with the marque, later to become one of the most successful imports on the British market.

FORTY-TWO

ROVER 3-LITRE COUPÉ

'Your speedometer,' I told the police sergeant, with the confidence of feeling sure that I was right, 'must be faulty. When did you last check it?'

For motoring journalists accustomed to testing cars at high speeds and often cruising fast cars at 120mph when the motorway was clear, the news that there was to be a mandatory overall speed limit of 70mph was devastating. It was brought in by the Transport Minister, Hugh Fraser, a dour Scotsman with little experience or knowledge of cars and modern driving conditions. It would start on 22 December 1965, and run for four months as an 'experiment', but we all knew that once in force, it would never be lifted. Before the start date arrived, Fraser was removed from office and replaced by Mrs Barbara Castle, who didn't even have a driving licence. One of her first acts was to extend the experimental period for a further two months, and then this was followed by a six-month extension, before it was finally made permanent. But there was a silver lining – a compensation, which all of us on the road-test staff welcomed.

This good news was the editor's announcement that we would still go on testing the maximum speeds of road-test cars by taking many of the faster ones to the Continent, as we used to do before the opening of the M1. A special budget was allocated to cover the additional expenses that this would involve, and by chance I was involved in the first of these expeditions, which were always called 'testing for max'. In company with colleague Geoffrey Howard, we were to take two cars to Holland, where at that time there was no speed limit. One was a Rover 3-litre Coupé Mark III, and Geoff's test car was a Fiat 2300S Coupé.

We crossed the North Sea on the night ferry from Harwich to the Hook of Holland, and soon knocked off the maximum speed runs and upper acceleration times. The Rover didn't manage the high speeds we had been promised, giving a mean maximum of only 107mph, with 112mph in the best direction. It could almost have been tested at the MIRA proving ground at Nuneaton, but the high-speed circuit there had three banked bends, which always tended to scrub off some of the upper speeds, resulting in dubious top-speed figures. The Fiat 2300S managed 120mph. The test runs were always done with the trailing fifth wheel and dead accurate electric speedometer. As part of the test, each car's speedometer readings were written down on the road-test log cards to give the true value every 10mph. The Fiat's speedo was grossly optimistic.

With the high-speed parts of the test in the bag we drove down to Calais, swapping cars half way, then we took the afternoon ferry back to Dover. I didn't like the Fiat much, with its terribly fussy 6-cylinder engine. I described its valve gear at tickover as like 'hearing a hundred grannies in a knitting competition.'

At Dover we went our separate ways, and as Geoff was not available next day I arranged for another colleague to meet me at the Toddington service area on the M1 to leave his car there and accompany me to MIRA as observer to complete the acceleration, braking and fuel-consumption tests on the Rover.

During the night, the weather broke. It was January, with sleet blowing about and turning to wet as it landed on the motorway. The 70mph-limit experiment was in its fourth week. As we cruised north on the M1, I became aware of a white car far behind, keeping station with us. Was it police, I wondered? We were in the

Northampton police admitted that they could never have caught the Rover 3-litre Coupé if I had not slowed down. Photographed here in Holland the day before the M1 adventure, it was an elegant car and made light work of the horrid weather.

Northampton area, where I knew the police used white Ford Zephyr estate cars to patrol the motorway.

Even with the diminishing effect of the Rover's panoramic mirror, I became convinced that we were the object of attention. The road-test cards with all the previous day's data written down were lying in that useful full-width tray below the Rover's central fascia panel, and I asked my colleague to look and see what the speedometer had been reading at true 70mph.

'Seventy-nine,' he replied, so I made sure that the Rover's speedometer needle was exactly on 79mph. In due course, the white car caught up and slowly overtook. As I had feared, it was one of the police Zephyrs, but they didn't have the blue lights and illuminated signs reading 'STOP' in those days. Instead, the arm came out of the window, indicating a halt on the hard shoulder and desire to have words.

Only when I left the comfort of the Rover's heated leather-clad lounge did I realise quite what a horrid day it was, with a strong headwind and this wet snow blowing about, the road streaming water, and passing vehicles trailing clouds of soaking spray.

I was informed that I had been exceeding the new 70mph speed limit, my driving licence was inspected and a ticket written out, with due warning that a summons would follow.

I was furious, and pointed out that I knew exactly how fast I had been going because I had a corrected speedometer. I had taken the car to Holland to test it and had trailed a fifth wheel operating an electric speedometer, which was exactly accurate.

'Your speedometer,' I told the police sergeant, with the confidence of feeling sure that I was right, 'must be faulty. When did you last check it?' At the same moment I opened the boot of the Rover revealing the fifth wheel and all the other test equipment. It looked pretty scruffy, but I could see that they were impressed, and I detected the first seeds of doubt appearing.

'You go along at 70 again, and we'll check you once more,' said the sergeant. Again we motored along the third lane with the speedometer at 79mph, and the police Ford Zephyr almost touching the Rover's back bumper. I could imagine drivers we passed thinking: 'Doesn't he realise the police are after him?'

Eventually the Zephyr's lights were flashed, and I pulled in again. 'We checked you that time at 76mph,' I was told.

Further argument ensued. We were getting nowhere, except very wet and cold, when to my delight I heard the officer say: 'Give me the ticket back, and we'll ignore this one in view of the doubt about your speed. But keep it down in future; we've got to observe the new limit while it's an experiment, haven't we, otherwise they'll never know whether the experiment worked or not.'

There was a frantic search, the ticket found and handed back, then a more friendly discussion about the stupidity of this new limit, and they revealed that with the wind blowing they had been flat out and only just able to catch up the Rover Coupé.

We parted amicably and drove on to MIRA. There wasn't much that could be done in this weather, but perhaps some low-speed testing might be possible. I picked up the road-test log cards to see what needed to be done and immediately saw the heading: 'TEST CAR: Fiat 2300S Coupé'. The speedometer correction I had been given was the one for the Fiat, and the Rover's card was underneath, revealing that at 70mph its speedometer needle was on 73. I was a little humiliated to realise that the police had been right after all.

FORTY-THREE

Jaguar 240

≡ I looked at the rev counter and thought at first that the needle must have
≡ fallen off. Then I saw it, right off the scale and almost on the clock situated at
≡ the bottom of the rev counter

A stroke during the weekend removed the assistant editor, Len Ayton, to hospital, from which he never returned. I was sad about what had happened to him, and several times went to visit him in hospital at Barnet. When it was clear that he was not going to come back to work, I was promoted from features editor to assistant editor. At much the same time, the Audi Super 90, which I had so enjoyed, was returned to Mercedes-Benz, and in its place I was to take on one of the new Jaguar 240 saloons.

It was actually a bit of a mixture, because although it had the improved engine, with power increased to 133bhp, it didn't have the new more slender bumpers introduced at the same time in September 1967, which identified the new model as the 240, instead of the Mk II 2.4. I enjoyed driving it enormously, but it was not without its problems, one of which was the very heavy and not very accurate steering. Another was that I was now living in a house at Radlett with a very steep drive, to be taken uphill in the morning. Every test car hated this, the one exception being the Jensen C-V8, whose enormous power took it up the slope without the slightest trouble, even one morning when it was covered in snow. In contrast, the Jaguar was particularly reluctant to lift its heavy weight up a slope of about 1 in 5 on a cold engine. It had a manual choke control, and the routine I had to adopt was to start the engine, reduce the mixture enrichment, and run the engine for a little while, then put the mixture back on rich and climb the gradient with much clutch slipping.

But in most other respects I found this Jaguar immensely enjoyable with its sleek looks, its beautiful fascia in walnut veneer, and its lovely instruments, with large, clear rev counter and very accurate speedometer seen through the top half of the steering wheel. For any long distance journey such as the drive to Glasgow to cover the Scottish Show, I always took the 240 if I could avoid taking anything else. It was also in the Jaguar 240 that I experienced being driven by one of the most wonderful drivers it was ever my pleasure to enjoy as passenger.

His name was Innes Ireland, an ex-Formula 1 racing driver of considerable experience, who had recently been appointed *Autocar's* sports editor. He brought a breath of fresh air and *joie de vivre* into the journal, and being well off financially it was all a great joke, which he didn't take too seriously. He made the job fun, and he also wrote entertainingly. His predecessor, Peter Garnier, was quite miffed at the way Innes enjoyed going out to Formula 1 races and phoning in his story in the middle of the night, which Peter had always found a great and onerous labour, never to be taken as pleasurable.

With my great interest in long-distance rallies, I had covered several times the great Spa–Liège–Sofia rally, organised by the Belgian Touring Club. Increasing restrictions due to accidents and high speeds on ordinary roads made it impossible for the rally through Yugoslavia to continue, so the organisers decided to replace it with a reliability trial – effectively four days and three nights round the 17.6-mile Nürburgring racing circuit.

I was down to cover this great event in August 1968, and planned to drive out there in the Jaguar, taking with me the very industrious photographer Peter Cramer, who was to accompany me on many events in the future. Peter was always good company. Shortly before departure, Innes Ireland told me that he had been chosen by Lancia to drive one of their Fulvia Coupés, teamed up with Stirling Moss, on what was now called the *Marathon de la Route*, and could he have a lift out there with 'you fellas'? Of course I agreed, and we arranged to meet in the company's car park at 8 a.m. We were booked with the car on the 10 a.m. Air Charter flight from Southend to Ostend.

Although a little lacking in power for its size, the Jaguar 240 was comfortable and a great pleasure to drive. It was also quiet, after an electric fan conversion was fitted. (Peter Cramer)

It was a beautiful sunny morning, and only a few minutes late Innes's personally owned Aston Martin DB6 swept into the car park. We exchanged pleasantries, then piled into the Jaguar and set off to Southend. On arrival at the airport the customary request for passports left Innes nonplussed for a moment, as he said: 'Where's my jacket? Didn't you fellas put my jacket in?' It turned out that he had left it hanging up in his Aston, with his passport in the pocket.

Responding promptly, I rang the office, using the number of colleague Martin Lewis, who was always noted for being in early, and explained the situation.

'Right,' said Martin, 'I'll drop everything and bring it right away.' Even with the best time he could make, we had no hope of catching the 10 a.m. flight, but I was able to rebook the whole party on the 11 o' clock.

'It's OK,' I said to Innes and Peter, as I emerged from the airport office, 'Martin Lewis is bringing your jacket over and I've rebooked us on the 11 o' clock.'

'Did you tell him about my racing kit as well?'

'What?' I exclaimed. It turned out that Innes had wafted into the car park and left his Aston with his racing helmet and overalls in the boot, the windows down, and the keys in the ignition! I always said he was a carefree happy-go-lucky chap.

Immediately I got back on the phone and rang the number of grumpy old Mr Heedon, the car-park attendant, and told him to stop Mr Lewis who would soon be driving out of the car park. 'Sorry sir,' he replied, 'he's just left.'

By now my secretary had arrived in the office, and I arranged for her to get a minicab to bring everything else out of this damned Aston Martin over to Southend Airport. The airport officials must have thought we were crazy when I asked to be transferred to the 1 o'clock flight, but it turned out that there was no room for the car on that one, although there was space for passengers. So Peter and I had to take the 11 o'clock, and leave Innes to come over alone on the 1 o' clock. We waited there patiently for his belated arrival.

At last, some five hours behind schedule, we were away, and Innes was now driving the Jaguar. I admired the lovely smooth, controlled way in which he drove, and on the *autoroute* to Liège he cruised smoothly along at between 90 and 100mph. As we caught up each car, he drove past on whichever side was free, frequently passing them on the inside. 'Never disturb them,' he said. 'Once you go flashing the lights and trying to make them move over you can be stuck behind them for miles.'

He adopted the same policy in Britain where, of course in the late 1960s, many drivers were enjoying acting as policemen to enforce the new 70mph speed limit, and didn't like being passed on the inside. One of these nasty people reported Innes and he finished up being taken to court for it, but escaped without penalty. He used the strategy that I suggested to him, namely to say that he had been obstructed, so waited in the left lane, and the person in the right-hand lane suddenly braked hard, leaving him no choice but to go past on the inside.

After a while on our journey to the Nürburgring we had to stop for fuel, and I then took to the back seat and dozed off, with Innes still driving. Some time later, I was suddenly aware of a smell of hot oil. I opened my eyes and focused on the instruments. Oil pressure OK, temperature a bit high but nothing to worry about, and then I looked at the rev counter and thought at first that the needle must have fallen off. Then I saw it, right off the scale and almost on the clock situated at the bottom of the rev counter.

'Innes,' I yelled, 'you're not in bloody overdrive!'

'Oh, sorry fella,' he said and worked the switch, immediately taking the revs back from 6,300 to 4,900rpm. No harm was done, but on this Jaguar overdrive top was very much top gear, and direct fourth had a maximum speed of 93mph at 5,500rpm.

This carefree lackadaisical attitude in Innes was part of his charm, but it ran him into trouble again later when he was driving for Mercedes-Benz in the great London–Sydney rally, when a stone holed the radiator. He didn't notice the thermometer going off the scale and pressed on at full speed until the engine blew a head gasket.

Later, on our journey to Adenau for the Marathon, after we had left the *Autobahn*, Innes's normally beautifully controlled cornering suddenly went wild, to such an extent that I thought at one time we were going off the road. But he recovered control, and stopped the car saying that something was wrong. Sure enough we had a flat tyre at the rear, and lost a further half hour unloading all the luggage and changing the wheel.

Very late indeed we arrived at Adenau, dropped Innes with all his kit at the hotel booked for him by Lancia, and went down to our hotel where a message told us what room was reserved for us. Lancia finished third and seventh, but the Moss-Ireland-Maglioli Fulvia lost its gearbox oil and had to retire when lying second. Innes was soon making his own way back to England, while Peter Cramer and I stayed on to cover the event to the finish. It was full of drama, and finally won convincingly by two 2-litre Porsche 911s crossing the line together in a tie. On one night there was thick fog, and as we drove up to the circuit in the dark, unable to see much in the murk, we were staggered at the speed of the leading Porsche, where the road passed under the circuit.

The rules laid down for the Marathon were very strict about service, only twenty minutes being allowed every seventy-five laps. MG had entered a team of two MGCs, the first of which had to retire after overheating caused by coolant loss.

The other one was going very well and lying third behind the two Porsches, but when it came in for the permitted routine service the mechanics unwisely decided that the brake pads would last through to the next service interval. But when the car came in, with the driver Andrew Hedges complaining that the brakes were now very poor, the mechanics couldn't release the pads, which had almost welded themselves in place with the heat. There was much hammering and cursing, while team manager Peter Browning anxiously studied his watch. Eventually he said: 'He'll have to go.'

'Can't,' came the reply. 'It's only got one brake pad in.'

'He'll have to go, or we're disqualified,' insisted Browning. The relief driver, Tony Fall, jumped into the driving seat and with the strict instruction 'Don't touch the brake pedal whatever you do,' he set off round the 17.6-mile circuit in the dark with no brakes.

When he arrived back at the pits, of course he couldn't stop. Browning and several mechanics tried to grab the car and bring it to a halt, and it simply bounced over a wheel chock thrown in front of it. When Fall eventually managed to crunch into reverse and stop the car, it was well past its pit area. 'You'll have to go round again,' yelled Peter Browning. He knew that to reverse in the pit area meant instant disqualification. When Tony Fall arrived next time we were all ready for him, and he came in more slowly.

'It got a bit hairy going down to the Adenau bridge,' said Tony Fall. 'I was in first gear and running out of revs; it went to 8,000rpm and was still going faster. I'm glad no one got in the way when I was doing 125 along the back straight.'

The two laps without using the brakes had helped to cool everything off, and this time the mechanics were able to get the seized pad out, quickly bleed the brakes and get the MGC back into reasonable trim. Time penalties (one lap deducted for every minute in the pits) dropped the MGC back from third to eighth, but in the last few hours it managed to regain two more places and finished sixth. It all made for exciting copy, enhanced by Cramer's night pictures. Tony Fall sadly died in 2008.

On our long journey back to England, the 240 again ran beautifully, and we had managed to get the punctured tyre repaired, but I was a little disappointed by the noise of the Jaguar engine, which seemed much louder than I remembered from that first 2.4, which had been one of my earliest road-test experiences. I eagerly accepted the offer by Kenlowe to fit one of their electric fans in place of the huge multi-blade standard fan, which didn't even have a viscous coupling. It made a big improvement to the noise level, and also increased the top speed from 106mph to 111mph. The only problem with it was that its mounting was weak, and the carrier arm tended to slip down until a modification was carried out. A persistent reader wrote in to insist that removal of the belt-driven standard fan could not have made such an increase in the power required to raise the maximum speed by such a large amount, but the facts remained indisputable.

Jaguar were well pleased with the publicity given to the 240 in the journal, and were happy for me to retain it for a second year, and because the report of the Marathon de la Route had been full of interest, as a reliability trial for ordinary standard production cars, I was asked to cover it again in 1969.

'Why don't we,' I said to Peter Cramer, 'take our wives and children over and leave them in Belgium on the way through to the Nürburgring? They can have a few days' holiday at the seaside – it'll be a bit of a squash in the Jaguar, but we can make it OK.' Peter was enthusiastic, and it was all arranged unofficially. He had two little girls, and my wife Jennetta and I had our son, Bruce, who was then four, and daughter Rachel at eight months. We arranged to cross by the new Hovercraft service from Ramsgate to Calais, which had the advantage that the booking for the car included any number of passengers.

It all worked very well, and the Marathon was particularly exciting. Innes Ireland was booked by Lancia again as lead driver in one of three Fulvia HF Coupés, and was flown out to the circuit, but his drive ended abruptly when the third driver Paganelli lost control in torrential rain and finished up in the shrubbery down a bank far from the track. But Lancia had their just reward when one of their three cars, with Tony Fall as one of the three drivers, won the event.

It showed how important reliability was in this eighty-four-hour endurance event, that a Triumph TR6 was thirty-third on Wednesday, had moved up to thirteenth early on Thursday, and was eighth on Friday, finally coming in third at the finish on Saturday.

We had our own little adventure on the return trip, after picking up our respective families in Blankenburg. We had saved up some expenses and brought money of our own to settle their bill. 'Will you take German marks?' I asked the manager.

'Oh, certainly,' he replied, 'a hedge against the devaluation.' It was widely expected then that the Belgian franc would have to be devalued, but it didn't happen.

Short of cash, I thought we could avoid buying any more petrol for the Jaguar until we were back in England where it would not have to go down as overseas expenses, but the fuel warning light had been on for a long time, and as I drove up the ramp on to the Hovercraft I heard the electric fuel pump rattling frantically. The Hovercraft was pretty full, and we had to go into one of those horrid inner compartments with no window and lots of paraffin fumes. Soon the children were ill and so was Peter's wife Marion. I was nursing the girls, one on each shoulder, and Jennetta, also not feeling very well, had Bruce on hers, when suddenly came the announcement that one of the four engines had failed, and the captain regretted that the crossing would take much longer than usual. It did – in what seemed to be a never-ending nightmare, the Hovercraft rocked its way over a very rough sea.

Eventually we docked, and there was just enough fuel in the Jaguar to limp to the Ramsgate Point. It was an exciting journey in the 240, but its days with me were coming to an end. Jaguar had launched the new XJ saloon, and were keen for us to take one of these for long-term assessment, and my beloved 240 had to go back.

FORTY-FOUR

ROVER 3.5

The oncoming driver took panic and threw both hands up off the wheel.
His car veered straight off the road into the adjacent field

On my first visit to Sweden, in 1960, I noticed that nearly all local cars had left-hand drive. As Sweden, like Britain, drove on the left this seemed very odd, and I asked several people why it was. Most Swedes speak good English, and the answer was always the same: 'We are going to change one day, and drive on the right, like they do in Norway and on the Continent. Then you British will be on your own, and you will have to change the rule of the road also.'

No way, I thought, and I also wondered if the changeover would ever occur in Sweden, but they all seemed determined that it was going to happen; and in the end, it did.

In July 1967 an invitation came from the Swedish authorities for the journal to witness the changeover, and the necessary passes were enclosed. The editor asked me to take on the job of covering the event, which would take place on Sunday 3 September, and it was arranged that I would take the new Rover 3.5-litre saloon and do the road test on it at the same time. Photographer Peter Cramer was to accompany me.

I was delighted with the car when it arrived, with the familiar sumptuous leather and polished wood interior, while under the bonnet was the big change: the worthy old 6-cylinder engine was replaced by the Buick-derived V8 all-alloy engine of 3,528cc capacity, fitted with BorgWarner Type 35 automatic transmission as standard.

I decided that we would cross on the night ferry from Harwich to Esbjerg in Denmark, then drive across Denmark and take the ferry again to Hälsingborg in Sweden. Long journeys in Sweden would give us plenty of opportunity to assess the smoothness of the changeover from driving on the left (*vanster*) to the right (*höger*). But on the ferry I had an adventure of my own.

We crossed on the magnificent ferry *Winston Churchill*, and enjoyed a reasonably comfortable night although the sea was evidently quite choppy. In the morning I took a shower, and the cubicle had a surrounding lip about 2ft high to prevent any water from slopping over, with the usual instruction to make sure the shower curtain was inside the surround. While I was showering, the ship took a sudden sharp lurch to the left. I tried to grab the sturdy vertical bar, but missed it, and as I was flung backwards the top of the lip contacted my legs just behind the knee joint, which left me hurtling backwards. I grabbed the shower curtain but its pop mountings all released and I landed on my back on the floor of the washroom, giving my head a resounding wallop, which knocked me out.

I don't know how long I was unconscious, but when I came round, the shower had soaked the floor because of the lack of a curtain. Only afterwards did it occur to me that if I had been more seriously injured, anyone who found me might have wondered what I was doing, naked, with a plastic sheet wrapped round me!

Once we had arrived in Sweden it was at once evident that immense work had been done in preparation for the rule of the road changeover. Wherever we went there were wrapped-up gantry signs, arrows on the road pointing the wrong way with just the fragments of the black covering still clinging to them, traffic lights in the wrong places, filter lanes which you turned into *after* making your turn instead of before, and direction signs on the other side of the road in towns.

It was all highly amusing, and would come right on Sunday; this was Saturday (*höger* day -1). We spent a lot of time in Gothenburg taking pictures at identifiable sites, which we would photograph again after the changeover, but at about 2.30 p.m. I noticed that we were having to wait longer and longer for traffic to come and be photographed, and suddenly we had the streets to ourselves. There were plenty of people about, and the odd taxi or bus, but otherwise no traffic.

The press information had advised that there would be a traffic close-down from 3 p.m. on Saturday in Gothenburg, but I hadn't expected it to be so sudden or so complete. With mounting panic I called to Peter, who tumbled into the Rover, and we headed out of the city in the direction of Stockholm where we wanted to be at the *Höger Press* HQ.

Those direction signs on the opposite side of the road were very difficult to follow, and we took a wrong turn and lost some time, with the result that when we reached a police checkpoint on the outskirts of the city, the pole was across the road. The policeman looked at his watch and resolutely refused to allow us past. Traffic had finished, we were told, and our press passes proved meaningless. Suddenly the police were talking together and pointing at the Rover, and I guessed we were in danger of having the car impounded. I did a rapid U-turn, ignored the shouts from one of the policemen and we headed back towards Gothenburg.

It was now dark, as we turned off the main road, followed a general northerly direction until we came to another main road, and again turned away from the city, but with the same frustrating result. This time we didn't argue but turned hurriedly away again, wondering what to do, but I noticed that this checkpoint had been much farther out from the city than the previous one. If we could only get across, we would be on the far side of the barrier and could escape, but there was a railway line running roughly parallel between the two roads.

Many false turns were made before we located a track down to a siding and a coal yard, but there was no level crossing. It wasn't a major railway line as one could

In their advertising, Rover apologised for making their new big saloon quieter still; and it certainly was a magnificent car for a long journey, thanks to the Buick-derived V8 engine.

tell from the rust, but I was still a bit terrified about what would happen if we were stuck halfway across the line when a train came along. There was much checking of ground clearance and listening for trains before I summoned up enough courage to bounce the Rover over the railway lines, using the sleepers as a ramp.

There was a sickening thud and graunching noise underneath as the chassis came down on to the line at one point, but I knew I mustn't stop and risk getting grounded straddling the lines. I applied some extra power and the back wheels clambered over the second line and we were safely across. Peter had a torch and we inspected the underneath but could see no sign of any damage; the trick had worked. When we reached a main road we could see the lights of the police checkpoint and we were now on the outside of the closed traffic area. We were soon making record time to Stockholm, the Rover's lights soaring through the darkness on roads almost completely free of any other moving vehicles.

On arrival at Stockholm it was all very different from Gothenburg. Our passes were accepted and we were allowed to drive through the city. It was a fascinating experience, as there were people everywhere but no traffic other than the odd taxi. One heard laughter, a distant clock chiming 10 p.m., the swish of the Rover's tyres and the burble of the V8 exhaust – all sounds that would normally be lost in the hubbub of the traffic.

We located the *Höger* HQ and spent some time talking to people and reading the numerous ticker-tape reports coming in from all over Sweden about preparations for the changeover and how it was going. I was thumbing through these and suddenly shocked to read one that said: 'British registered Rover seen travelling down centre of road at enormous speeds – police still searching.' Then I saw Peter's grinning face and realised that he had typed it.

Changeover time in Stockholm was 5 a.m. on Sunday morning. Anyone on the road at that remote hour had to stop, check for other vehicles, then drive across the road and continue on the right, but if they had any sense they were like me, fast asleep and letting *Höger Dag* get under way on its own.

After a quick breakfast Peter took a few pictures including some of the new left-hand-drive Leyland buses on the road for the first time, and then we headed out of Stockholm, retracing our route to Gothenburg. But we soon ran into appalling traffic problems. Apparently the king had been on television and advised people to get out in their cars on Sunday and try driving on the right while police surveillance was at its highest. A miserably slow journey followed. The official speed limit was 60kph (37mph), but queues of traffic were proceeding at about 20mph with drivers becoming almost apoplectic if overtaken.

Unlike the locals, who were just driving round a circuit, which had all right-hand turns, we had a long way to go, and felt justified in ignoring hooting, light flashing and gesticulations whenever we overtook anyone at whatever speed.

A particular Volvo driver was so obviously incensed at what he saw as violation of the sacred rights of *Höger Dag* that I hurriedly had to overtake a few more for fear of being rammed. We were short of fuel, and pulled into a garage, only to find it was closed, so rejoined the queue and had to pass this aggressive Volvo man again. But we had been going for 30 miles with the T-handle fuel reserve switch pulled out, and when the engine suddenly died there was no alternative but to draw in and swill the contents of our reserve jerrycan into the tank, watching that furious red face go past us again.

'You can't overtake him again, he'll have a heart attack,' said Peter, so we had a look at the map and I could see a possible minor road going in roughly the right direction. We found the turn-off and were going quite well, hustling the Rover round a right-hand bend on the rough water-bound gravel surface, when we met a Ford Taunus coming the other way. I pulled the Rover almost into the ditch on the right to make our intentions plain, but the oncoming driver took panic and threw both hands up off the wheel. His car veered straight off the road, and came to rest harmlessly in a field.

Eventually we rejoined the main road, and realised that the big traffic congestion was just at villages, with all drivers going round the same little right-hand route. Once clear of each village we could get some speed up again. Several times we saw women passengers in cars wearing crash helmets, and it was amusing to see the passenger's head moving about as the wives were so accustomed to being the ones who made the decision as to whether it was safe to overtake when their left-hand-drive car was being driven on the left. Now that they were on the right, their help was redundant, but they couldn't shake off the habit of many years.

We saw a young boy hitch-hiking with a small Union Jack on his kitbag, so took pity on him and gave him a lift. He was so grateful, telling us that all the traffic was going nowhere; he had been given lifts in several cars but made only about 10 miles.

It was with great relief that we reached Gothenburg, revisited all our previous picture sites and photographed them again with the signs now making sense, direction boards uncovered, and traffic moving along on the right. Then we caught the ferry back to Denmark and drove south to Germany and Holland, returning on the Hook–Harwich ferry.

The Swedish authorities had evidently put the fear of God into all motorists about the dangers of *Höger Dag*, and the very low speed limits in Sweden continued for many years. Also introduced at the same time was the rule to keep headlamps on by day, which I had found very irritating with the Rover, having to remember to put the switch across every time Peter got back into the car after taking his pictures. In fact, it wasn't until four to six months later that the accidents began to happen, when people relaxed and forgot for a moment which side to drive on, as happens to many British motorists when driving abroad. *Höger* had been fun before it happened, but was pretty dreary afterwards, and I returned to Britain hoping that we would never have a 'Right Day' over here. Iceland followed Sweden in changing to drive on the right a few years later, but of course with our volumes of traffic and the complex road infrastructure in Britain, the time when such a change could have been made is long past.

The Rover 3.5 had proved trouble-free and extremely comfortable for our long journey in which we covered 3,400 miles in six days. Its maximum speed was a fairly modest 108mph, but it had proved capable of cruising effortlessly at or close to 100mph. In the road test I commented that it was not difficult to put 85–90 miles into an hour when the road and traffic conditions were right, and praised the quietness of the Rover's new V8 engine. Its overall fuel consumption for the entire distance was 19.2mpg. I remember being impressed at how stable this big and not very aerodynamic car was in a day of very high winds coming back across Germany and Holland, but the really lasting memory is one of the great anxiety when driving it across that railway line in Sweden.

FORTY-FIVE

AUDI 100 AND MERCEDES-BENZ 250

As the moment of danger passed I was suddenly aware of headlamps
approaching fast from behind, and was back in first gear accelerating hard
when there was a tremendous thump at the back of the car

Usually the carefully planned launches introducing new models to the press go smoothly and with great efficiency, but just occasionally – often through no fault of the car firm concerned – things go badly wrong.

One such was the introduction of a new Russian Lada model in Ireland. I wasn't on this particular launch but heard all about it. The journalists were flown over, and then transported by coach to the hotel, only to be told with many regrets that the cars had not yet arrived. Never mind, plenty of food and drink, and the cars will be here in the morning. But they weren't. Eventually everyone had to pile into the coach for the return journey to the airport for the flight back home. Just as the

Wider and lower than the previous Super 90, the new Audi 100 was much improved, and came to Britain with a floor-mounted gear change.

coach was at the end of the hotel drive, the big transporter swung in with all the new Ladas on board.

'Does anyone want to stay on to drive our new Lada, and go back tomorrow?' called out the press officer. I gather there were no takers!

Another ill-fated launch in which I was very much involved happened in November 1968, when Audi arranged to launch in Bavaria the new 100 model, replacing the former Super 90. Assigned to cover the new car's introduction for *Autocar*, I made my way to Heathrow for the planned meeting with the press officer for Mercedes-Benz, Erik Johnson. At that time, the UK concession for Audi was handled by Mercedes. Later it was nearly humiliatingly snatched away from them by Octav Botnar, who had the concession for NSU. When the Audi factory was sold to Volkswagenwerk by Daimler-Benz AG, Thomas Tillings were desperate to retain the franchise, and paid Octav Botnar and his partner a sum believed to be £1.4 million for it – a lot of money in 1968. Botnar went on to set up the Datsun importing operation, later known as Nissan.

Back to our meeting at Heathrow in November 1968, where Erik greeted me with the depressing news that there was fog in Germany, and he feared that Munich airport might be closed. We would have to put down at Düsseldorf and continue by train. Nowadays, aircraft can cope in almost zero visibility, but some forty years ago the pilot trying to land an aircraft was quite keen to be able to see the ground.

A lifelong revulsion for trains, dating back to journeys made as a schoolboy during the war, sent me scurrying across to the Avis desk at Düsseldorf, and I returned a few minutes later clutching the documents for a Ford Taunus 17M, which I had hired.

There were about fifteen journalists in the group, including such notable stalwarts as the late Basil Cardew (*Daily Express*) and Courtenay Edwards (*Daily Mail*). I suggested to Erik that we only needed to hire two or three more cars and we could all continue by road, but he wasn't happy about this at all. 'The *Autobahn* gets very dangerous when it's foggy,' he replied.

It looked as if I would be on my own for the drive, until another eminent journalist, Charles Bulmer (editor of *Motor*, who sadly died in February 2012), asked if he could come with me. 'Delighted,' I replied, and then Doug Blain, editor of the recently started magazine *Car*, joined us.

'See you all at Ingolstadt,' I said with a cheery wave as we set off to find the Taunus, but it was destined not to happen.

The Taunus that I had hired was one of the last Fords to be produced for the Continent only and not marketed in Britain. Its replacement was the Cortina Mk IV, the first common European production from Ford. I took the first spell at the wheel, and was pleased to find that in this area of Germany the weather was good – very cold, and soon dark, but with crystal-clear visibility. We made good progress, cruising at about 130kph (80mph), and stopped after a couple of hours for a coffee.

Charles then took the wheel and I stretched out for a snooze on the back seat. After a while I woke up, focused on the instruments to see how far we had travelled and was astonished to see that we were doing only about 70kph (43mph).

'Why are we going so slowly?' I asked. They told me that the car had been getting slower and slower, presumably suffering from carburettor icing in the chill night air. Spotting a service area near Nuremberg, which also had a motel, we decided to have a meal and spend the night there.

'Did you manage to fix the car alright during the night?' I asked Charles jokingly at breakfast next morning. In fact, it had cured itself, and the carburettor icing did not recur.

We arrived early at Ingolstadt and attended a very informative briefing on the car, helped by a cutaway example with all its innards revealed. Although these are commonplace now it was one of the first sectioned display cars I had seen. Where they had cut through the tyre they had filled the space where the air would be and coloured it blue. We were going to tease the gullible Basil Cardew that the new Audi had special *Blau Luft* tyres with blue air in them! But the opportunity didn't arise because there was no sign of the rest of the British contingent.

The briefing over we were given directions to a fine *Schloss* some way over to the east where we were able to start driving the new 100. It had the same high-swirl 1,760cc engine as the previous Super 90, with exceptionally high compression ratio by the standards of those days. Power had been increased by 14 per cent to 103bhp (net – which was the old way of measuring power output, without such ancillaries as the dynamo).

Retained from the previous model was the steering-column gear change – a feature I quite liked, though many were very critical of it – but we were assured that imports for the funny people in Britain who drove on the left side of the road would have a floor-mounted gear change. The new Audi was wider and flatter looking than the previous Super 90 and I was very taken with its appearance. Audi had also taken steps to try to reduce the excessive understeer of the previous model, one move being to relocate the battery under the rear seat.

The test route was extraordinary, and I think Audi was lucky to get away without any major disasters. I was flagged off and followed a twisty minor road for about 10 miles. At every junction along the route somebody was on patrol. Audi had effectively closed the road to the German public. Suddenly there were marshals standing in the road flagging me down and I was informed that this was the end of the test route. 'Here you turn, please, and go back,' I was told.

This meant frequent confrontations – often quite frightening – with oncoming Audi 100s driven by rather wild Continental journalists being caught out by the understeer, which was still very marked with all the engine and transmission weight ahead of the front wheels. I took to sounding the pathetic beeper horn on every bend and was ready to have to steer off the road if someone coming the other way had 'lost it'.

After a couple of drives I was told that lunch was ready, and went into the *Schloss* to find that the remainder of Erik's fragmented group had arrived. On hearing of their adventures – waiting at stations, short of money after the unexpected purchase of railway tickets in the days before credit cards, late breakfast at Munich in the hotel where they should have spent the night, and finally a coach trip to Ingolstadt only to find that everyone had gone and they'd missed the briefing – I was jolly glad to have baled out into a hire car. But worse was to come for them.

Lunch was just starting to be served, but even as the first bite neared the mouth, one of the Audi team came bustling round with the news that Munich airport was open, followed by, '*Schnell, bitte,* your coach goes. You must come now!' I heard later that by the time the coach reached the airport, the fog had come down and closed it again. They then had to trundle 100 miles back to Nuremberg, whence they flew home late that evening, having had little chance to do more than grab a fleeting glimpse of the new Audi 100. Charles had to go back, too, but at least he had driven the car. It was never the intention that I would go back with the group. Instead, I was to make my way to Munich, then fly to Stuttgart and pick up a Mercedes-Benz 250 automatic for an *Autocar* road test.

Erik was going to come with me, and hearing that we were going to Munich by car, the late Maxwell Boyd, then motoring writer for the *Sunday Times*, elected to join us so that he could stay over and at least drive and photograph the new Audi in the sunshine of the afternoon. Doug Blain had to get back, so had rejoined the main group, leaving just three of us again in the Taunus.

By the time we left the launch venue, darkness had descended, and as we made our way south to Munich on ordinary roads, we ran into dense fog. Going as fast as seemed prudent, I was a little surprised to see behind us the lights of a car catching up and, as it drew alongside to overtake, saw that it was a Mercedes-Benz 230SL.

'He's pushing his luck,' said Maxwell, and almost immediately an unlit tractor appeared from the right and crossed the road in front of us. An accident seemed inevitable, but the Mercedes driver braked violently, swerved and nearly spun, but just managed to avoid the tractor. My reaction had been to brake hard as well, to keep clear of the expected shrapnel. As the moment of danger passed I was suddenly aware of headlamps approaching fast from behind, and was back in first gear accelerating hard when there was a tremendous thump at the back of the car.

'There goes all our kit,' said Max Boyd, who had put his expensive photographic gear in the boot, but in fact the damage to the Taunus was not too bad. We had been hit by a rear-engined NSU Prinz, which was in a sorry state at the front. Its two occupants were bloodied, especially the passenger (no seat belts, of course), and they both remained in the car.

Other cars stopped at the scene, and Erik went off in one of them to try to find the tractor that had caused it all, but it had disappeared; the Mercedes SL, after its narrow escape, had also gone. I learned a new German word: *ein Schlepper*,

Like all Mercedes at the time, the 250 was under-geared and fussy when cruising. The test car was collected in Germany, already with British registration.

meaning a tractor. Like magic, only a few minutes after the accident another Ford Taunus arrived with a more familiar German word, *Polizei,* on the side.

I couldn't understand why the NSU had collided with us; it had been a long way behind. But then the police showed me a breathalyser with which they had tested its driver. I had heard about them, but never seen one before, and they had not yet arrived in Britain. It was the early type, with crystals that changed colour on contact with alcohol fumes. When the driver of the NSU was tested, the crystals had changed colour all the way up the tube.

Eventually we were free to continue to Munich, where we spent the night at the superb *Bayerischer Hof.* After dinner, Erik said we deserved more drinks down in the nightclub in the basement of the hotel, where far too much was consumed. Next morning I had an almighty hangover. We had checked out, and were walking away when the receptionist called out: 'Oh, Herr Johnson, there is another bill here.' It was the damage for our drinks in the nightclub, and Erik's signature looked as if a spider had climbed out of the ink well and crawled across the bill.

Money was an ongoing problem. One forgets what it was like in the days when you either had cash with you or were broke, with no recourse to plastic. Erik had borrowed some from his friends at Audi, but the *Bayerische Hof* had devoured it, and my funds had been demolished by the car-hire charges.

We had already decided to drive to Stuttgart, as we certainly couldn't afford to fly, and I reckoned we would make it without having to buy more fuel. Then we would be OK – we should be able to borrow from the Mercedes press officer. Max Boyd elected to stay on and take a chance on the airport re-opening.

Apart from its buckled rear bumper, the Taunus didn't look too bad, and as I had paid extra for full insurance they were not concerned about it when I checked it in at Stuttgart airport. A taxi took us to the home of Dirk Strassl who was then the very popular press officer for Mercedes-Benz. It was now Saturday and Erik greeted him with, 'Could you please pay for our taxi?' And then asked, 'How much cash can you lend us?' Later Erik told me that he wondered how he was able to claim back on expenses the money he had borrowed all around Germany to repay all those kind people who had come to our rescue.

Dirk's wife kindly gave us lunch, though I was still suffering from the excesses of the previous evening and never liked *sauerkraut* anyway, so I didn't do much justice to it. Erik told me he had always wanted to see a road test started with the car supplied straight from the factory, and that was why he had arranged for me to collect the car from Dirk Strassl on the Saturday. It had right-hand drive and was fully run-in. For its time, this Mercedes-Benz was a very elegant and functional car, called the 250 with Daimler-Benz four-speed automatic transmission. It had a 2½-litre 6-cylinder engine giving 130bhp.

Considering that they had the best road system in Europe, it was surprising that Mercedes-Benz engineers turned out cars with very low gearing, making them very fussy at speed. The 250 ran at 4,500rpm when doing 80mph – you could hardly call it cruising – and the resultant fuel economy was very poor. It gave only 17.3mpg, but I have to admit to driving it very hard indeed.

In the money again, we spent the night at Cologne. Then, after a late start, we ran into a tremendous Sunday morning jam at the Belgian border at Aachen. It cost us nearly an hour, and from then on I held the Mercedes at its maximum of 108mph wherever possible (four years were to pass before Belgium put speed limits on its motorways), but it was all to no avail. We arrived at Ostend airport just in time to see the Bristol freighter on which the Mercedes was booked lumber into the air without us. Oh, for a mobile phone!

It was a Sunday in November, there were no more car air ferry flights that day, and fifty years ago you didn't get a sea ferry every half hour or so. I had to be back at the office first thing on Monday morning with the three-page description and road impressions of the new Audi 100 written and ready to go to press. The next ship was the night boat from Dunkirk to Dover at 12.30 a.m. We had a cabin, and although it was a very rough crossing I wrote my 1,500-word Audi report using a typewriter borrowed from the purser.

It was an ancient machine (probably worth a lot now as an antique), with keys coming down sideways on double arms. One of the letters kept sticking, and the next ones would jam down on top of it. Eventually, exasperated, I made my way to the car deck and returned brandishing the Mercedes's dipstick. A drop of oil at each end of the offending key worked wonders, enabling me to finish the report and grab a couple of hours of sleep before making my weary way back to the office.

F O R T Y - S I X

JENSEN INTERCEPTOR AND FF

Soaring along the Heads of the Valleys road at 125mph we passed what we thought was yet another competitor. 'That wasn't a competitor,' murmured my co-driver; 'that was a police car.'

It may seem an extraordinary choice for an economy run: a car with a Chrysler V8 6.3-litre engine and automatic transmission, but there was method in the madness. As well as dividing the cars into classes based on engine size, the Hants & Berks Motor Club, who organised the Mobil Economy Run, contrived a 'formula of efficiency' with good prizes going for the top three cars. Each car was given a 'bogey' mpg target, based on engine size, weight and gearing. Beat the formula: that was the idea behind entering such a potentially thirsty car as the Jensen Interceptor. We had noted how the formula for the Holland Birkett Memorial Trophy seemed to favour a big engine in a heavy car, and I think that if it hadn't been for an unfortunate and unexpected fiasco, we might have won.

It was well into the second night of the 1,000-mile route, after the Leominster refuelling stop, when I began to notice that the lights seemed rather poor, and then saw for the first time the appalling reading on the voltmeter. We were down to 9 volts. I should have been paying more attention to the instruments, but on those narrow Welsh lanes, the very wide Interceptor was quite a handful and needed full concentration on the road ahead.

At the top of a hill where there was sufficient road width for other competitors to pass by, we pulled in to investigate. Leaving the engine ticking over, we opened the bonnet and saw by torchlight the alternator drive belt. It had broken, and was lying on the under tray. The alternator was not turning and we were not getting any charge.

Hindsight is wonderful. We realised later that what we should have done was to kill all electrical loads, tuck in behind another competitor, and press on without lights to the next refuelling point where repairs could have been carried out in dead time. Instead we made the fateful decision to stop the engine and fit the replacement belt, which we were wisely carrying.

Then came the moment of truth – would it start? At the third try, the big 6.3-litre V8 almost caught, but not quite, and subsequent attempts just produced that infuriating clicking of the starter solenoid, familiar to anyone who has ever been dogged by a flat battery. The next idea was to try getting up speed down the hill and put the automatic transmission selector into Low, in the hope that this would jerk the engine into life. That descent by moonlight with no lights on at 30mph was one of the most terrifying drives of my life. But it didn't work – with Chrysler Torqueflite automatic transmission you can't start an engine this way no matter how fast you go.

At the bottom of the hill there was a little cottage with lights on, and they kindly allowed me to use the phone (no mobiles in those days). I called rally driver Bill Bengry, whose garage we had used for the previous refuelling and explained the position. He was not far away, and Bill was an experienced rally driver; I hoped he would be with us quite quickly. Unfortunately he spent a lot of time gathering up mechanics, tools, batteries and jump leads before coming out to help. It was only the last of these things that we needed, and although he covered the 16 miles to us in record time, three quarters of an hour had passed, and the whole field had gone by. We had spent twenty-one minutes fitting the new alternator drive belt, so in total had over an hour's lost time to recover.

There was the usual jolly fireworks display as the live jump lead touched an earth point, but we were soon better organised and the jump start had the engine running again. I then had a fantastic drive to try to make up time. Extra fuel used was much less important than avoiding lateness penalties on the scale of 0.5mpg deduction from the final result per whole minute late. The Jensen responded so magnificently that we nearly made it. Every two or three minutes we would snatch the tail lights of another competitor and hurl them behind us. One of my few claims to fame might be that I went faster than any other competitor has ever driven on an economy run. At one time we were soaring along the Heads of the Valleys road showing 125mph when the tail lights of what we thought was yet another competitor were swallowed up.

'That wasn't a competitor,' murmured my co-driver, Jeff Daniels, 'that was a police car. Never mind, I don't think he'll catch us.'

And where was the observer, who was supposed to be enforcing strict adherence to the law all this time? The answer, he told us later, was keeping mum and thoroughly enjoying it.

We had another refuelling control at Merthyr Tydfil, where in dead time we were able to tighten the new alternator belt, which had started slipping, and we needed a jump start again from another car as there still wasn't enough juice in the battery

Although a bit of a handful on the narrow Welsh lanes, the Jensen Interceptor provided superb motoring and was doing very well on economy until the disaster on the second night.

to fire up. Unwisely I then handed over the driving to Jeff, who didn't respond to the occasion and went much too slowly for the last few miles to the time control where we arrived three minutes late. If I had continued at the wheel, I think we would have made it, and avoiding the 1.5mpg penalty deduction would have raised our mpg figure from 14.8mpg to 16.3mpg and given us third place in the class.

It was not only for us that it was a night of great adventure, as the section from Llanbister to Llangollen over the Bwlch-y-Groes mountain road formed a very tight stage of only 87 miles and although it was easy for the Jensen with all that latent power, even now driving again for optimum economy, it was very hard for some of the more ordinary family cars. In my report of the event, I wrote: 'At last the Mobil Run has become more like a rally, and any who doubt this had only to stand at the Llangollen time control and smell the stench of burning brake linings as each car came in, to realise how tight it had been.'

It was certainly a memorable economy run for all competitors, and for me and my crew it was particularly exciting. People who used to imagine that the

Skiers were amazed to see the Jensen FF climbing the piste at Gstaad, demonstrating the terrific traction that you get with four-wheel drive even on ordinary tyres.

Mobil Economy Run, with its 30mph average speed, was a boring doddle have no conception of how difficult it was to maintain that average over the tough terrain of the route.

There were time penalties for seventeen competitors, and six retirements, three of them due to accidents. A Saab 99 won the coveted Holland Birkett Memorial Trophy, which we might have achieved if it hadn't been for the disaster.

I absolutely loved that Jensen with its fine handling and effortless power, but the great experience had come two years earlier when the four-wheel drive Jensen FF came in for road test, and I was sent off with a colleague to 'go and find some snow'. It was early March, but the weather was very mild as we headed south to Switzerland. In Germany, we measured the maximum speed at 130mph, and knocked off the high-speed acceleration figures, which were pretty amazing by the standards of those days. The FF was able to accelerate from rest to 120mph in just over half a minute (37.2 seconds), despite its enormous weight of 1,800kg. But of course, the penalty was a formidable rate of fuel consumption. Our overall figure for the 1,500 miles of the test was 13.6mpg!

Identified by its double air grilles on the side, the FF's main distinction from the Interceptor was that it had four-wheel drive and, almost unique in those days, it had anti-lock braking. The idea of finding some snow was to see how the FF responded on really slippery surfaces.

On the way to Switzerland we cruised along the magnificently straight and (then) traffic-free *Autobahn* towards Basle, keeping the speed down to about 100mph so as not to be too hard on the FF's fuel consumption, but we did allow ourselves a few miles at 120mph to shake off a police helicopter, which had been following the Jensen and sitting almost on the roof. These were the carefree days before speed limits.

On arrival in Switzerland we went to the local tourist office and asked which was the nearest pass that was closed, so that we could try driving over it. The girl gave us an odd look, but then advised us to try the Col des Diablerets and the Col du Pillon. At the top of the Diablerets we found a triangular circuit of deeply snow-covered roads between high banks of packed snow left by the snow ploughs. With blue sky and brilliant sunshine it gave ideal photographs, one of which I later had mounted and sent to the Jensen directors.

Diablerets had been fun but no real test for the car, but at the foot of the Col du Pillon we came to Gstaad, which was thronged with skiers. At about 5 p.m., the sun dropped behind the peaks and as the temperature started falling rapidly, the skiers soon disappeared, and I had the idea for a little bravado: 'Let's try the car on the ski run,' I suggested. We found a way on without difficulty, and although prepared for four-wheel-drive traction, we were quite stunned at the way the Jensen on ordinary Dunlop RS5 cross-ply tyres would climb and even stop and restart on a 1-in-4 gradient on snow polished and compressed by skiers.

It was too dark for photography, so we resolved to stay the night at Gstaad, putting a rather large hole in our expense funds, and next morning we were back on the ski run with the FF. We were at once surrounded by skiers, amazed to see a car on the slopes, and before anyone could come and order us off we had taken enough pictures to secure an ideal shot as the heading picture for the road test in the 28 March 1968 issue, showing the Jensen on the snow, surrounded by skiers.

Lunchtime found us still lingering at Gstaad, but as we were booked with the car on the flight from Ostend next morning, we eventually had to get going and prove that Switzerland to the Channel port in an afternoon was possible with a little help from what was then one of the fastest and safest saloon cars in the world. In fact we made it easily in time to book into a hotel and have dinner at Ostend, having covered 522 miles in 6½ hours – an average of just over 80mph.

FORTY-SEVEN

Volvo 164

I'd had a little wine with the meal, so I was ordered out of the car to sit on the collapsed back seat of the police Volvo 122S and submit to the breath test

Whenever there's a heavy fall of snow in Britain, as happened in 2009, the usual storm of protest breaks out: 'Why is it that snow brings travel chaos in Britain, while other countries are able to cope so marvellously?' Well, of course, part of the explanation is that if the authorities know that severe wintry weather will descend every year they can justify spending the enormous funds necessary to deal with it. When it's once in about ten years, it's not so easy. But there's another aspect not generally appreciated, and this is that a heavy snowfall settling on the roads, even if they have been salted and gritted, causes chaos in any country. I have witnessed and been involved in such disruption in France, Belgium, Germany, Austria, Switzerland and Sweden; and indeed it was in Sweden that I experienced the worst shambles that snow can throw at us, no matter how we wish to travel.

It happened in February 1970, three years after Sweden had changed the rule of the road to come into line with the Continent and drive on the right. I was allocated to go over to cover the Swedish Rally, accompanied by photographer Ron Easton. 'Don't worry,' I said to Ron, 'it never snows when I go anywhere.' On the rare occasions when it did, I rather enjoyed the challenge it presented, but I was destined to have to eat my words on this occasion.

We flew to Gothenburg where Volvo had kindly provided a 164 for us to use for covering the rally. I said that I would write an article about the car, and did so later, but within a couple of months we had a right-hand drive version delivered to the office for road test. The 164 was a stately, comfortable saloon with 3-litre 6-cylinder engine, having pushrod overhead valve gear and delivering quite a generous output, for those days, of 130bhp. On test, with automatic transmission, the 164 gave a top speed of 107mph and averaged 17.9mpg.

Our left-hand-drive model for the rally coverage had a manual gearbox, and on motorways in Sweden it cruised in relaxed style at around 80mph – a speed that would probably have one sent to prison in Sweden nowadays. Checking the car over in the airport car park I noticed that a folding spade was provided in the boot – all part of the Swedish driver's essential winter equipment.

We drove 150 miles north to Karlstad, which was the headquarters of the rally. It had been chilly in Gothenburg, but as night fell in Karlstad it became bitterly cold. Roads were all snow-covered, but there hadn't been any snow for some days, and the roads tended to have two wheel tracks along each lane, with a shallow track of compressed snow between them like a broad white line.

We soon adapted to the Swedish driver's way of life, which began with getting 'togged up' for the rigours of the early morning. My garb comprised two pairs of socks plus sockets in rubber boots, two pairs of trousers, two thick pullovers and an anorak, plus gloves and the inevitable Swedish hat with let-down ear muffs.

So equipped we would totter out to the car, unlock, pull the mixture control right out (these were days before fuel injection took control of cold-starting fuel control), switch off the heater fan and electric rear window, depress the clutch pedal, and work the starter. The Volvo never failed to start on about the third or fourth try, but the laboured sound of the starter motor made one realise that even a Volvo is not impervious to the drop of battery voltage in severe low temperatures. I fitted a little thermometer on the front bumper, and in the morning it was off the Fahrenheit scale, reading below zero, equivalent to $-22°C$. After a few seconds the mixture control could be pushed in a little way, and we would then leave the engine warming up while we packed photographic gear and luggage in the boot.

Often there had been a light sprinkle of snow during the night, but it was very powdery and could just be dusted off or left to blow away the first time the speed went over about 30mph. The air was so dry that no ice formed on the windscreen overnight.

After a couple of miles the mixture control could be pushed in and the heater be opened up, at first admitting a blast of icy air, but after about 10 miles it would be starting to warm up nicely, and about 10 miles later we would make a quick stop to take off some of the outer garments. Finally, after about three-quarters of an hour, one could begin to think about reducing the heater setting.

All the time each car trailed a cloud of powdery snow blowing about and ours was always seen in the rear mirror, mixed with the vapour from the exhaust.

We checked in at the rally headquarters, and on the Thursday night at 6 p.m. the convoy of 150 starters began to be flagged away at one-minute intervals. Within a couple of hours they were racing and sliding over the first of some forty special stages, most of them little more than forest tracks. Cars that went off the road – which dozens did – usually didn't come to much harm, but they tended to finish buried deep in snow and irretrievable except with heavy lifting equipment.

The first eighteen stages took competitors through twenty-seven hours of tough driving, and then they had Friday night off. It all started again on Saturday morning when they covered the same stages, this time in daylight. There were no end of incidents for an industrious reporter to cover, and I was glad I had been allocated three pages for the report.

The team of three works Ford Escorts driven by Makinen, Andersson and Mikkola suffered damaged sumps over the severe bumps and dips of some of the stages. Movement of the engine was sufficient to bring the sump in contact with the steering rack, and the first sign of trouble for the driver was a high-pitched vibration as the indignant crankshaft bashed it clear again. Then came the loss of oil pressure, which put all three cars out of the rally. Those who were superstitious were quick to note that Timo Makinen, running in car number 13, went out on the 13th stage on Friday 13 February! He was able to coast to the end of the stage where the service car was waiting, but the damage was too severe for a quick repair.

We had an ideal vantage point for the last of the eighteen stages, which was on the Travbana Arena, an oval circuit normally used for pony-trotting races, but now covered with packed snow. Bjorn Waldegaard came round the bend at the north end with his Porsche 911S apparently completely out of control, but in fact it was in a beautifully held slide giving a lasting memory of the Swedish driver's mastery of fast driving on ice.

After a busy day chasing the rally we felt we had deserved a meal – Ron had been pleading for it for some hours – and we found a restaurant in town, but I was shocked at the poor quality of the food and the terribly slow service. On the way back to the hotel I was driving slowly so as not to miss the entrance to the hotel, which was simply an unmarked hole in the snow bank, and pulled in to let the car behind go past. Immediately a hand came out of the side window waving a *'Polis'* sign.

Swedish police are apparently ready for any driver they stop to attempt to make a run for it, and we had barely come to rest when one of the policemen was at the door. There was no language problem, of course, since anyone in any responsible position in Sweden speaks good English. We went through the usual rigmarole: who were we, whose car was it, where's your licence, and then the key question: have you had anything to drink.

I was a bit worried about this, because I'd had a little wine with the meal, so I was ordered out of the car to sit on the collapsed back seat of the police Volvo 122S and submit to the breath test – still a novelty in Europe and not yet introduced in Britain. It was a relief to see that the crystals didn't change colour at all – you couldn't tell the difference from one of the new ones. We then had an interesting conversation in which I learned that the Swedish driver over the limit would be sent off to a kind of labour camp and have to pay a stiff fine as well. The foreign driver would be taken straight to jail, have to pay what was then a horrendous fine of about £60, and be escorted to the airport with the details endorsed in the passport.

It remained bitterly cold next day but still there was no snow. Ron took a picture of a sign in the town, which read *Dam Friesering*, and said it was very appropriate. It meant, of course, ladies' hairdressing! Everyone was commenting that it had been a very fast rally due to the snow-free conditions. 'I told you,' I said to Ron, 'it never snows when I go anywhere.'

There were more excitements on the rally next day, and we were well placed to see Svensson's Saab come over a rise too fast, mount the snow bank, roll right over and then come to rest on its side. At least a gallon of petrol poured out, probably from the breather, but fortunately there was no spark to ignite it. The co-driver climbed out of the window, but Svensson remained inside while the British journalist and photographer, helped by the co-driver and another spectator, put it back on its wheels. He restarted the engine and was all set to press on, but his steering was completely broken. The steering wheel spun round uselessly.

It was good to see the Swedish-entered Triumph team doing well. Determination was shown by one of the Triumph drivers, who rolled his 2.5PI but managed to get it back on its wheels and continued for 20 miles through the bitter cold with no windscreen and having to hold the door closed. Frozen condensation in the fuel lines stopped another of the Triumphs, and mechanics had to heat the pipes and fuel tank with hot water. Watching, I made the cheerful suggestion: 'Why don't you use a blow-torch?' The resulting glare told me without words, we are not amused.

Waldegaard with the Porsche 911S won the rally for the third time in succession, and the Saab V4 of Stig Blomqvist was second. Triumph won the team prize.

Next day, unable to find another one, we went back to the same restaurant in the evening and this time I thought I had better play safe and have only one carafe of wine. I then realised that the carafe was nearly all glass, and that the contents scarcely filled a glass, so it was not surprising that, taken with a meal spread over about two hours due to the rotten service, it hadn't registered on the police breathalyser.

I worked late into the night and again on Sunday morning typing the rally report and then Ron and I went out to take some pictures of the 164. Sweden is not very good for backgrounds because it's all either trees or built up, and everywhere was snow-covered, but we were taking shots of the Volvo in front of an attractive house when suddenly another Volvo 122S with the now-familiar word *Polis* on the side pulled up. 'Why,' they asked, 'are you taking pictures of a policeman's house?' I responded that I had no idea it was a policeman's house and we were just getting scenic pictures of the car borrowed from Volvo. Rather grudgingly, after inspecting our press passes, they were convinced. I decided I would not like to fall foul of the Swedish police.

With everything done, results list typed out, and Ron happy with his pictures, we had a final breakfast in the hotel on the Monday morning, before our return flight to Heathrow. Suddenly we noticed that it had started snowing. 'It would do that, now that the rally's over,' I commented, and we agreed that we had better get going to the airport, and we allowed half an hour for the short journey that had previously taken only fifteen minutes.

A huge covering of snow had to be cleared off the Volvo before we could move it, but once we set off the conditions were appalling. Traffic had already built up and was proceeding at a crawl, and coming to rest on the slightest incline as lorries tried to find some grip. The Volvo's heated back window couldn't cope, snow built up on the side windows, and it was extremely difficult to tell in the white confusion what was road and what was snow bank.

About half an hour after our flight was due to have left we did a magnificent slide into a parking space, cleared all our kit out of the 164 and rushed in to hand the key to the Avis desk as agreed. 'No need to hurry,' we were told. 'All flights are delayed.'

We then had a most frustrating day. I kept threatening to hire a car and drive to an airport that was open, but it would have meant crossing the ferry from Helsingborg to Helsinger and going down to Copenhagen. All the time we were reassured that flights would be leaving soon. Then suddenly there was an announcement that bookings were being taken on an aircraft that would depart in half an hour. Never mind where it was going to, there was a terrific scrum to try to get a place on it. We didn't join the struggle, thinking that all flights would be going soon although the blanket of snow was still descending relentlessly.

Later, we heard the aircraft engines starting up, and we could see the amber flashing lights of two snow ploughs battling along the runway. Their drivers were obviously in radio contact, because simultaneously they turned off, and a cloud of snow went up as they ploughed off into the snow bank, and then the aircraft was zooming along the runway. Every person in the departure lounge – including us, I am ashamed to say – was crammed against the windows, not to miss the crash if it happened. But it didn't, and that brave pilot made it safely into the air.

We'll be next, we thought, but no, the news was that we were to be taken by coach to Gothenburg station and onwards by train, but it didn't happen. We sat for two hours in the coach with engine and wipers going, listening to endless reports over the radio in Swedish about the traffic conditions, windows streaming condensation and the time for our 5.40 p.m. train long past. 'Don't worry,' we were told, 'you'll be taken to a nice hotel for dinner and then we'll be able to fly you out tomorrow.' The traffic was as complete a shambles as ever seen in Britain, with the fifteen-minute journey taking nearly two hours.

I had been in touch with the office repeatedly and they were screaming for the rally report, due to go to press next day. While we had dinner, an efficient girl at the hotel sent it all over by telex, and I was most impressed later to see how few mistakes she had made.

The real irony of the situation, though, was that the hotel they chose to take us to was the very same one we had left ten hours earlier!

FORTY-EIGHT

NSU Ro80

'Well, Stuart,' asked Harry Mundy, 'what's your erudite opinion of the Wankel engine now you've been running one for – how long is it?'

On that long and sometimes rather fraught launch of the Audi 100 in Germany in 1968, in the very amiable company of Press Officer Erik Johnson, we discussed the idea that Mercedes-Benz might like to provide an Audi 100 for long-term test by *Autocar*. Erik had been very pleased with the results of the Audi Super 90, which had preceded it as my long-term test car, and was very receptive to the idea, but it was a long time in coming. I finally received my new Audi 100 in 1971 and began all the elaborate procedures of checking delivery condition and so on, which always started any long-term test. But only a few weeks later came the 'coup' when the Shoreham-based concessionaires for NSU laid claim to the Audi franchise.

Immediately, Mercedes-Benz were obliged to remove all Audi sales material from their Brentford showrooms and, like being caught up in a hostile takeover, the 100, which I had run for only a few weeks, had to be returned. It was very humiliating for all concerned, and left me without a permanent car – not that there was ever any shortage of test cars at the office, but it was still rather a nuisance. A short time later, however, there was a friendly call from the newly formed Audi-NSU (GB) Ltd saying that they felt I had been rather let down, and what they would really like to do would be to supply one of the new Ro80s on extended loan so that we could gain experience of the latest version of the Wankel rotary engine.

I had some misgivings about running another Wankel-powered car, remembering the problems experienced with that first single-rotor unit in the Spider, but the Ro80 was a much more advanced car with twin-rotor engine installed in a very attractively designed saloon. Nearly forty years later my friend and colleague Paul Harris, editor of *Audi Driver* magazine for which I contributed a lot of work, purchased a very well-preserved example of the Ro80 and it brought back many memories to sit in one of these spacious and attractive cars again. Sadly Paul died of cancer in July 2015.

The example that I was to run was taken over on 22 March 1971, already with 1,651 miles recorded, and only two days later I set off in it to drive to the NSU and Audi factories in Germany to research a big Audi-NSU supplement for *Autocar*. It was arranged that their publicity chief, whose name I am pleased to say I don't remember, but we'll call him Mr Bean, would come with me to show me round, and my erstwhile photographer Peter Cramer came along to do the pictures. A day or two before departure, Bean rang to ask if his son could come along with us for the ride. The boy was about 10 or 11, and although I wasn't too pleased about it, I could hardly decline since NSU were picking up all the expenses.

We had little trouble with the Ro80 on this 1,000-mile journey except for a bad wind whistle from the passenger door, and a trace of misfiring, which developed on the return journey. I was not to know then that misfiring was to be one of the problems of the Ro80. But there was no end of trouble with the inadequate plans of Mr Bean.

On this first long journey I came to like the Ro80 very much indeed, appreciating the excellent visibility afforded by its deep windscreen and narrow screen pillars – something you don't get on any car these days – and the impressive stability, ride comfort and ventilation. It took the substantial load, which included enough luggage for the heavyweight Mr Bean and his son to have sufficed for a month's holiday, very well indeed.

The first bad misunderstanding happened when we arrived at Neckarsulm, where the twin-rotor Wankel engine was being built and the Ro80 assembled. There was special interest in the Wankel concerning its possibilities for mechanical assembly, and we were supposed to take pictures of every stage of the process. So it was not very pleasing news to learn that Bean had not done his homework, and the factory was closed for a holiday.

'Never mind,' said Bean, 'it's time for lunch anyway. We'll get them to send you some pictures.' Bean loved his food, as we were already discovering. But we continued on to Ingolstadt where I had some instructive interviews with Audi personnel about the future arrangements now that Audi and NSU were merged.

On the *Autobahn* north from Frankfurt we ran into torrential rain. There was also a strong wind, and it was dark, but the lamps were very effective and I was most impressed by the feeling of security the car gave. I felt we were well equipped to keep out of trouble if the Germans, hurrying home after work, had the inevitable motorway pile-up, but we cruised on to Cologne without incident. Mr Bean made it abundantly plain that he didn't appreciate being overtaken by other cars, but Peter kindly calmed him down with words to the effect that he could leave it to me to get us there in one piece and that I would go fast only when it was safe to do so.

What I also did not discover until the last day of the trip was that Bean knew that he had already been given the sack, and this task was to be his last assignment. He was determined to make NSU pay dearly, so we were put up in the best hotel in Cologne on the way back, and given top-class meals and wine. Next day he kept marching off with his son round the beautiful Cologne shopping centre and returning with armfuls of luxurious silver purchases to be stowed away in the boot, and I wondered whether these, too, were going down on his expenses as 'entertaining those very expensive *Autocar* people'. Customs were still tight at Dover in those days, and I was a bit shocked when he calmly put the 'nothing to declare' sign up on the windscreen. If we had been stopped and searched they might well have confiscated the car, but I felt I could claim ignorance of his extravagant purchases, and mercifully we were just waved through. Apart from an increasing tendency for the engine to misfire, we had an uneventful journey back to London where we were pleased to see the back of Mr Bean with all his expensive shopping.

Suspension on the Ro80 was by MacPherson struts at the front, with trailing arms and struts at the rear, and the engine lay in line ahead of the front wheels, which took the drive and had inboard disc brakes. I thought this arrangement of having

NSU's Ro80 was a very futuristic car but was doomed by the inefficiency and unreliability of its Wankel rotary engine. It is seen here on the left, alongside the excellent Opel Commodore GS Coupé that replaced it.

the front brakes well away from the wheels was very sensible; at least there was never any problem of brake dust on the wheels, and drive shafts that could take the engine torque were well able to cope with braking loads as well.

NSU had been well aware of the inherent roughness of the Wankel engine at low revs, in contrast to its legendary smoothness at high revs, and to counter this the car was available only with the semi-automatic transmission, which was popular at the time. It had both clutch and torque converter, with a three-speed manual gearbox but no clutch pedal. A micro-switch in the top of the gear-lever knob actuated a clutch release servo in response to the lightest touch. This would catch out the practice of many drivers, to go along with one hand on the wheel and the other resting on the gear lever. Do that, and the clutch would operate and the engine rev furiously.

Official recommendation for town driving was to leave the gear in second, but getaway was very slow like that and I always drove it completely as a manual car except that I would select first gear in advance at traffic halts and hold the car back with a light touch on the brakes until ready for the off.

What used to fox many drivers was that it seemed odd to change gear without pushing a clutch pedal down, so they used to press the brake pedal instead! Considering how many drivers, unfamiliar with the Ro80, would set off from traffic lights and then do a tyre-shrieking crash stop as they trod on the brake pedal when going from first to second, it is remarkable that the Ro80 was never clouted in the back. With familiarity, though, this was no problem and I used to brake with the left foot, as I do with all automatics, yet never used the brake pedal in error.

After running this car for six weeks, it was booked to go into the NSU depot at Shoreham to see if they could do anything about the misfiring and an increasingly worrying problem, the excessive smoking from the exhaust when the engine was cold. I also asked for the nearside windscreen wiper to be replaced as it had a habit of coming adrift. Later, I wrote in my notebook 'Never seen again'. This referred not to the wiper, but to the whole car!

No explanation was given, but I was simply advised that a new car was being supplied and I never did find out what had gone wrong with the previous one. The newcomer, in what I thought was a horrid orange colour, arrived on 2 July 1971. An improvement was that the left door fitted properly, eliminating the bad wind roar that the other one had suffered, but it offset this with a number of new irritating faults, which the earlier car didn't have, such as a slightly loose driving seat, a bad flat spot in acceleration response, and very stiff steering. ZF power-assisted steering was standard so this was a surprising weak point. On top of it all, the cold-start smoking was as bad as with the previous car. I used to be quite ashamed when driving off in the morning, to see in the mirror the clouds of blue haze pouring out behind.

After 1,400 miles the clutch started to remain engaged. This wasn't as bad a problem as on an ordinary manual gearbox car, and it was still possible to drive provided one remembered to knock the gear lever into neutral before coming to rest. If it was left in third (top gear on this three-speed unit) the only way to get out of gear was to stop the engine first.

Normand Continental were the NSU dealers for London, and the Ro80 went to them for numerous attentions. They rectified the heavy steering and fitted a new clutch at 2,124 miles. The flat spot remained, as did the smoking.

In due course I made a new date to take the car to Shoreham where the excellent engineer Mike Hoppis said he would have a look at it. He meticulously stripped down the formidable big Solex carburettors, used a forceps to extract two tiny springs, and measured them. Finding that they were 8mm long, he stretched them slightly, making them 9mm, and like magic the flat spot was cured, but sadly not so the cold-start smoking. We were burning oil at the rate of a pint every 400 miles. I used to dread being stuck in slow traffic because this could result in oiling up one of the sparking plugs, and once this had happened it would never clear of its own accord in the way a performance engine can 'blow the smuts out' and be brought back on full song when given a blast at high revs. With the Ro80 engine, the only solution to an oiled plug was to change it.

Once a plug had oiled, the car became almost undriveable, with power reduced to about 30 per cent of normal. I always carried spare plugs and the necessary articulated spanner, and changed them as a pair. With practice, I was able to do it in about three minutes. After sand blasting, they were re-usable, which was as well since new ones cost £3.84 for a pair, at a time when ordinary piston-engine sparking plugs were about 30p each.

Despite its problems, the Ro80 was a great long-journey car, and I remember a lovely run up to Glasgow to cover the 1971 Scottish Motor Show when the car showed its ability to cruise at 80–85mph with a wonderfully low level of mechanical noise and near total absence of vibration.

As mileage increased, so the problems seemed to diminish, or perhaps it was that I had learned more about how to rectify them, such as the ease with which one could unscrew the slow-running jets, blow them through and refit them in a couple of minutes, getting a better tickover. But in June 1972, with the car now nearly a year old and 20,000 miles on the clock, I began to notice a knock from the engine when it was pulling.

By chance, NSU gave a press conference in London to explain all the improvements that had been made to the Ro80 to make it more reliable. They had now overcome all the problems, they assured us, including reducing the smoking when cold. The engineer Mike Hoppis was there, and I asked him to come down to the basement car park and listen to the noise my engine was making. He diagnosed straight away that it had a bearing failure.

Another 240 miles had been covered by the time I took the car down to Shoreham where it had been arranged that we would take the engine out and go through a complete strip-down, with photographic coverage. By then, the knock had become very bad, and I had to take the last few miles extremely gently.

It took just over an hour to get the engine out of the car, and a further hour saw it stripped down to the centre plate. When the rotor was revealed, a piece of metal swarf was spotted, which had broken off the failed bearing. It was found that the crankshaft was of the earlier type; a subsequent modification had been made to increase the oil flow to the bearing and avoid this failure.

It was all put together again, with new rotor seals, although the ones removed were still within production tolerances for a new engine, and I drove it home the same night enjoying the advantage of the Wankel engine that, even when new, no running-in was needed.

Apart from some details like a new front wheel bearing at 25,000 miles, and the usual problems of blocked carburettor jets and the disgraceful smoke after cold starting, the Ro80 served well until November 1972 when, with a mileage of 26,286, it was felt that we had no more to learn about the Wankel engine, and the car was handed back gratefully to NSU. In its place I took over an Opel Commodore, and it was certainly good to drive without being ashamed of the pollution every time I looked in the mirror soon after a cold start.

The Ro80 was certainly a wonderful test bed for the engine, making the best of its advantages of smoothness at speed, compactness, and low weight. It was a very safe, comfortable and enjoyable car to drive, with the good balance and handling owing much to the lightness of the engine. But the engine let the car down with heavy fuel and oil consumption in relation to the performance.

At the launch of the Jaguar XJ V12, the late Harry Mundy, who had previously been the magazine's technical editor before moving on to Jaguar as engineer in charge of power units, asked solemnly: 'Well, Stuart, what's your erudite opinion of the Wankel engine now you've been running one for – how long is it?'

'Four years, on and off,' I replied, and I had to add: 'I'm afraid it hasn't come up to the initial high expectations. The disadvantages of smelly exhaust, disappointing economy, lumpy low-speed running and lack of bottom-end torque far outweigh the advantages of compactness, low weight and smoothness at high speeds.'

Harry was always argumentative, but this was one of relatively few occasions when I heard him reply: 'I agree.'

FORTY-NINE

FORD FIESTA AND ESCORT, AUDI 100

Ford's managing director said he was anxious to flag us away, as he had a
board meeting starting at 9 a.m. Rather cheekily I commented, 'Don't worry,
sir, I'm sure they won't start without you!'

It all started with a casual discussion in the office. We had arranged for our staff
Austin Princess 1800 to be converted to run on LPG (liquefied petroleum gas) to
explore the new idea of running cars on gas instead of petrol. It had a 15-gallon
LPG tank in the boot, and the Princess already had a large 16-gallon petrol tank.
With both fuels it would surely run 'forever and a day' without running out. 'Why,
yes,' someone commented, 'it would probably go all the way from Land's End to
John o' Groats.' The idea sparked interest, so with my colleague Martin Lewis and
photographer Peter Cramer, we set off for Land's End on a sunny day in 1976.

Ford Managing Director Roger Humm ready to flag the Fiesta away from the
Brentwood HQ on its way to Berlin, which was reached for £8 worth of fuel.

In advance we had arranged sponsorship involving all the firms who had anything to do with the construction of the Princess, including its tyres and the LPG conversion. So much per mile from Inverness was the request, and when the car reached Groats early next morning, having gone all the way for 860 miles through the night without refuelling, we raised £1,006 for charities, divided between the Graham Hill memorial fund and the Motor Industry Benevolent Fund (BEN).

More economy assignments followed, and then in 1984 when the new Audi 100 was launched with a huge 17.6-gallon fuel tank, I reckoned we at last had a car that could cover the end-to-end distance in standard form. My son Bruce was keen to come along as navigator, and the RAC sent its engineer Bob Proctor down to Penzance, where we met him at the station, to act as observer. We had lovely weather for the run, and the Audi made it easily, to such extent that we determined to head back south, still driving for economy, until it ran out. This happened just short of Falkirk, and the RAC confirmed that we had covered 1,150.3 miles at 51.1mph and fuel consumption of 59.27mpg. After a lot of persuading, the editors of the *Guinness Book of Records* agreed to accept it as an official record for the longest distance travelled by a standard production car without refuelling.

Only afterwards did I learn that Paul Buckett, who was then press officer for Citroën, was planning to try to achieve this with a CX DTR, and we had 'spiked his guns'. However, three years later I was asked by Citroën to see if the big CX model could beat the Audi's figure. This time, my daughter Rachel joined us with the

Escorts lined up and waiting for the early morning start on Westminster Bridge.

RAC observer, and the Lucas engineers were supporting the effort because the car was fitted with their diesel fuel-injection system called Epic. It certainly proved its worth, reaching John o' Groats with plenty of fuel left at an average consumption of 63.9mpg, although at lower speed than the Audi 100, averaging 42.6mph.

Ford was next on the economy idea, and in 1988 wanted to show that its latest Fiesta 1.6 diesel could go from their Brentwood headquarters to Berlin, where they also have a factory, at low cost on fuel. The RAC sent engineer Richard Waterhouse to be official observer. We were to be flagged away by the managing director of Ford GB, Roger Humm. As we were making our final checks he was anxious for us to get under way, and said that he had a board meeting starting at 9 a.m. Rather cheekily I commented: 'Don't worry, sir, I'm sure they won't start without you!'

My little joke evidently didn't upset the MD, because the following year Roger Humm awarded me a special environmental award as part of the Segrave Trophy, which Ford supports, for 1989.

We crossed the Channel on the midday ferry from Harwich to the Hook, and spent the night in Holland. Next morning we were away promptly and were soon joining the queue at the Helmstedt checkpoint for the humiliating business of handing over passports and seeing them disappear in a box on the little conveyor belt system to take them to the immigration official so that he had time to check identity details before our turn in the queue about an hour later.

From then on it was easy going to Checkpoint Charlie and back into the west, where Richard Waterhouse supervised the careful refilling of the Fiesta's tank. It had not quite made 90mpg, but 89.1 was near enough after 513 miles, and Ford was delighted by the news that the fuel cost had been only £8. They made a lot of use of this in subsequent advertising, and in advance a competition had been arranged with *Practical Motorist* and *ITV Oracle*, offering the Fiesta used for the run as the first prize for the nearest guess at the car's mpg figure for the distance. Entries closed, of course, before the finish. The car was won by K.C. Peach of Solihull, and handed over at the Birmingham Motor Show. The runner-up received a cheque from Shell to cover the cost of the amount of fuel that would take the Fiesta 30,000 miles. I don't think they would do that these days!

We took the Fiesta to the Berlin Wall, and pictures, now somewhat historic since the wall came down, were taken with the graffiti-laden wall in the background (see color section).

A different kind of economy venture came in 1991 when I was asked by Ford to organise an economy run from London to Moscow.

It was a great event, starting with a prelim drive in a Ford Sierra with two Ford mechanics to plot the route and draw up route instructions, which I did on a tape recorder and then keyed on to a computer in the evenings. I left the Ford team at Moscow and flew back ready for the great event in July 1991, which was sponsored by Ford in conjunction with Saga.

Ready for the start from John o' Groats on Sunday morning, the
Audi 100 2.5 had been filled to the brim and everything was reset.

Twelve competitors had been carefully selected by eliminating contests, and we
had six Ford Escort Ghias with 1.8-litre diesel engines, plus two back-up cars, one
of which was for me to drive. We covered 1,860 miles over six days, at the end of
which everyone was flown home and motoring writers were flown out to bring the
cars back on a less-controlled economy drive. Best result by the Saga team was that
of Alf Charlton, who had previously competed in Mobil Economy Runs, but the mpg
figures were somewhat distorted by the chaotic refuelling conditions on the way.

After all the fuss the *Guinness Book of Records* people had made before they would accept that my 1984 run with the Audi 100 was an official record for the longest distance travelled without refuelling, I was dismayed to find that it had been displaced by some Australians driving a Toyota fitted with an optional extra fuel tank. So when the new Audi 100 TDI with 5-cylinder 2½-litre turbo diesel engine was launched, I was determined to try to get the record back.

Could we do the end-to-end trip twice on a tankful, I wondered? Probably not, but we would have a go, and Audi was enthusiastic about the attempt. I suggested that we should do it in reverse order, starting at Groats, going to Land's End and then back again, and the Audi 100 TDI was delivered by low-loader to Inverness airport, to which I flew with the long-suffering Bob Proctor as RAC observer. We set off early on a Sunday in July 1992, but ran into terrible weather in the Glasgow area. When we stopped at my favourite hotel, the Auchen Castle, I did some calculations. The industrious fuel expert Peter de Nayer had fitted the car with a fuel flow meter, so we knew exactly how much diesel had gone through, and the result was disappointing. I realised that I would have to squeeze the utmost economy out of the Audi to achieve the target.

Next day we trickled quietly on to Plymouth, where we enjoyed a quick meal stop before pressing on to Land's End and arrived at the hotel at 11 p.m. Despite our late arrival, the patient RAC observer was ready for the off at 6 a.m. next morning. It was late evening when a loud cheer from Bob announced that we had done it – beaten the twin-tank Australians, and we were still running although the fuel warning light had been on for three hours!

When the Audi finally came to a stop, with the fuel meter clicking like mad as air went through the system, we were back in Scotland on the A74 at what was until recently a little-known village called Lockerbie. Three years earlier, in December 1988, the sabotaged airliner came down at exactly that spot. The RAC man produced his measuring equipment and established that we had covered 1,338.1 miles at average fuel consumption of 75.9mpg, and speed overall was 37.9mph. Accepting the RAC's certificate, by coincidence Trial No. 1000, the Guinness people recognised this as a new record for the longest distance travelled without refueling.

Many more fuel-stretching efforts and economy-driving records followed, and are listed in the Appendix at the end of this book. Many of them were sponsored by Lucas and their energetic marketing manager, Don Hiett, in a vigorous bid to promote the company's Epic diesel-injection system. I also became involved in more fuel-economy competitions when I was appointed clerk of the course for the *Fleet World* contest called the MPG Marathon in 2000–2002. It involved a lot of time and hard work plotting the routes and the detailed route instructions, but it was all a lot of fun and I enjoyed taking the competitors over parts of the country many of them had never seen before.

FIFTY

ROLLS-ROYCE SILVER SHADOW

I reckoned we could just squeeze the Rolls through between the trees at one point, albeit at a frightening angle

As our tenth wedding anniversary drew near in 1972, hints were dropped by my wife, Jennetta, that something very special was required to mark the occasion, and there was no question of being allowed to forget this important celebration. In fact, as the date approached, I had clear plans for the event because just by chance the latest version of the Rolls-Royce Silver Shadow was due for road test that very week, and I put my name down, being the one member of the road-test team anxious to be allocated this one.

It was all kept very secret, and Granny, living near Nuneaton, was briefed in great confidence to expect arrival of the two children and the dog to be looked after for five days. Unfortunately, my secretary unwittingly let the cat out of the bag by leaving a message at home to please tell Stuart that 'the green card for the Rolls has arrived'. Those were the days when you needed that important insurance document to take a car abroad, and one benefit of the 70mph speed limit introduced seven years earlier was that *Autocar* had a special budget for taking high-performance road-test cars to the Continent for maximum-speed testing. The Silver Shadow, expected to do over 110mph, was definitely in the permitted category. A few days sloshing about in luxury in Belgium, Holland and Germany was going to be our way of celebrating the great tenth anniversary on 25 August 1972.

On the previous day, Thursday, we set off to drive north up the M1 to deliver the children, but as we neared what used to be called the Blue Boar service area at Watford Gap, traffic came to a standstill. Long motorway hold-ups were still quite rare in the 1970s, so after we had stood for half an hour with the engine off it became evident that there must have been a substantial accident. A man tapped on the window and asked me to move the Shadow forward a little so that he could squeeze his truck out on to the hard shoulder and escape.

'You shouldn't do that, you know,' I advised. 'The police will catch you.' But I obliged, he made his escape, and half an hour later I followed suit. After 2 miles on the hard shoulder, and an illegal exit from the service area on to the A5, we arrived at Granny's much later than expected. No time for the offered cup of tea – we had a hovercraft to catch at Ramsgate, so we hurried on our way. From where we left the motorway to the grandparental home at Sharnford and back was 50 miles, but when we rejoined the M1 heading south, the block of stationary traffic on the northbound carriageway remained solid. We saw the same car with two canoes on the roof, and another distinctive vehicle, which had been alongside us, still in the same positions, so our naughty diversion had been worthwhile. Later we learned that the accident had been very bad indeed, with a massive acid spillage in which a woman fell over and died from horrific acid burns, and the carriageway remained closed for many hours.

What I had forgotten when making the plans was that Jennetta's passport, new on 25 August 1962, and handed over after the wedding ceremony, had expired on 24 August 1972. Never mind, I thought, no one will notice, but they did. At the French border into Belgium we explained what had happened, and the customs officer smiled knowingly, said it was *romantique* and let us through. From Belgium we crossed into Holland, and here again the expired date was noticed but the explanation was accepted. We spent the night in Amsterdam, did a boat tour having left the Silver Shadow with its front wheels right on the edge of one of the canals with the front overhanging to accommodate its length, and took advantage of a Dutch motorway with little traffic and (in those days) no speed limits to knock off the essential high-speed test runs before heading down to Germany.

The Silver Shadow was proving superbly comfortable and luxurious, and Jennetta did not mind playing the part of road-test observer while we did the high-speed

The Silver Shadow was the first Rolls-Royce with unitary construction, disc brakes and self-levelling suspension, but even in 1972 it still had vague steering. (Warren Allport)

acceleration tests (everything above 70mph) and the maximum-speed runs. It reached 119mph in one direction, and gave an average top speed of 117. Fuel consumption was running at 12.4mpg, but who cared in 1972?

We had enjoyed a pleasant time in Holland and spent the night at a lovely hotel right on the edge of the Rhine where we could see the barges going along from the bedroom window, but now we planned a little excursion farther down the Rhine, in Germany.

Anticipating trouble at the border I chose a minor road crossing, but here it was all very different. The lapsed date in the passport was spotted, and we were commanded to leave the car and go into the office to explain the problem to the chief of police. I heard the conversation going on in the inner office, and the senior policeman said: 'Spricht er Deutsch?' [Does he speak German?]

'Ja, aber schlecht.' [Yes, but badly]

At this I piped up loudly from the outer office: 'Aber nicht so schlecht dass er nicht verstehen kann.' [But not so badly that he can't understand!]

The police chief then emerged from the office holding the rogue passport and began a long school-masterly ticking-off that we were trying to travel with an obsolete passport. Turning to my wife he then said in good English: 'You will be stateless; no country will have you. You must remain here in Holland while your husband goes to Düsseldorf to get the passport renewed at the consul's office.'

We returned to the Silver Shadow, made a U-turn and pondered what to do. Going to Düsseldorf was ridiculous. I began to wonder if there might be another unmanned way across. We followed one or two tiny lanes and found a place where there was a wood with trees well apart. The barbed wire barriers of thirty years earlier had long since been removed, and I reckoned we could just squeeze the Rolls through between the trees at one point, albeit at a frightening angle. Unfortunately it was not to be. If the car had been 4in lower we could have made it, but a substantial branch was just too low.

'Well, you'll have to walk through and wait for me,' I said, and left Jennetta there as I drove back to the frontier and passed through without difficulty. But on the other side the roads were very different and I had a job to find the point where we had tried to get through the wood. In the end, there she was, having walked some way from the wood, and we were together again.

Now unofficially in Germany we meandered pleasantly along the road parallel to the Rhine and stopped for the night at Bad Breisig in a pleasant hotel, which turned out to be a health resort full of old ladies there to take the waters. We parked the car in the dark and walked towards the hotel entrance where a man was standing outside under the hotel lights. As we approached, his mouth opened and I guessed what he was going to say: 'You've left the lights on in your car,' but he didn't say a word and I knew that they had switched themselves off. Common on many cars these days, the 7-second delay before the courtesy lights went out was a novel refinement of the Silver Shadow.

Next day we toured around more, and then made our way back by *Autobahn* to Holland and at the much busier frontier post the out-of-date passport slipped through unnoticed. A magnificent dinner at my favourite restaurant, the De Ridderhof at Maassluis, was followed by the night crossing from the Hook to Harwich, which was also the route I most liked to take once the car air ferries ceased operations, since it saved on time and reduced the expenses. It concluded a memorable and thoroughly enjoyable anniversary celebration.

Normally road-test cars were delivered to and collected from our offices at Waterloo, but I opted to take the Silver Shadow back to Crewe, and arranged for the next test car to be delivered there so that I wouldn't have to suffer the indignity of a train journey back to London. As soon as I arrived, I was told: 'Mr Plastow would like to see you.'

David Plastow, now Sir David, was managing director of Rolls-Royce, and later of the Vickers Engineering Group, which owned the company. He met me in his grand office, and after greetings sat back in his chair with his hands clasped behind his neck and said: 'What's wrong with our cars?'

I was quite taken aback, and replied meekly: 'Who said there was anything wrong with them?' But then I took the opportunity to say what I really thought, and responded: 'Well, if you really want me to be frank, I have to say that the steering is absolutely frightful. There's anything up to half a turn of the wheel that does nothing, and you can drive like an American film star, constantly jogging the wheel to left and right while the car proceeds straight. It needs to be replaced with a rack-and-pinion system. In my experience of testing all these cars, whenever it's rack and pinion it's always precise;' the Silver Shadow still used a recirculating ball system.

I went on to suggest some other possible improvements: that the appearance would be enhanced by making the wipers hide from view when not in use, that there should be a rev counter, and that the seats should give more lateral support.

Plastow listened with keen interest to my comments, but none of the changes I mentioned ever came to fruition until after four more years when the Silver Shadow II was introduced in February 1977, and one of the most significant changes was that it now had rack-and-pinion steering. I'm sure that this important design improvement would have happened anyway, but perhaps that conversation at the top in 1972 helped to move things in the right direction, resulting in a car that was much more pleasant – and safer – to drive.

LAMBORGHINI MIURA AND MERCEDES-BENZ 280SL

≡ They had told us it should do 170, and they weren't talking kilometres

As I hope these chapters have revealed, my twenty-six years on the staff of *Autocar*, and subsequent time as a freelance motoring writer, provided some magnificent motoring, and among the richest memories was a wonderful journey to Italy in June 1970. I was to drive out with a colleague in the Mercedes-Benz 280SL that we had on an extended loan, and carry out the full road test on that fabulous sports car, the Lamborghini Miura. The Mercedes had been provided absolutely new on a six-week assessment, and we had to do the very tediously slow running-in required for the first 600 miles. By the time we took it to Italy it had done 6,000 miles. We packed all the test and photographic equipment into the Mercedes, removed and stowed its hardtop, and trickled quietly out of the firm's car park on a sunny afternoon, destination Bologna.

Adding interest to the journey, we plotted a fascinating route through Switzerland and stopped for the night at a hotel in Interlaken where I knew that my father and stepmother were enjoying a couple of weeks' holiday, and surprised them by turning up at their table for dinner.

The drive across Switzerland in beautiful sunshine with the hood of the Mercedes neatly folded away was absolutely magnificent, but I was not entirely pleased with the 280SL. It was at a time when all Mercedes-Benz cars were tending to be too low-geared, which surprised me in view of their excellent *Autobahn* network and their customarily high cruising speeds. The 280SL had only a four-speed automatic transmission – the Daimler-Benz system with fluid coupling. It was not the best of automatics, and the car speed at 1,000rpm was ridiculously low at 18.6mph, which was much the same as my old 1949 Vauxhall Velox. It meant that when cruising at 90mph, the 6-cylinder engine was storming away at nearly 5,000rpm, and the maximum speed of 121mph was achieved with the engine turning at 6,500rpm, well over its power peak.

It also meant that it walloped through quite a lot of fuel, though one didn't worry much about that in 1970, before the second big oil crisis, and the overall 19mpg consumption didn't delay us too much with fuel stops thanks to the generous 18-gallon (82-litre) capacity of the fuel tank.

We made very quick time to Bologna where we met the very helpful English chief engineer, Bob Wallace, and transferred our test equipment and personal

Mercedes-Benz 280SL in a picture taken by my late father just as we were about to leave for Bologna after a night at Interlaken.

possessions, squeezing them into every available bit of space in the Miura. We had to accommodate that incredibly awkward fifth wheel, like a big auto cycle wheel with fixing bracket to drive the electric speedometer, and there was the fuel meter as well, to measure constant speed consumption up to 140mph. Our dead accurate electric speedometer was calibrated to only 140mph, so for speeds above that we were going to have to rely on stopwatch timing and rev counter readings. We didn't have satellites and electronic speed displays in those days.

We spent the night at Bologna, which was perhaps a mistake because when we ventured out at 4.30 next morning we had no experience of driving the car, but we wanted to get that very high maximum speed in the bag while the roads were still devoid of traffic. Several high speed runs were made, showing that 160mph was quite quickly attainable, but finding an adequate straight to be able to keep the foot down long enough to be sure that maximum speed had been reached was not easy.

One rather alarming moment came when I suddenly found myself hurtling towards one of those very tight bends that often take one by surprise on the *autostrada*, and when I took my foot abruptly off the accelerator the sudden torque reversal sent the mid-engined Miura into a terrifying snake. I think that if I had touched the brakes the car would have spun, but after a few seconds it sorted itself out, by which time all that Armco at the bend was getting frighteningly near, and what a lot of distance it takes to bring the speed down from the upper 160s!

By now, the appearance of occasional early morning traffic was beginning to make any further attempts at such a high maximum speed too hazardous, so we concentrated on getting the acceleration testing done, but with such an enormous span of revs from the fabulous V12 engine, testing seemed to go on forever. As the day warmed up, it became almost unbearably hot inside the Miura, since the ventilation seemed to depend on having the windows open, and we had to keep them closed to avoid spoiling the aerodynamics. .

Up and down the *autostrada* we went, recording such times as fourth gear, 120 to 140mph in 8 seconds, and 100 to 120 in third in 5.8 seconds. Each time as the car came to rest for the figures to be written down, both doors were flung open like a couple of air brakes, to let in some cool air.

At last, it was all over. We had fitted the fuel meter and done those irritating fuel consumption figures, showing that the Miura went from 23.4mpg at 30mph to 12.1mpg at a constant 140mph, and the brake tests were also completed. We returned to our hotel for baths and lunch in lieu of the breakfast we had missed, and settled on a plan of campaign. It was Friday, and my colleague was keen to go to the island of Elba where a girlfriend was receptionist at some tourist villas and would be able to find us a room for the night. The island would make a good venue for our pictures and we could leave early on Sunday morning and try again for our 'max' on the Pisa-Florence *autostrada* before the Italians started to clutter up their fine roads.

The fastest car we had ever tested, and a record that stood for a long time, was the exciting Lamborghini Miura. It was a car for really rapid travel in the era of no speed limits.

Using the Miura for grand touring to cut across from the north down to Pisa instead of just blasting up and down on full throttle showed it in a very different light. It really was a fabulous machine in which to cover the ground at simply appalling speeds, to which one became more and more accustomed. There were no open-road speed limits in 1970, of course, and we made a very rapid traverse of Italy, with a long stay at Florence where we almost had to fight our way back to the car through the crowd of admirers, and spent Friday night at Siena before going on next morning to catch the ferry at Piombino.

There was no problem in getting across to Elba, but we were warned that the only return ferry on Sunday morning not fully booked was the 6 a.m. crossing. We decided to risk it but would have to make jolly sure that we caught that ferry.

Elba provided all we could have wished for in the way of photographic backgrounds, and we were also able to finish off the 'fiddly' parts of the road test such as measuring the turning circle. We joined the mainly young holidaymakers staying at the villas for a riotous and very enjoyable dinner, and frequently had to respond to questions about the 'fabulous black and red sports car'. They all wanted to know 'what does it do?' meaning mph (no one worried about mpg in 1970). I always responded with: 'Well, we've managed 168 so far but we think there's more to come; we're going to have another go tomorrow.' When they heard we were planning to leave at 5 a.m., the response was: 'Oh, please don't wake us up.' And we very nearly didn't.

I had set the alarm clock carefully but there had been several days of dawn and pre-dawn starts, and it unwound its spring in a vane attempt to rouse us. Suddenly I was awake and stared at the clock and my wristwatch in disbelief before yelling: 'Mike, we've overslept; it's half past five.'

There followed a frantic six minutes of dressing and packing and I kept saying: 'If you leave anything behind you've lost it.' Fortunately the bill had been settled in advance, and we tumbled out hurling bags, cameras and belongings into a Miura boot scarcely designed for pit-stop loading. Mike had the key and jumped into the driving seat while I squeezed into the passenger seat with our two suitcases on my lap.

From cold, the V12 engine needs three stabs at the throttle to prime the six carburettors, and then it bursts into life with a crescendo of sound – just the thing for a Sunday morning. We roared away through the gears, and as most of the corners were left-handers I had the early view from the passenger seat on the right and called out 'go, go, go' every time I had a clear sight through the bend.

There were some heart-stopping moments on the way and then suddenly we were in the big square at Portoferraio. The previous day it had been full of parked cars but was now virtually deserted as we drove straight across at an angle. 'Yes,' I yelled, 'the ferry's still there, but he's putting the pole down, go, go, go...' I could imagine the futile arguments with a grumpy ferry operator who wouldn't let us on once he had lowered the barrier.

'Hoot,' I shouted. The Miura had strident air horns, but they weren't needed. The ferryman heard and saw the red projectile hurtling towards him with the engine roaring at 50mph in first gear, and at the last second he flung the pole upwards just as we shot beneath it. We could never have stopped in time, but we might just have cleared it, so low was the Miura. As we climbed out I noticed the black marks on the ferry deck where we had slithered to a halt.

The rest of the day went well. We had the Pisa *autostrada* practically to ourselves at that hour of a Sunday morning, and did a reconnaissance run north checking that there were no obstructions on the southbound carriageway visible across the Armco. Prominent advertising hoardings were noted as the position to get ready for the end of the straights. Then came the very exciting runs for maximum speed. Southbound, the Miura reached 7,600rpm in fifth, which worked out at 173mph. After scribbling down the data we turned back at the next flyover, blasted past a little Fiat 500 at 130mph, and went on to see the rev counter stabilised at 7,500rpm. The average of two-way runs came to a satisfying 172mph.

It was a record that stood for a long time in the *Autocar* road-test annals; in fact I don't think the staff ever actually tested any high-performance car to a speed higher than that although of course even faster cars were on the way. But also on the way was the second oil crisis, bringing speed limits everywhere.

We called at Bologna to hand the fly-spattered Miura back and transfer everything to the Mercedes-Benz 280SL. It was good to have more space and not to be roasted as we had been in the closed Miura with no air conditioning, but it did seem slow after the electrifying performance of the Lamborghini. We took the ferry next day back to England and arrived at the office where everyone was eagerly awaiting the outcome of one of the most exciting road tests ever, safely in the bag.

FIFTY-TWO

MAZDA RX7

≡ The launch coincided with a record snowfall – almost unheard of in Rome

On a lovely sunny morning in May 1981 I was walking up from the car park to the office and met coming the other way one of our photographers, the late Ron Easton. The company's long-threatened move from Waterloo to Sutton in Surrey had taken place at last in the previous year, and for those living more than 30 miles from the new office premises there was a very fair arrangement that we could try commuting for up to a year and then decide either to stay on or take voluntary redundancy. With a cheery 'Hello' Ron said: 'Have you seen what the Government have done in the Budget? They've doubled the tax-free limit for redundancy payments.'

Ron had worked for the firm even longer than my twenty-six years, and he lived about the same distance away. By the end of the day I had decided to leave and take the redundancy settlement offered to me, and set up as a freelance motoring writer. It was not only the attraction of the money as a firm base on which to set out alone, nor was it the longer commute that decided me. In fact, I preferred the drive from my home at Radlett in Hertfordshire to Sutton instead of the ever more dreary fight to drive and crawl my way into London. For the longer trip to Sutton, I needed to be in the car and driving by five minutes to seven and could then be at the office soon after 7.30. Everyone on the road at that hour was keen to get a move on. When the lights changed on the North Circular Road we would all zoom away and soon the block of traffic would be cruising along at 80, notwithstanding the 40mph speed limit, before speed cameras spoiled the fun! I also enjoyed the drive through Richmond Park, seeing the deer, but the down side was coming back. No matter what time I left, those 35 miles were always a dreary procession taking well over an hour.

No, what decided me to go freelance was that the job had lost its interest. I was still actively involved in road-testing, but was finding it harder and harder to get away from the office on assignments while working under a new editor who seemed to be away more often than he was there. As deputy editor I was increasingly doing the editor's job without either the authority or the pay. Ron Easton also decided to leave and take redundancy, so we both had a joint farewell staff party on 11 September 1981.

Setting up as a freelance was an exacting task, and I was still carrying out road tests for *Autocar* but soon realised that writing anonymous articles was a mistake. I needed to build up my own network of signed outlets. This was brought home to me when I went out to the 1981 Frankfurt Motor Show soon after leaving and met Erik Johnson, the press officer for Mercedes. An elegant new Mercedes 380SEC Coupé was launched at the show and, forgetting for a moment that I was no longer on the staff, I asked, 'When do we get it for road test?'

'*You* don't get it,' he replied half jokingly. 'You're bottom of the list now!" Ironically, when it came in for road test in July the following year it was allocated to me to carry out the test.

It was good to be finished with the rush-hour London commuting and be able to spend more time at home with my wife, as well as being able to decide my own work schedule. When I left *Autocar* for the last time I had to hand back the BMW 732i that had been my long-term test car, and also sadly went the firm's credit card for fuel, but I could still charge for expenses incurred working for the old firm. I had my Triumph Dolomite 1850, later changed to a Triumph Acclaim HL, but almost at once I set up a rolling road-test programme with a fresh car coming in for assessment every week.

The work became different and no longer was I involved in the procedure of editorial work. Instead I wrote test reports and articles with pictures, posted them off, and next time I saw them they were in print. I registered for VAT, which was a good move, otherwise my accounts would have become a shambles, so the quarterly schedule of getting it all typed out and accounted for was a good discipline.

As the number of magazines for which I was writing increased, I was invited to more and more new model launches, which were always most enjoyable and an excellent way to keep up to date with developments. My portfolio of outlets included *Practical Motorist, Volkswagen Audi Car* (later changed to *Audi Driver and Volkswagen Driver*), *Diesel Car, Transport Engineer, Oracle* (ITV), *Auto Zeitung* (Germany), *Maxpress* (Japan), *Asian Auto* (Malaysia), *New Zealand Car* and *Car* (Singapore).

Launches were invariably spread over two days with a night away and sometimes a flight to some distant location where the cars would be awaiting us, usually with a specified driving route to be followed. I was flown to America a few times, but usually launches were in Europe and mainly the UK.

Naturally we were required to pair up, two to each car, and finding a suitable driving partner was difficult at first. I was quite shocked at the poor standard of driving of some colleagues who were then going to write about the car's behaviour. Sometimes, too, there was danger, as happened on a Mercedes-Benz launch when an irresponsible journalist drove far too fast, well beyond his capabilities and had a serious crash. As luck would have it, he escaped injury, but his passenger, Gordon Cruickshank suffered a back injury leaving him paraplegic for life. Fortunately, I wasn't on that launch.

A little later, on a Škoda launch I shared with Graham Fryer, who had founded the Driving Instructors' Association and was editor of the Association's magazine *Driving*. He is an excellent driver, and after that first meeting we always contrived to attend launches on the same date and drive together.

In February 1986, there was a launch for the new Mazda RX7 with improved Wankel rotary engine, and it was based at Rome. We were sitting enjoying dinner when someone came in and reported that it was snowing, which is exceptionally rare that far south in Italy. I was afraid that there would be no driving next day, but bravely they let us go out in the cars and the only part cancelled was the track driving. It was very wet snow, thawing fast, and on the main road into the centre of Rome many branches of the trees beside the road had broken under the sheer weight of snow. One of these had landed on a parked Fiat 600 and was sticking out of the roof – an unpleasant find when its owner returned.

Driving around Rome in such conditions was very exciting, and I enjoyed the RX7 but it was annoying that during the night thieves had broken into the Mazda test cars and stolen the radios, leaving ugly holes in the fascia.

The RX7 was on chunky tyres, and with the snow so wet one had only to let the rear wheels spin a little to claw their way down to the firm ground beneath. Sadly, though, Mazda's efforts to make a success of the Wankel engine were doomed by its inefficiency and high fuel consumption.

FIFTY-THREE

Peugeot 605

We cruised at about 110–120mph and covered the 204 miles back to Aswan in just one minute under two hours

During my years as a freelance motoring writer there were many superb launches of new models, and one that was particularly memorable was the 1990 introduction of Peugeot's new big car, the 605. Peugeot's industrious chief of the press department in Paris favoured Egypt for his new model introductions, and when we were flown out there it was easy to understand why, since about 90 per cent of the cars on the roads of Egypt are Peugeots.

One needs a fast car for the long straight roads of southern Egypt, and the Peugeot 605 fitted the bill admirably, offering three-figure cruising speeds.

Our five-hour flight in March 1990 in a Boeing 727 landed in Aswan where we were transferred by coach to our floating hotel on the Nile, the *Nile Ritz*, for dinner and the first night's stay in a comfortable cabin on the boat. Next morning there was a briefing at which we were urged to take care on the return journey as the long fast drive across the desert ended at a roundabout where we had to turn left. Later we learned that a journalist from another country on a previous group had arrived at the roundabout still doing about 100mph. The occupants were not seriously hurt but the car was very badly damaged.

We were then led out to the fleet of 605s, all with 3-litre V6 12-valve engines, and set off for the long 200-mile drive across the desert to Abu Simbel where the ancient monuments built to honour the Egyptian king Ramesses II many thousands of years ago had been moved in 1968–72 in a fantastic UNESCO project to prevent them from being flooded and lost for all time when the new dam at Aswan was built, raising the level of the Nile. The monuments were dismantled, moved higher up the hillside, and then rebuilt by Swedish engineers.

It was pleasant to relax in the very comfortable and quiet 605 on the seemingly endless stretch of tarmac, almost totally devoid of other traffic, and only on about three occasions was it necessary to slow down from the 90mph cruising speed where sand had blown across the road. At the briefing, someone had asked about the speed limit and we were told 'we have special dispensation'.

Destination for the first day of the Peugeot launch was the famous monument to King Ramesses at Abu Simbel, and going by car was the best way to get there.

At Abu Simbel a magnificent lunch awaited us, enjoyed in the open under a cloudless sky, and then we were taken on a short ride on a boat giving an impressive view of the monuments from the water, followed by a conducted tour. We were shown how on the birthday of the ancient Pharaoh, Ramesses II, the sun shone directly through the opening in the monument and lit up his carving.

It was then time for the return journey and we were transferred to the more powerful version of the 605 with 24-valve engine, which proved enormously fast. We cruised at about 110–120mph, and covered the 204 miles back to Aswan in just one minute under two hours, and we did remember to slow down for that roundabout, where the skid marks of the earlier accident were an additional reminder to take care.

The following day was very different, with a drive in the 3-litre automatic along the bumpy and very busy road to Luxor where lunch was provided, followed by a fascinating tour of the Luxor monuments and burial chambers of the kings. A 605 turbo diesel was then provided for our return drive back to our floating hotel, before next morning's return flight back to Gatwick.

It had certainly been a most impressive demonstration of the ability, performance and ruggedness of the new 605, and the Peugeot press officer impressed on us that no other manufacturer would dare to expose its cars to these roads and driving conditions.

Hearing about our adventures on this remarkable four-day Peugeot launch, my wife Jennetta declared that she had always wanted to see Abu Simbel and I readily agreed that we would, though it was not until three years later that we went back to Egypt, already our fourth holiday there, and this time had booked into the Isis Island hotel at Aswan. The flight landed at Luxor and from there it was a slow trundle in a coach taking three hours followed by the free ferry service to the hotel on an island in the middle of the Nile. It was rather sad to find that this huge and very attractive hotel with 430 rooms had only about thirty-five residents, so most of the time we had the magnificent swimming pool entirely to ourselves.

'Now, if we're going to Abu Simbel, we'll do it properly,' I said. I knew that most people take a flight to get there, but it gives only about half an hour for a hurried visit to the monuments. We couldn't hire a self-drive car, so we booked a one-day trip with driver to include lunch and a tour guide, all for £100, which was about the same as the cost of flying there. For anyone wishing to visit Abu Simbel I strongly recommend to do it this way.

We leave at 6 a.m., we were told, which was equivalent to 4 a.m. British time, but we were on the ferry at the right time and pleased to see our taxi waiting for us. It was a Peugeot 505 Estate car, probably about 15 years old, and with 608,681km indicated on the speedometer, which had long since stopped working. The driver was a bit surprised to see me going round and checking the condition of the car, especially when I made him open the bonnet. But I knew we were going to do

400 miles of desert travel, and I was quite relieved to see a Toyota diesel engine, so felt we should be OK.

There was a stop for a drink at a little café about halfway, and after about three hours in which we saw only about four other cars on the road, we arrived at Abu Simbel. The English-speaking guide provided for us proved first rate and very informative, and after a short while all the other visitors departed to get their return flight so we had the tour of the monuments almost entirely to ourselves. This was followed by a very good lunch at a nearby restaurant and then it was time to start our rather weary return drive.

We were following a coach and beginning to look forward to the stop at the café we had visited on the way out, but were surprised to see people rushing out carrying furniture. Then we saw the reason: the kitchen was on fire. The coach driver produced a small fire extinguisher, but it was soon exhausted without quenching the flames, and we felt sorry for the poor man who ran the café, seeing his livelihood in danger, though the flames did soon die down. No use ringing the fire brigade, which were 80 miles away, and the café wasn't on the phone anyway!

We continued our journey and were quite glad to get back to our hotel, but it absolutely confirmed that if one wanted to see the amazing monuments of Abu Simbel this was the best way to do it.

FIFTY-FOUR

RENAULT 21 GTD

We popped through the hole in the wall and stepped into no-man's land between West and East Germany, but a guard on the other side shouted at us. 'You are lucky,' said a man on the west side as we stepped back. 'Two weeks ago he would have shot you.'

'Right, let's just check that we've got everything: passports, tickets, money, hammer, chisel.' We were off to Berlin for a long weekend, and the immediate reaction of friends and relatives when they heard where we were going was: 'Bring us back a piece of the wall.' So the implements with which to attack it were essential equipment.

It was 1990. Communism had begun to collapse in 1989, and all the news was full of the West Germans' assault on the hated Berlin wall. 'We ought to go and see Berlin before it changes too much,' said my wife. I agreed at once. A Renault 21 GTD was with me for test, and it needed only a quick call to Renault to get permission to take it abroad and arrange insurance.

Although with an 'atmo' engine of only 1,870cc, the Renault 21 GTD provided good transport for our hurried weekend trip to East Berlin.

John Kerswill, editor of *Diesel Car*, which was one of my outlets, was keen to take a feature on the trip but he pointed out that the letters GTD on the side of the Renault didn't mean that it had a turbo. It was the same 'atmo' engine of 1,870cc as first appeared in the Renault 19, with a rather modest output of 65bhp.

It was just a couple of years since I had driven a Ford Fiesta 1.6D to Berlin on an RAC-observed economy test, achieving 89.1mpg, and I was interested to see how much things had changed. But this was to be no economy run: we crossed on the P&O night boat from Felixstowe to Zeebrugge on Friday night, and were on the road soon after 7 a.m. next morning. The miles slipped away easily with the Renault cruising at about 90mph, and we crossed from Belgium into Holland with no delay, although the crossing into Germany at Venlo was slow.

Noon found us passing Bielefeld, and after a fairly leisurely lunch we reached the Helmstedt checkpoint just after 3 p.m. It was there that the relaxation in East Germany border formalities was most evident. When I had crossed two years earlier – and the time before that in 1964 – I was made to hand over passports, which were put into a little container and travelled forward 50 yards on a moving conveyor belt, to be checked before one arrived at the frontier. When the Wall was breached in 1989 there must have been some violence at Helmstedt that was not reported. One of the conveyors was reduced to a jumble of twisted girders and the other had been ripped off by Germans venting their fury against this bureaucracy.

Now they were no longer used, and instead passports were passed through the car window, 10 German marks (£3.70) paid for the visa required by all non-Germans, and we were on our way in a couple of minutes. Previously it had taken nearly an hour to clear the border.

The next surprise was the dramatic change on the corridor motorway. Compared with two years earlier, traffic had increased tenfold and there were now parking areas and service stations where previously no stopping had been the rule. Gone, too, were the East German guards looking at us through binoculars.

West Berlin was entered at Checkpoint Bravo, and we soon found the Hotel Schweizerhof where we had wisely booked a room; hotel space in Berlin was under pressure as a result of the tourist boom that followed the dismantling of the wall.

Jennetta (in black trousers) stands on the battered remains of the Berlin wall.

It was with some relief that we headed back to the West at Allied Checkpoint Charlie.

Next day, Sunday, we had no difficulty finding the Wall; we had only to head for the noise of hammering. Hundreds of Germans were standing on the Wall; others were hammering at it and in places had broken right through and twisted away the steel reinforcement. At one of these points we stepped through into no-man's-land between West and East, but immediately a guard shouted at us. 'You are lucky,' said a man on the west side as we stepped back. 'Two weeks ago he would have shot you.' We spent a little while with our hammer and chisel, and were surprised how easily great chunks of the roughly cemented wall tumbled down.

Seeing the number of cars pouring into the east side I decided we could risk taking the car over, and we made our way to the Allied crossing point, Checkpoint Charlie, where we paid 5 marks each plus 10 for the car (total £7.40). After only a few minutes delay we found ourselves driving in the East.

First impressions were of the grim, forbidding and run-down apartment blocks that looked like a condemned barracks, but almost immediately we came round a corner and a truly beautiful city came into sight with wide promenades and magnificent old buildings. Many of them were pockmarked with the evidence of ferocious fighting, and there were simply thousands of bullet marks on the walls.

After a fascinating afternoon wandering around East Berlin, it was a pleasant relief to hand over our transit visas and drive back to the comfort and freedom from austerity in the West.

We enjoyed another day in the spacious parks of West Berlin, and then next morning, Tuesday, we were up early in the hope of catching the 6.15 p.m. P&O ferry out of Calais. We spotted both the radar traps on the 60mph corridor through East Germany, but not until the second one had flashed as we passed the unmanned camera. I pulled in and waited for several minutes until a big lorry came along and tucked in behind it. About a mile later we came to the police checkpoint, but successfully passed it without being noticed!

We reached the Helmstedt crossing at 10 a.m. and were then able to start motoring in earnest. The Renault 21GTD kept throbbing along with its speedo needle often hovering either side of 90mph according to whether the road was uphill or down, and averaged just over 70mph for the 456 miles from Helmstedt to Calais. In spite of hard driving, the Renault's average fuel consumption was 38.4mpg.

The remnants of the wall we had brought back were a jumble of bits of slate with fragments of cement attached, but as requested I mounted some pieces neatly on cards and labelled them: PART OF THE BERLIN WALL, REMOVED AND BROUGHT TO UK, 1st APRIL 1990. Not surprisingly, in view of the date, no one believed they were genuine!

FIFTY-FIVE

JAGUAR XJ6 AND DAIMLER SOVEREIGN

'What!' I exclaimed. 'We'll never make it. It's seventeen minutes past three already. Well, I'll do my best.'

A memorable 'dash for the flight' occurred in September 1994, when I was invited to Scotland for the launch of the new Jaguar XJ6 and Daimler Sovereign. I had a Rover Vitesse Sport on test, and as the launch coincided with the annual caravan trade show at Hull I decided to drive up, enjoy a pleasant lunch as guest of ABI Caravans, later doomed to go into administration, and carry on to Scotland next day. Jaguar kindly agreed to put the flight ticket in my wife's name so that she could fly up to Inverness after the launch and join me on a leisurely scenic drive back south spread over a few days. This was the sort of thing I could enjoy with my freedom as a freelance writer.

After the caravan show at Hull, I drove on north for a while and stayed the night at the Anglers Arms near Morpeth. Next day I motored on to the magnificent

The combination of Scotland's lovely clear roads, the sumptuous Skibo Castle as base, and the superb new Jaguars and Daimlers made this a most memorable launch.

Skibo Castle, north of Inverness, where the launch was based. Most journalists flew to Inverness and were then shuttled to Skibo in a fleet of chauffeur-driven Daimler limousines.

It was just after 3 p.m. when I arrived at Skibo and saw the late David Boole, then Jaguar press officer, and asked if, having arrived early, I could take out one of the cars for a drive, ahead of the main test-driving scheduled for the following morning. He readily agreed but said that he was worried about three Dutch journalists who hadn't returned.

'They should have left for the airport ages ago,' he said, but almost as he uttered the words, one of the new Daimler Sovereigns arrived with the missing Dutchmen. The shuttle service to the airport in Daimler Limousines had long since finished so there was some discussion as to who would take them to the airport, at which I intervened with: 'Would you like me to do it? I might as well have a journey with a purpose.'

The offer was eagerly accepted, the three Dutchmen put their luggage in the boot of the Sovereign, which they had been driving and all three of them settled down in the back, leaving the front passenger seat vacant. We trickled quietly away down the drive, and almost as a conversation topic I asked what time their flight was due to leave.

The magnificent interior of the Daimler with its part wood steering wheel. The big arrow on the left was a reminder for the many foreign journalists being brought over for the launch to drive on the left.

'Four o'clock,' came the reply.

'What!' I exclaimed. 'We'll never make it. It's seventeen minutes past three already. Well, I'll do my best.' I put the headlamps on and moved the excellent J-shape transmission selector over to the left ready for instant down changes to third, and we accelerated away on the main road.

It wasn't the best weather for a fast drive, with steady Scottish drizzle coming down, but fortunately there wasn't a lot of traffic and the road, although single carriageway, has some long straights, and we saw 110mph three times. Luckily there were no police about, and no one could have read the number plate with sheets of spray flying up behind. We hit 85mph going over the Inverness Bridge, but from then on there are few opportunities to go fast with airport traffic almost constantly coming the other way. But we made it, and arrived at the airport at exactly one minute to 4 p.m. We had covered 45 miles in forty-two minutes, an average of 64mph, but if the last slow miles were excluded it would have been nearer 70. As we arrived at the airport I asked the Dutch journalists if they had realised that the new Jaguar and Daimler were as fast as this. They all spoke good English and in unison replied, 'No!'

Colin Cook, product affairs manager, was waiting anxiously at the entrance and heartily relieved, he said afterwards, to see his last three passengers arrive for their charter flight. I put the window down and said jokingly, 'I'll forward the speeding tickets to you direct!' It wouldn't have happened, of course, but in any case this was before the 2013 prosecution of Chris Huhne and his ex-wife made one realise what a serious offence it is to get someone else to take your speeding points.

I trickled quietly back to Skibo and arrived with the fuel warning light glowing ominously. Next morning there was a test route drive in which I enjoyed the new XJ6 3.2 and especially the supercharged XJR before saying farewell and remembering again to say 'Sir John' to the always friendly Jaguar boss, John Egan who had just been knighted, before getting back into the Rover Vitesse and hurrying back to Inverness Airport to meet Jennetta. We then spent a couple of days touring quietly south and eventually back to our home near London. It was a most entertaining and highly memorable launch.

FIFTY-SIX

MITSUBISHI LANCER, GALANT AND CARISMA

'Come on, they're waiting for you.' The police had stopped the traffic in Warwick Road and they were waiting for us to drive out

As well as writing about cars, one of my prime occupations as a freelance motoring journalist was driving cars to establish economy records or to confirm manufacturers' claims that their new model was the best and most frugal in its class. The more of these I did, the more I was asked to drive another one, and the details of some of the more significant ones are in the Appendix at the end. The first one was for Colt Cars, later named Mitsubishi. I was asked to drive the new Colt Lancer 2000 Turbo from London to Munich in 1981. The target was to show that it could average 60mph while returning over 30mpg, and was also capable of averaging over 100mph.

It was also the first long journey I did with the RAC's observer, Bob Proctor. We suffered awful weather on the way out, and had a strange adventure on the *Autobahn*. I saw an object lying in the middle of the carriageway, and as we drew near it was obvious that it was a jerrycan. Farther along, there was another one, and the temptation to stop and pick it up was resisted to avoid upsetting

On the opening day of the London Motor Show on 15 October 1997 we were allowed to park the Mitsubishi Carisma for the economy run in the front of Earls Court. Here we are ready for the send-off by Mitsubishi's MD.

Bob's meticulous timing of the journey. Another kilometre passed and there was another jerrycan lying on the road, but this time it was on fire, and three American servicemen were doing a kind of war dance around it, trying not very effectively to put the flames out. It was kerosene, not petrol. Then came the real disaster, where a large articulated truck had hit one of the jerrycans, burst it, and caught fire. The driver was standing looking helpless as the truck blazed and it looked as if the fire would soon spread to his trailer. Traffic had all come to a halt in a long queue behind it, and although Bob stopped the watch every time the engine was stopped, the delays played havoc with our timing.

We were eventually clear of the holdups and pressed on to the agreed meeting point, the Hotel Deutscher Kaiser in Munich where we met and had dinner with racing driver Barrie 'Whizzo' Williams who was going to drive the Colt back to London at record speeds to give the other side of the picture – the 100mph average speed – to tie in with our economy run. He suffered appalling weather – it was November with snow beginning to fall – but in spite of this he managed to cover the 736 miles back to London in eight hours and thirty-five minutes' running time, to give an average of 85.6mph. I'm sure the Belgian police will have stopped looking for him by now!

After this demonstration, Mitsubishi called on me three more times for long drives showing the efficiency of their cars. The next one was in January 1995, when I took a Galant 1.8 petrol automatic from Westminster to the centres of Brussels, Luxembourg and Paris – four capitals on a tankful. The car averaged 44.22mpg for 586 miles at an average speed of 46.39mph. We were flagged away from Westminster Bridge at 11.45 a.m. on Thursday 19 January, and arrived at the Eifel Tower at 11.16 a.m. on Saturday, two days later. The results were heavily quoted by Mitsubishi in their advertising.

The advertising department were delighted to have positive results to promote, so I was asked to do another run later in the year, using the new Carisma 1.6 model, and taking it back to Holland, where it was built. The run was in October 1995, ahead of the car's launch scheduled for January the following year. The route started at the South Mimms service area on M25, and thence to Harwich for the overnight ferry to the Hook of Holland. We then headed north to the Dutch town Zurich – no connection with the one in Switzerland – and back south to Belgium and France, returning on the Calais–Dover ferry.

After a rather frightening run through the Purfleet-Dartford tunnel with the fuel warning light shining brightly – not the best place in which to run out of fuel – the tank finally ran dry just 10 miles short of our original starting point. We had covered 716 miles in thirteen hours and forty-two minutes' running time. The consumption worked out at 51.26mpg, and the average speed of 52.25mph showed that we hadn't been hanging about. The proud boast that the car had

Mitsubishi's Carisma was the first car to feature direct petrol injection into the cylinders. Seen here in Spain on its way to Morocco, it averaged 65.06mpg

managed 'over 700 miles on a tankful' gave the advertising department a good 'handle' on which to base their promotion for the new Carisma.

Just two years later, a more ambitious project was arranged, to promote the later version of the Carisma with the first direct-injection petrol engine. It was called the Carisma GDI, which I didn't like at all because it sounded as if it were a diesel engine, rather than a petrol one. It actually stood for Gasoline Direct Injection. We were to start from the Earls Court Motor Show in October 1997, and drive to Morocco, part of the objective being to drive across France without buying any French petrol, which at that time was relatively expensive.

'Come on, they're waiting for you,' came a shout as we were getting organised for the start at the front of the Earls Court building on the opening day of the Motor

Show. They couldn't spare an RAC observer for this long run, and my wife Jennetta came along to act as navigator and timekeeper, and she was being given instructions in how to work the video camera on loan for the event. The police had stopped the traffic in Warwick Road and they were waiting for us to drive out, so a hurried departure was made.

On this event I came to curse what was then the fairly new innovation of mobile phones, because the team making a video film of the event kept ringing up asking us to wait for them, and the first of these infuriating calls came within ten minutes telling us that they were 'parked miles away' and asking us to stop and let them catch up. It was tempting to say 'no, we're on a timed run and can't wait,' but we had to co-operate with the film team.

The maddening result was that we missed the 2.15 p.m. boat on which we were booked and instead crossed at 3.45 p.m. On arrival at Paris there had been an accident and the *peripherique* was closed, resulting in the most appalling traffic shambles – not quite what one wants for an economy run! As a result of the diversion we couldn't go to the Novotel we were booked into without adding unnecessary extra mileage, and several other hotels tried along the route were full, so it was 3.30 a.m. before a rather weary team was able to find somewhere to spend the night.

We had filled the tank to the brim at Dover before boarding the ferry and in spite of the wastage of time and petrol in Paris, made it to Spain without buying any French petrol, and the fill-up at Irun, just over the border into Spain, showed consumption of 63.56mpg. At the pretty Spanish town of Ronda the video team urged me to drive the car among the tables at a small café for filming with the map spread out. The inevitable happened – police arrived, were not interested in 'film for publicity' and imposed a 6,000 peseta (£25) fine!

We found a good British-run hotel at Estepona where the manager next morning said that we had 'made very good time.'

It turned out that he had seen us leaving Earls Court on TV news only the night before (Saturday) and didn't realise that we had actually departed on the Thursday. Fuel was very low when we reached the ferry terminal at Algeciras, but there was enough left to take us off the ferry at Tangier and into the first scruffy garage to fill up, which showed that we had just topped 65mpg overall for 1,260 miles. We had said goodbye to the video team with great relief, as they had to leave their hire car and catch a return flight from Gibraltar, so Jennetta took over, managing our borrowed video camera with great aplomb except at the port when a Tangier local took a swipe at the camera and nearly knocked it out of her hands.

We then enjoyed a couple of days in Tangier and a very pleasant run back at normal speeds across Spain and France, back to Dover. We had covered a total of 5,459 miles.

FIFTY-SEVEN

Mazda 626

≡ It's always a worry when driving on an economy run that calls for the tank to
≡ be run dry; where will the car be when the last of the fuel goes through and
≡ the engine power is suddenly chopped off?

'Zeal what?'

'Monachorum. It's somewhere down in Devon.'

Zeal Monachorum was chosen to be the middle destination. Among various suggestions of possible routes for a 1,000-mile economy run in Britain, Mazda liked best the idea of visiting five places whose first letters would make up the name M-A-Z-D-A.

Choosing a place beginning with M was easy enough. Maidstone, Maidenhead, Marlborough, and so on. Finding two beginning with A was also easy, and Dover was the obvious target for the letter D. It was just the Z that was tricky.

Well known is Zeals, which used to be traversed by the West Country road the A303 but is now bypassed, and the Ordnance Survey lists only three others. Zelah and Zennor are both down in Cornwall, which was not a good idea for an economy run at the height of the holiday period. So Zeal Monachorum won the day and was to be honoured by a visit from the economy-seeking Mazda 626.

When the project was first suggested to me, I felt it wise to point out the snags. 'It's a bit of a tall order,' I warned in a fax. 'It has a good fuel tank, holding 14 gallons, but it's still going to have to do well over 70mpg to make the thousand.'

Then I did some more research. The new 626 2.0 DI has, as the name suggests, a direct-injection diesel engine, and unlike many diesels it's a 16-valve unit. Power is 100bhp, and the engine torque reaches maximum at only 1,800rpm. The gearing is very high, giving 56mph at only 2,000rpm in fifth.

Reassured, I began to think it might make it. We'd certainly have a jolly good try anyway, and perhaps even if it just made a figure in the 900s it would be sufficient to vindicate Mazda's claim that the new 626 diesel made it possible to achieve 'in excess of 750 miles between fill-ups in mixed driving.'

It was certainly going to be mixed driving alright, and by no means just trickling along easy fast roads and motorways. My wife Jennetta was going to come with me to navigate, and her map-reading skills were going to be tested especially in the maze of narrow Devon lanes to seek out the elusive Zeal Monachorum, high up on the edge of Dartmoor while the third leg of the journey would take us right along the South Coast from Exeter to Dover, passing through such congested holiday resorts as Bexhill, Hastings, Hythe, Sandgate and Folkestone. It was going to be a grand tour of England, from the Midlands almost to the Scottish border, then down to the West Country, followed by Kent, and finishing in the London area, all to be done in three days.

To reduce the amount of mileage not included in the economy run, Melton Mowbray was selected as the M for our start point, and many lesser places beginning with A such as Ashbourne, Abridge and Acton were spurned in favour of Alnwick, up in the far north of England. Gradually I became accustomed to the idea that it's pronounced 'Annic', rather like the space in your roof, the attic.

This was not to be a creepy-crawly economy run, with the lorries trying to tread on our rear bumper, but at the same time I was obviously out to get the best economy from the 626 by avoiding all the things that waste fuel, such as erratic throttle control, heavy acceleration, high cruising speeds and needless use of the brakes. A first step was to set the tyre pressures to the permitted maximum.

That's 'Z' in the bag! On an economy run to prove that the new Mazda 626 diesel could cover 1,000 miles on a tankful, we visited towns beginning with the letters MAZDA, and Z was the difficult one; here the Mazda is at Zeal Monachorum.

Five hours after completing photography to prove our presence at Melton Mowbray, we had traversed the Tyne Tunnel and were on the A1 heading north with 219 miles covered and the fuel gauge still pointing confidently at the full mark. On the A1 north of Newcastle you keep seeing signs warning that there have been forty-six deaths and injuries in the area over the past three years, and then they trot out the ministerial panacea for all accidents: 'Don't speed'. One would have thought that the long-overdue dualling of the road would have been a more effective solution.

The military were there at historic Alnwick, as we took pictures with the castle in the background. 'What's going on?' we asked, and learned that they were building a Bailey bridge in the castle grounds ready for a competition, and we were told that the castle itself was being restored under a privately financed budget, which has expanded from the original £5m to £10m. Well pleased with our Alnwick destination as the farthest point north, only 30 miles from the Scottish border, we headed back south and round Newcastle-upon-Tyne by way of the still fairly new western bypass.

Knaresborough was the destination for our first overnight halt, reached with 356 miles covered in running time of less than eight hours, and the gauge still encouragingly above what one might read as the two-thirds mark. It was still above the half mark when 500 miles came up on the trip recorder at 1 p.m. next day, but we were under no illusions: the second half of the run was going to be much tougher than the first.

Our route cut across to the A42, avoiding the dreaded Birmingham snarl-ups by using the M42, and then down to the M5. Jennetta's impeccable navigation made the sole slip of the whole journey when a minor lane was missed in Devon, but it added only a third of a mile. Progress was frequently thwarted by tractor confrontations in Devon, but eventually Zeal Monachorum was reached.

Sporting a fine signboard in the centre, explaining that the peculiar name comes from its history as the Cell of the Monks, it is a pretty village with attractive thatched cottages. Progress had been good, and we checked into a hotel in the heart of Exeter in time for a welcome meal. The fuel gauge was reading slightly below the mid-point between quarter-full and half; but with 678.9 miles indicated, we were more than two-thirds of the way to the thousand.

Calculations that evening revealed that we had a secret weapon in reserve, and all might not be lost even if the tank ran dry before 1,000 miles had been covered.

It's always a worry when driving on an economy run calling for the tank to be run dry: where will the car be when the last of the fuel goes through and the engine power is suddenly chopped off? One place where it could not be allowed to happen was in the narrow and congested northbound lanes of the Dartford Tunnel on the M25. So I decided that we would have to head clockwise round the M26 and M25 to avoid any risk of this potential disaster.

We had visited Dover and taken what pictures were possible although it was forbidden by both traffic laws and the demands of safety to stop almost anywhere, and had scored the final 'A' by a diversion into Ashford. I don't think I have been there since I went as a young motoring writer in July 1957 to cover the opening of the Ashford bypass, long since absorbed into the M20.

The weather had been perfect throughout, and all was going well when the fuel warning light came on near Polegate, just before Hastings was reached, at a mileage reading of 884. A further 116 should be possible, I thought, on the remaining fuel, but we had done quite a lot of local running in both Dover and Ashford, all using up precious derv.

So it was no surprise when there was the first telltale sign of hesitation. Oh, what a shame, I thought: it's going to run out at 998, and not quite make it. But then we crested a rise on the M26, another egg cup full of fuel found its way to the pipe, and took the Mazda quietly on for another 2 miles. When I stopped the car on the hard shoulder the distance recorder was reading 0.6, the figures having reverted to zero after 999.9.

It was still slightly downhill and the car might have run on a little more, but you're not allowed to coast at 15mph, or to drive along the hard shoulder, are you? Anyway, it was unnecessary. Honour had been satisfied by covering an indicated 1,000.6 miles on a tankful. There was also the 'secret weapon' referred to earlier. This was that checks of the distance recorder had shown it to be slightly under-reading. The Mazda doesn't, like so many cars, exaggerate the true distance covered, and in fact the 1,000.6 miles recorded convert to a true distance of 1,022.6.

By the time the emergency 5-litre can had been poured in, and the car driven on to the Clackett Lane service area, a true distance of 1,031.9 miles had been covered, and a further 58.14 litres to fill the tank gave a fuel consumption of 74.29mpg. In spite of the towns such as Hastings and Folkestone traversed, and the considerable mileage on minor roads, the running average speed was 45.96mph. Impressive car, this new Mazda 626 DI.

FIFTY-EIGHT

Mazda 323

☰ The American policeman thought it was the funniest thing he had ever seen

Mazda's industrious press officer David Palmer had an ingenious idea to obtain topical coverage for his new models. He arranged for the cars in right-hand-drive

Mazda had the 323s shipped to California with right-hand drive and already on British registration. The American policeman spoke to us through the open sunroof.

form to be imported from Japan to the west coast of America and for journalists to fly there direct. The cars were then shipped to England and arrived just as journalists were back and writing their stories. It was September 1989, and we flew in one hop from Gatwick to Los Angeles in a DC10, arrived in ten hours, thirty-one minutes and stayed at the Ritz-Carlton hotel at Monarch Beach.

The car Mazda was launching was the new 323, and next day in beautiful weather I shared one with the late Tom Leake. It was my turn to drive when we came over the brow of a hill and saw what was obviously a police traffic check at the bottom of the hill. I kept the speed very low, but in spite of this we were signalled to pull over.

The policeman who halted us wandered over, and speaking through the open sunroof asked for 'you's driver's licence'. At that moment another car appeared, so he went off to deal with it and then came back, saying: 'You found that driver's licence yet?'

'Sorry,' I replied. 'I've left it in the hotel.'

Then looking down through the sunroof of the right-hand-drive car, he said; 'I don't wanna see you's driver's licence, I wanna see you's driver's licence," pointing down at my companion, Tom. Then in amazement, he exclaimed: 'Oh hell, you ain't got a wheel!' He walked away roaring with laughter, and we drove off without any problem over the forgotten licence.

Long-distance Drives and Economy Achievements

1966   Second in Class in Mobil Economy Run in Mercedes-Benz 230 automatic.

1967   Won Class in Mobil Economy Run in Daimler 2½-litre.

1969   Won Class in Mobil Economy Run in Audi Super 90 at 40.42mpg.

1972   Won Class in Mobil Economy Run in Triumph Dolomite 1850 at 40.55mpg.

1974   Won Class in Total Economy Drive in Citroën Dyane 6 at 58.0mpg.

1975   Won Class in Total Economy Drive in Triumph Dolomite at 39.7mpg.

1976   Won Class in Total Economy Drive in Morris Marina Super at 38.35mpg.

1976   Drove with colleagues in an Austin Princess from Land's End to John o' Groats without refuelling; car was equipped with optional 15-gallon LPG tank. Raised £1,006 for charity.

1981   Drove Colt (later known as Mitsubishi) Lancer 2000 Turbo from the RAC in Pall Mall to Munich, aiming to average over 60mph and 30mpg. Average achieved was 61.3mph and 30.99mpg.*

1982   Drove Renault 9 GTL diesel from London to Geneva and round Lake Leman for 'Guess where it ran out of fuel' competition, averaging 57.66mpg at 39.85mph.

1983   Drove Daihatsu Charade diesel on 197-mile test route at average 83.76mpg.

1984   Set *Guinness Book of Records* entry for car with longest fuel range by driving standard Audi 100 with son Bruce and RAC observer on board from Land's End to John o' Groats and back to Falkirk, 1,150.3 miles at 59.27mpg and 51.1mph.*

1985   Drove Renault 5 TL petrol round Britain, 878.7 miles at 75.6mpg.*

1986   Drove Daihatsu Charade turbo diesel from John o' Groats to Dover at average 103.8mpg.*

1987   Drove Citroën AX diesel from John o' Groats to the NEC for the model's launch, without refuelling its 9½-gallon tank, at 75.3mpg; 593.4 miles.*

1987   Drove Renault 5 GTD diesel from Calais to Nice without refuelling, and then back north for 6 miles until the tank ran dry. The result, 75.35mpg at average 40.47mph, was used for two Renault competitions, each with a similar 5 GTD as the prize.*

1987	Drove Citroën CX DTR Turbo from Land's End to John o' Groats without refuelling, 862 miles at 63.9mpg, average speed 42.6mph, with daughter Rachel and RAC observer on board.*
1988	Drove Ford Fiesta from Brentwood to Berlin on £8 worth of diesel, 512.7 miles at 89.1mpg.*
1988	Drove Peugeot 405 diesel from England to Monaco passing through nine countries on the way, 1,118 miles at 73.4mpg, as part of Lucas 'Epic' injection system evaluation.*
1989	Drove Citroën AX diesel from England to Spain, covering 1,057 miles on 10 gallons. In the same Citroën AX diesel, then set new world economy record for standard car covering 110.1 miles on a single gallon.*
1989	Awarded Segrave Trophy special environmental award for efforts to economy driving.
1989	Drove Austin Montego from Land's End to John o' Groats, but car ran out north of Inverness, having covered 750 miles at 64.9mpg
1990	Drove the first car to break the 100mpg/100mph barrier, though obviously not at the same time; a Vauxhall Nova Merit TD covered 105.59 miles on a gallon, and I then drove it flat out for an hour from a standing start at Millbrook Proving Ground, covering 103.82 miles.*
1992	Drove the first Toyota Carina made in Britain at the Burnaston plant on a 1,901-mile round Britain journey visiting Toyota dealers in England, Scotland, Northern Ireland and Wales, raising funds for the Anthony Nolan Bone Marrow Trust. Car was a Carina E 1.6 GLi, which averaged 51.9mph and 40.7mpg. The car was priced at £13,099, and the drive raised over £20,000 for the Trust.
1992	Raised the 'longest fuel range' record in the *Guinness Book of Records* to 1,338.1 miles from John o' Groats to Land's End and back to run-out on the A74 at Lockerbie, in an Audi 100 TDI at 75.94mpg. This was the 1,000th RAC observed trial, and I had driven on twelve of them.*
1993	Raised the world economy record for standard production car to 116.16mpg with later version of Citroën AX D, again promoted by Lucas for their 'Epic' injection.*
1995	Drove Mitsubishi Galant from London to Brussels, Luxembourg, Paris and back to London on 13.26gal of petrol. The Galant averaged 48.36mph, and 46.09mpg.
1995	Drove Mitsubishi Carisma 1.6 GLX 5-door from M25 at South Mimms to Harwich then to Hook of Holland (on overnight ferry), The Hague, Dan Halden (north west point of Holland) and back via Utrecht, Breda and South Mimms, covering 715.8 miles on a tankful at 51.26mpg and average speed 52.25mph.

1997   Drove Mitsubishi Carisma GDI direct-injection petrol car from Earls Court to Tangier at 65.06mpg for 1,658.4 miles; total fuel cost £75.

1998   Drove Mazda 626 DI for 1,031 miles round England to establish that it could do 'over a thousand miles on a tankful.' Average speed was 45.96mph, and economy 74.29mpg.

* Indicates event observed and ratified by the RAC

Acknowledgments

The author is grateful to *Autocar* for providing the basis for a most interesting career driving the world's cars and travelling to fascinating destinations, and thanks for the use of some of the pictures from the early days. He is also indebted to the friendliness and hospitality of many firms in the motor industry who over the years have taken him to often exotic locations.

Other titles published by The History Press

0-60 in 120 Years: A Timeline of British Motoring
KEITH RAY

Looking back over the past 120 years of British motoring, there have been milestones, setbacks and world-class engagements. Motoring in Britain held the world stage on numerous occasions in terms of car design, innovation and outstanding sporting achievement. Here Keith Ray explores every aspect of the motoring world, from its humble beginnings to the vital importance it has today in all of our lives, chronicling the industry's history.

978 0 7524 9757 0

Around the World in a Napier
ANDREW M. JEPSON

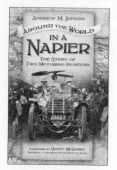

At the start of the twentieth century, American millionaire Charles J. Glidden undertook a journey around the world. Assisted by Sussex engineer Charles Thomas, the millionaire took his Napier car across thirty-nine countries on four continents, to places that had never seen a motor vehicle before. Andrew Jepson tells the fascinating story of these ground-breaking journeys with the aid of images taken from Charles Thomas' own photograph albums.

978 0 7524 9773 0

The Bentley Story
REG ABBISS

Bentley's huge, snarling British race cars dominated motor racing for years. Driven by hard-partying young men known as the Bentley Boys, they consistently beat all comers, winning the Le Mans 24 Hour Race five years out of six; they were the world's most admired and feared sporting cars in their heyday. After languishing in semiobscurity for decades, in the 1980s Bentley was back, and today is the world's leading performance luxury car.

978 0 7509 5462 4

The Aston Martin Story
JOHN CHRISTOPHER

John Christopher takes a fresh look at 100 years of Britain's most iconic car company, Aston Martin. Its first car was produced in 1915 but war and financial troubles often tempered progress and the company went through various changes in ownership. Today the company is best know for its numerous James Bond appearances and its prestigious super-cars, which continue to be market leaders throughout the world.

978 0 7524 7133 4

Visit our website and discover thousands of other History Press books.
www.thehistorypress.co.uk